WITHDRAWN

MRS. G.B.S.: A PORTRAIT

Books by Janet Dunbar

MRS. G.B.S.: *A Portrait*

A JOB IN TELEVISION

FLORA ROBSON: *A Biography*

FIVE FESTIVAL PLAYS

GOLDEN INTERLUDE: *The Edens in India, 1836-42*

THE RADIO TALK

EARLY VICTORIAN WOMAN: *A Study of Social Life, 1837-57*

Mrs. G. B. S.

A PORTRAIT

BY

Janet Dunbar

HARPER & ROW, PUBLISHERS

NEW YORK AND EVANSTON

For Lysbeth

CONTENTS

[vii]

ACKNOWLEDGMENTS

I wish to record my indebtedness to the following, for permission to use unpublished letters and to quote from copyright material:

Mrs. S. Combe, Mrs. P. Hillyard, and the Executors and Trustees of Charlotte Shaw's estate; the Trustees of the British Museum; the Public Trustee and Society of Authors; Professor A. W. Lawrence and the T. E. Lawrence Trust; the Passfield Trust; Dr. Warren Roberts and the Humanities Research Center, University of Texas; the Henry W. & Albert A. Berg Collection of the New York Public Library; Mr. and Mrs. St. John Ervine; Mr. Hesketh Pearson.

I acknowledge with grateful thanks the help given to me by many people during the preparation of this book, especially by Mr. C. G. Prestige, Mr. Dan H. Laurence (Shaw's authorized bibliographer), Mr. Geoffry Allen (British Library of Political and Economic Science), Mr. and Mrs. Julian Brown, Miss M. L. Hoyle (Department of Manuscripts, British Museum), Mrs. Georgina Musters (nee Gilmore), Mrs. Hilda Munthe, Dr. Octavia Wilberforce, Mr. Gene Tunney, Mrs. Vincent Sheean (Diana Forbes Robertson), Mrs. August Belmont, Miss Dorothy Walker, Miss Phyllis Bottome, Miss Blanche Patch.

I was also given invaluable assistance by the late Sir Barry Jackson, the late Sir Sydney Cockerell, and the late Dowager Countess St. Germans, who was a stepdaughter of Arthur Smith Barry and was thus a link with Charlotte's early life.

I wish to thank Lysbeth Merrifield for much patient help and the excellent index, Ralph Merrifield for his care in making copies of very old photographs so that they could be reproduced, and Mrs. Winifred Clark for devoted secretarial assistance.

NOTE: The spelling, punctuation and idiosyncratic locutions in the letters quoted throughout this book have been retained.

PREFACE

After his wife's death in 1943, George Bernard Shaw found a collection of her private papers which he did not know existed. He read a number of them, and later said to his half-cousin, Georgina Musters:

"I lived with Charlotte for forty years, and I see now that there was a great deal about her that I didn't know. It has been a shock."

To an old friend, Eleanor O'Connell, he said in 1944:

"It takes a long time for two people to get to know each other, and from a diary I discovered lately, and some letters which she wrote to T. E. Lawrence, I realize that there were many parts of her character that even I did not know, for she poured out her soul to Lawrence."

Charlotte Payne-Townshend married George Bernard Shaw on June 1, 1898, at the West Strand Register Office, in London. They had known each other for two years, and their courtship had been full of uncertainties from the beginning. Each had had very strong objections to the institution of marriage as such, and had intended to remain single. Charlotte had refused many suitors, and Shaw, after several philandering episodes, had managed to keep out of the net.

What made them change their minds? Both were highly individual people, not easily swayed; both were over forty and should have known their own minds. Was the marriage a success? Their friends in later life thought them an ideal pair, devoted to each other and to the same causes, a supreme example of married companionship on the highest plane. In fact, the older Charlotte grew the lonelier she became as far as intellectual companionship was concerned; her letters to T. E. Lawrence clearly bring this out, though she never said so explicitly. Her early life, with its miseries and frustrations, forced her in on herself, so that her restless, highly intelligent mind became preoccupied with profound questions of religion and philosophy which, with her inadequate education in those subjects, were quite beyond her range. Her life at home had given her a suppressed horror of marriage, but her attractiveness as a young woman made many men want to marry her, and as she had perfectly normal instincts she was often torn by the most appalling conflicts. Her strongest desire was to be *free*. She would not, she determined, again be in bondage to anyone.

Yet she married Shaw. He, at the end of his life, said that he should have remained a bachelor: he was not the marrying kind. It is probable that he was right. He also said that Charlotte was the only woman he *could* have married, and that may have some truth, too, though it is possible that had he married someone less fastidious and sensitive, less willing to fall in with his romantic notions of an idealized union—someone who was a mixture of Jenny Patterson, Orinthia, Mrs. Pat Campbell, Eliza, and a dash of the astringent Beatrice Webb—he would have been happier in the essentials of what makes a good marriage.

Charlotte was descended from a line of Protestant clergy in Ireland, and she was herself intensely interested in religions, though she was not a pious church-goer in the conventional sense of the term. She was a rebel by nature, beating passionately against the straightjackets of her era, yet unable to come to terms with the complexities of her own nature. Her marriage resolved these conflicts for a time, but she was always aware of them, and they were probably the underlying cause of her continual urge to travel—an urge which drove Shaw almost frantic at times, for what he wanted most was to stay in one place and get on with his work.

Almost as strong as Charlotte's quest for spiritual truth was her deep love of Ireland. She was English on her mother's side, but she never thought of herself as anything but Irish, for her roots were in County Cork, and she was very proud of her lineage.

This book is based on Charlotte's Annuary, private notebooks, writings in manuscript, and a vast collection of family papers and correspondence, made available by her surviving close relatives and the executors of her estate. Charlotte had none of the brilliance of Shaw, but she could write well, and from her early years she filled notebooks with her thoughts and comments.

Shaw's love-letters to Charlotte before their marriage are very revealing, especially if they are studied together with his letters to Ellen Terry written at about the same time. Unfortunately, few of Charlotte's letters to him have survived: he does not appear to have kept them, as she did his. She had, however, a habit of drafting letters in pencil before she wrote them in ink, and as these tally closely with the relevant letters which exist, it is reasonable to use similar pencilled drafts as basic material.

It is a great pity that T. E. Lawrence should have destroyed so many of the letters which Charlotte wrote to him when he was in India, though here, again, some pencilled notes survive. One must be thankful that he did not destroy the dozen or so extremely revealing letters in which her habitual reserve vanishes, and she does indeed pour out her heart to him, and a great deal of bitterness, too. These were the letters of which G.B.S. knew nothing, and which gave him such a shock after her death.

The book is in two parts because that was the way her life divided itself. To understand Charlotte, one must begin with her eighteenth-century forebears, for she inherited many strands of her nature from the kind, gentle Townsends, as well as less admirable qualities from her mother's family, the Kirbys.

NOTES: Charlotte was born a Townsend; the "h" was added to her surname when she was a girl. (See Chapter 2.)

The punctuation in Charlotte's and G.B.S.'s letters has been followed, except in the case of Shaw's signature. He sometimes used full points, but usually signed his initials without points. All his signatures have been given points for the sake of consistency.

PART ONE

Charlotte Payne-Townshend

1

THE TOWNSENDS

(1757–1855)

For over a century, happiness had been woven into the Townsend marriages, a bright continuing thread. Old letters, loving and charming, were handed down in the family, to be treasured by successive generations.

"My dearest Dear Life," wrote Philip Townsend to his wife from New York in February, 1757. "After a long tedious passage of almost fourteen weeks and a great deal of bad weather we (God be praised) arrived safe Wednesday last . . .

"This town is very large with spacious streets and buildings . . . some here tell me that it is as large as Cork, but in my apprehension it is not ⅔ of Cork. We cannot yet guess at our destination . . . it is now said that 10,000 men are expected from England to make a descent on some of the French settlements . . . I have been in good health as ever I was in my life and, God be praised, I still continue to want nothing but returning to my heart's delight again, and I shall never have true comfort or satisfaction until I do. Could I but hear from you, I should think myself happy as I can be at this distance from you—and I trust in God as he has delivered me from this very dangerous passage at this season of the year, he will also still protect and send me safe back to the arms of my dearest dear life till which I can have no real comfort or satisfaction . . .

"Blessings, ten thousand blessings, on you and my dear children. I am my dearest dear life

"Yours most

"Phil^p Townsend

"To Mrs. Elizabeth Townsend, at the Rev^d. Horatio Townsend's at Coolmona, to be forwarded by Mr. Zackery Mannis, Merchant in Cork, Ireland."

Philip was a brother of Horatio Townsend, Vicar of Coolmona in the County of Cork. Philip's wife, Elizabeth, lived at Coolmona with her children while her husband was away with the Army in America and Canada. Philip came home from the war and took his family to live in a roomy country house in West Cork. Horatio Townsend missed his sister-in-law and her merry family. A Bachelor of Arts of Trinity College, Dublin, Horatio was a gentle, scholarly man whose life was bounded by his books, his relations and his parish. The duties of his charge of souls were not onerous, for the Protestant families in the neighbourhood were a tiny minority in a countryside predominantly Roman Catholic. Horatio led a pleasant, leisurely social life, reading the Dublin and London newspapers, which reached Cork regularly though late; visiting friends at the Big Houses in their walled demesnes throughout the country, riding and hunting, attending balls and parties. He was kind to his servants, courteous and tolerant, treating them well and not doubting that they were content with their lot.

It was the ambition of the average villager to obtain a position for himself and for as many members of his numerous family as possible in the household of such a good master, where at least they would be sure of food. The eighteenth-century Irish peasant lived in a state of appalling poverty. Ragged, half-starved, he was totally uneducated, except for the bare smattering he sometimes received from itinerant "teachers" who set up hedge-schools in a dry ditch in summer. The grip of the alien conqueror across the water was harsh. The small tenant farmers could only pay the extortionate rents of their holdings by working from dawn to dusk, rearing pigs and poultry for market, and living themselves on potatoes and buttermilk. It did not occur to Horatio to question the work of Providence in dividing mankind into the rich and the wretchedly poor; he had been brought up to accept his little world. As he was kind and charitable, his servants paid him respect and made him laugh with their homely witticisms. He had little idea of the resentments which bubbled beneath the surface of the country people's good manners, or of the widespread hatred which had been growing in the hearts of the oppressed Catholic peasantry everywhere.

The Protestant Ascendancy in the eighteenth century stemmed from the Penal Laws of Queen Anne's reign. The Irish Roman Catholics had been adherents of the Stuart cause, and when that failed, had been viciously punished. England was determined that never again would the Irish help a Pretender, and imposed laws which took care that they would not get the chance. The two harshest laws were those which denied them the franchise and forbade them to own land (most of which had been confiscated from their forebears). They were completely in the power of their landlords, who could evict them if they did not pay their rents—a power which was used.

Horatio was not a landlord; he had a sufficient private income which, together with tithes—levied on the Roman Catholics as well as on the Protestants in a parish—enabled him to live his pleasant life in comfort. He made several moves during the next few years, then settled down and married a Miss Corker. It was the usual successful Townsend marriage, with instinctive "give-and-take" on both sides, and a foundation of genuine piety and goodness. A son and three daughters were born, the boy being given the curious name of Chambre, with Corker as his second name. The children were taught by their parents and by visiting governesses, Chambre's education being supplemented by tutors in the classics. When he was old enough, he was sent to Dublin, where he entered Trinity College and took his Bachelor of Arts degree in 1818. Five years later he was inducted into Holy Orders by the Bishop of Cork and Ross in the Cathedral Church of St. Finbarr, and became curate to his father, who was now Vicar of Castrum Ventry in the diocese of Ross.

Chambre married and took the living of Clonakilty. Horatio's home was soon broken up entirely by the deaths of his wife and a beloved daughter, Fanny. The other two daughters, Charlotte and Ann, were married, and Horatio felt that he wanted to be near Chambre. By 1825 he was living at Derry, a solid greystone house three miles out of the little market town of Rosscarbery, in County Cork. It is not clear whether Horatio built or bought Derry, but it was a house exactly to his liking, and was to remain the home of the Townsends for over a hundred years. Derry was magnificently situated on rising ground, enclosed in a wooded demesne, with ample stables, a terrace facing south, and gardens which sloped gently down to a lake. From the terrace one could look out on a great sweep of the bay, with a lighthouse rising like the stub of a pencil on the farthest point of land.

Horatio did not find it difficult to fill his days: riding, hunting, visiting his friends and being visited by them in turn. What he liked best was to drive in his brougham over to Clonakilty, where Chambre's growing family were as fond of him as he was devoted to them. Chambre had three children by now, Horatio—usually called Horace—Chambre and Lucy, whom their grandfather idolized. Between visits to Derry, Horace often wrote to the old man, who replied to him with the greatest affection.

"Many thanks to my dear Horatio for his sweet letter. Grantipa would rather have a letter from his Horatio than from the Lord Lieutenant, for he is only King of Dublin, but Horatio is Prince of Clonakilty."

Chambre's family increased to ten children; Mary Anne, Katherine, Nathaniel, Caroline, Anne, Susan and Richard followed the other three. His wife did not long survive the birth of her last child, dying when Horace was still in the schoolroom. Nurses and servants brought up the motherless children under Chambre's careful eye, with numerous female relations coming to stay for long periods. The children were given the usual education of the time by competent governesses, tutors being engaged for the boys.

Horace, like his father and grandfather before him, went up to Trinity College. He was aware that his father would have liked

him to enter the Church, but though he never doubted the faith
in which he had been brought up, he knew he had no vocation.
After taking his degree he read for the Bar, and began to take a
close interest in the world of business, especially the Stock Ex-
change. His father was now Rector of Kilmacabea, a village on
Glandore Harbour, in south Cork, and owned a modest estate.
There was a sufficiency of money for the upbringing of the ten
children, but not much over. Horace realized that if he wanted
money he would have to make it.

Chambre Corker Townsend died and Horace inherited the major
part of the estate, together with half his father's books and plate,
and a set of Hogarth cartoons. The rest of the available money was
to be divided equally between the other children, who were "to
get it at 21, and until then, the money to go to the child's education
and advancement in the world, the daughters to get theirs on marriage or at 21, whichever came first."

Horace took his responsibilities seriously. Old Horatio had died
some time before, and left Derry to him; the rents from that estate
made a useful addition to his patrimony. He carried out the instructions in his father's will with scrupulous care; he saw to it that his
brothers were established in their chosen professions and his sisters
had plenty of society—and opportunities of meeting possible husbands. Horace was shy and reserved, but he possessed a strong
sense of duty and an open, affectionate nature behind his quiet
manner. His brothers and sisters loved him dearly, and when the
time came for him to marry, they rejoiced.

The Kirbys were originally a Yorkshire family—a "goodish"
family for those days, lawyers and small country gentlemen. They
had an estate, Edstaston, near the country town of Wem in
Shropshire, and owned some land in southern Ireland.

In 1830, Thomas Cox Kirby entered the Army as a major in the
Horse Guards, the commission being signed by Melbourne and
countersigned "William R." He later sold his commission, intend-
ing to emigrate to Nova Scotia, but there is no evidence of his
going there. The Kirby records reveal very little personal or family

news: they are concerned almost entirely with money. Sales of land, marriage settlements, bills—the Kirbys kept receipted bills all their lives, and passed them on to their heirs.

Thomas Cox Kirby married Mary Ann, daughter of John Knight of Whitchurch, Shropshire. They had two daughters, Mary Susanna and Caroline. Their only son, Franklin Knight Kirby, was a soldier; he was commissioned in the 93rd Highlanders, and died in the Crimea in 1855.

Colonel Kirby, as he became, had business connections in County Cork, and the family came to live at Glandore. Thomas Kirby died in 1850, and his wife and daughters remained in County Cork. Caroline married Richard Webb, a naval officer. Horace Townsend met the Kirbys at parties, or dining at the houses of mutual friends. He found himself meeting Mary Susanna Kirby a great many times. She was elegant and quite handsome, with a cool, assured manner which the young barrister had not come across before, and which singled her out from the high-spirited, rather talkative young ladies whom he met in Cork society. He fell in love.

Horace Townsend of Derry and Mary Susanna Kirby of Glandore were married in Ross Cathedral on October 20, 1855. Of all the Townsend brothers and sisters, relations and friends, who crowded the Cathedral on that day, wishing the young couple well, few could have had the least doubt that this would be a happy marriage. All Townsend marriages were happy—why should this one be any different? Horace was a delightful, an estimable young man, who was known for his considerateness, generosity and kindness. Surely the best qualifications for the sweet bonds of wedlock?

They did not know Mary Susanna.

2

THE ENGLISHWOMAN

(1855—1874)

Horace took his bride to live at Derry. She had visited it several times, had admired the views, the gardens and the demesne, and had been gracious to the curtsying servants. Now that she was mistress of the house, she set about altering as much as she could in as short a time as possible. She could not do anything about the stables or the established lawns and gardens; in any case, these met with her approval, being large and well kept, with an adequate staff of grooms and gardeners to keep them up. The inside of the house was another matter. Mary Susanna planned redecorations, refurnishings. The Great Exhibition in London had let loose a number of new ideas, and young Mrs. Townsend liked to keep up with the fashion, especially English fashion. The Irish, she thought, had no fashion, either in clothes or in furniture.

Her husband considered her demands not unreasonable; after all, a bride was entitled to have her tastes carried out in her new home. For his own part, he was well content with the finely polished old furniture as it was; most of it had belonged to his grandfather, simple furniture with good lines, made by craftsmen. He kept back several pieces which had been used by Townsends for generations, and put them in his own library. For the rest, he gave way.

Having got the house to her liking, Mary Susanna was seized afresh with restlessness. She found social life around Derry limited. She had once spent a season in London, and though she had been only on the outer fringe of "Society," she had been taken to the outstanding events of the season. In any case, she had been used to the social life of Shropshire. The best families called frequently on each other in that county, and there was a pleasing formality in social relationships. English servants, too, were properly trained. Why, at Derry, Horace called his tenants "my people"! Mary Susanna disliked their easy manners, and she also objected to the friendliness of the Rosscarbery shopkeepers. Oh, they were perfectly polite, she could not deny that. But they were too . . . was "eloquent" the word? They had no idea how to keep their place.

Before a year was out Mary Susanna began to wonder, aloud, why her husband did not move to England, where they could participate in real social life—English social life. Horace, surprised, replied that he had no desire to live in England. He could not understand why his wife should be discontented with the social life in the neighbourhood: to him it had always seemed delightful. His many relations and the friends he had known all his life were, on the whole, cheerful and hospitable. They had their idiosyncrasies, of course, and the oddities among them provoked laughter at times, but it was good-natured laughter, with kindness in it. Hurt and astonished, Horace realized that his wife's laughter was not good natured: it was edged with scorn and contempt, something alien to any Townsend.

Her own family had returned to Shropshire and were living again at Edstaston. Mary Susanna used this as a reason for renewing her wish to leave Ireland and live in England. She began to press Horace once more to sell or let Derry, and make another home across the Channel. After all, she tried to point out, he was not really Irish; all Protestants in Ireland were of English stock.

This roused the gentle, unassuming Horace. His family had lived in Ireland for generations, and had intermarried with other Anglo-Irish families of similar descent. He told his wife that Derry was his home, Ireland was his country, and he did not propose to leave either. She could not shake him from that stand, and for a time she did not refer to the subject again. It was, however, always in the forefront of her mind.

Their first child, a daughter, was born at Derry on January 20, 1857, and christened Charlotte Frances in Rosscarbery Cathedral a month later. She was not a pretty baby, but by the time she was three months old her eyes had turned a beautiful, translucent green, so that from an early age people turned to look at her again.

Two years later, another daughter was born, and named Mary Stewart, the second name after a Townsend who had married a Stewart. Little Charlotte tried to say "sister" but got no further than "sissy," and from then on Mary Stewart Townsend was always called Sissy. Charlotte became Lottie. The children were looked after by carefully selected nurses and were taught to ride as soon as they could sit on a horse. Charlotte's earliest memories were of horses and dogs, and she was fearless with both. Sissy, too, liked animals, and their well-ordered lives were enlivened by the dogs they were allowed to own; their mother did not object to dogs.

The children went riding every day with their father or a groom, and after lessons played in the gardens or were rowed on the lake in the grounds by one of the gardeners. Lessons were important. Mrs. Townsend had engaged a resident English governess, who gave them a good grounding in the usual school subjects; and there were visiting language tutors. These specialized teachers travelled round the Big Houses, usually recommended from one family to another. They remained for a few weeks at a time, giving their pupils intensive teaching in the principles of grammar and paying particular attention to good pronunciation. A certain amount of homework was left each time—vocabulary exercises and reading—to be done under the supervision of the governess. The tutor then went on to the next Big House, to return some time later for the next lessons.

It was a surprisingly successful system. Charlotte and Sissy learned French, Italian and German, and by the time Charlotte reached her teens she was able to read French and Italian books in her father's library as easily as she read the English classics. The

sisters got on well enough, but they were entirely different in
temperament, and beyond their common love of dogs and horses,
had little to say to each other.

They were now the Misses Payne-Townsend. Horace had been
persuaded by his wife to take the additional name of Payne—a
family name on her side—and add it to his own. He was reluctant
at first, but Mary Susanna overruled him, and he adopted the name
by Royal Licence in 1863.

Horace had plenty of occupation. He was a Commissioner of the
Peace and took part in all the activities of a country gentleman. He
was also a keen student of the financial market, and increased his
yearly income steadily by shrewd investments. His name for probity
and honourable dealing stood high throughout the south. Charlotte
had inherited his love of the countryside. She liked walking in the
demesne, stopping to watch the men felling trees or cutting the
undergrowth. She knew everyone: the tenants in the low white
cottages, the villagers, the shopkeepers. She was perfectly aware of
the difference in station between herself and them, but it meant
nothing. They were her father's "people."

She loved, most of all, to go riding with her father by the little
rivers along the valley, where the banks were thick with balsam
and willowherb, coltsfoot and loosestrife. When they rode home
across open country, she would see the violet-blue smoke of the
turfcutters' fires, and would rein in her horse beside her father's
and listen while he talked to the men in his easy, quiet way. Sometimes they came across a horse sale, and that always absorbed her
close attention. The tinkers and itinerant dealers were adept at
their trade, the poetry on their tongues sugaring the sharp practice
which even she knew was going on.

When Charlotte went with her father into one of the peasants'
cabins on the estate, a chair would be dusted for her and she would
be shown the latest letters from sons and daughters in America—
that fabulous land of plenty. There was hardly a peasant family in
the district but had lost children in the inexorable tide of emigra-
tion; "lost" because it was rare for the young ones to come back on
the promised visit until long after the parents were dead, and they
themselves grown into grey-haired men and women. Money came,

however, and the dear ties of kinship held fast by a few poor letters
a year.

Charlotte somehow came to apprehend the lives of her father's
"people" from the time she could understand anything. The
terrible miseries of the potato crop failures in '45 and '46 were a
living memory, and she never, to the end of her life, forgot the
expressions on the old people's faces when they talked of it. The
name O'Connell, and his title, the Liberator, became familiar. Her
mother forbade all "talk" in the house; she tried to guard her
daughters from having more contact than necessary with the
servants, apart from the proper relationship between servant and
served. Nevertheless, Charlotte came to understand a good deal of
the life that went on outside the Big House.

Sissy was not so interested. Pretty, with neat, regular features
and a slender figure, she had become addicted to horses and hunting, and could always occupy herself in the stables or running
with the dogs, when she was not driving with her mother, or reading the journals from London, or sewing at fancywork, or planning
new clothes. She was as good a linguist as her sister, and being
unself-conscious and anxious to please, always shone in company.
Charlotte, too, rode to hounds, and took part in what social life
came her way, but her main interest was in reading. She spent a
great deal of time in her father's library, with its high bookcases,
old polished furniture, and the Hogarth prints on the walls. Horace
always welcomed her there; he was completely at ease with his
elder daughter, and he guessed that she was as anxious to escape
from the drawing-room as he was. He regarded his library as his
sanctum in every sense of the word: it was a sanctuary from Mary
Susanna.

His wife had revealed herself to be a nagger. Her strong will had
been apparent in the early years of their marriage, but as time went
on she became more and more domineering, more determined to
have her own way in everything, railing at him and nagging ceaselessly when she was refused anything which she demanded. She
could not bear opposition. If it was offered she made violent scenes,
and if these had no effect she began to weep, keeping up a spate
of sobs until she wore her husband down. But these displays were

carefully spaced—for everyday use she employed nagging to get what she wanted. This type of termagant had never been known in the family. None of the Townsend wives had ever been in the remotest degree like Mary Susanna. They had not been goody-goodies: each had her own share of temperament, and when there had been discussions on any subject, the ladies had been equal to their lords in spirited exchanges. But there had always been good nature, a willingness to listen to rational argument. There had always been courtesy—that endearing characteristic of the Irish quality. And there had been affection.

The effect of Mary Susanna's nagging was a slow withering of Horace's happiness. He had been genuinely in love with her when they married, and had been bewildered by the extraordinary change which came over her later, not realizing that the veneer of graciousness was thin and that the true nature of the woman now showed through.

It was in her father's library that Charlotte, in her fifteenth or sixteenth year, began to understand what had happened, and was still happening, in Ireland. Horace allowed her to read anything she liked, and was always ready to stop writing at his desk and answer her questions; she had a quick, probing mind, and she asked a great many. Horace was realistic about his country's wrongs, and he proceeded to enlighten his daughter in a way that would have roused the almighty wrath of Mary Susanna had she known of this extension to Charlotte's education.

Charlotte read Jonathan Swift's pamphlet, written over a century before, in which the eloquent Dean urged the Irish people to be self-reliant and improve their own condition. She read similar exhortations in Bishop Berkeley's *Querist* and the other pamphlets he wrote on the wretched condition of the eighteenth-century Irish peasantry. Berkeley had been influenced by Tom Paine, who had often pressed for an independent Irish republic. There was Theobald Wolfe Tone, the Dublin lawyer, who had led the rising in 1798. And the great Liberator himself, a Roman Catholic barrister, who had formed an Association to work for Catholic Emancipation after the famine of 1822.

Horace's habitual reserve disappeared when he talked of these men. He had never been antagonistic to the Catholics, and he was opposed to the iniquitous tithe laws, which compelled the Catholic peasants to pay tithes to the Irish Episcopal Church, a bitterly resented obligation, since they also had to support their own priests, and the Protestants were only a quarter of the entire population. The system was all the more detestable because of the tithe-jobbers, middlemen who bought tithe rights from such of the Protestant clergy as would sell them, and extorted a profit from the trade.

O'Connell had fought the law denying Catholics the franchise until, in the end, Wellington, the Prime Minister, supported by Sir Robert Peel, forced through the Catholic Relief Bill (Catholic Emancipation) and Irishmen were allowed to sit in Parliament. But the tithe scandal continued. The chief cry now was land reform. The agitation had been going on for decades; a movement for "the land for the people" had begun at the dawn of the century, and was never out of the people's minds. A burning sense of injustice was mixed with hopelessness that anything would ever get done, in spite of the continual efforts of patriots who were fighting for them in London.

The Anglo-Irish, the Protestants, descendants of the early English settlers put there by Cromwell, were the landlords. Some of them lived on their estates and tried to improve their land; they reclaimed bogland, planted trees, started home industries, such as weaving, to help their tenants, and built schools. For themselves, they built large houses and laid out their grounds, and as the estates were self-supporting, and servants' wages were low, they could indulge in a good social life and practise traditional hospitality on a lavish scale. They looked after their people and preserved their feudal privileges and responsibilities.

These landowners were in a minority. Most of the large Irish estates were owned by absentee English landlords who hardly ever visited Ireland, except for the shooting once a year. They found it more comfortable to live in England, or to travel abroad, and left it to a ruthless bailiff or agent to collect high rents from peas-

ants who were absolutely dependent on the land for a bare livelihood. The peasants had no security of tenure; they were not
allowed to own their farms and holdings. As their agricultural
implements were still primitive and they knew little of proper hus-
bandry or the planned rotation of crops, the potato harvest—which
gave twice the food yield of wheat—was their staple of life. If that
failed, starvation followed. Where the farmers owned horses and
cattle, conditions were a little better, but in the boggy districts
and in the mountains the people lived in unbelievable poverty,
working hard to earn enough to pay the rent, and living meagrely
themselves. If they fell into long arrears of rent they were evicted
from their cabins—rendered homeless as well as hungry.

The partial failure of the potato crop in 1845 and the total
failure of the crops in '46 and '47 were terrible disasters; over
200,000 people emigrated to the United States and thousands
more died from disease.

Quietly, without emphasis, Horace gave his daughter the facts
of the condition of Ireland and encouraged her to read his books.
He had no panacea, no plans for reform; he knew that one man
was powerless to alter the existing state of things—and in any case
he was a Protestant and therefore suspect. As a Commissioner of
the Peace, he did his best to be just and impartial when called
upon to arbitrate on local affairs. He was trusted. But he was aware
of the ferment going on beneath the surface of life around him.
Rosscarbery was in a district well known for intense allegiance to
the cause of Irish freedom; O'Donovan Rossa, the Fenian leader,
had been born here, and in the remotest hamlets the chief subject
of conversation was always of the past and its heroes. There were
still Moonlighters, men who took reprisals against harsh landlords and their agents by burning the Big Houses by night, and
maiming cattle. There were secret societies; Brotherhoods existed
everywhere. The Irish Republican Brotherhood, founded to fight
for political freedom, had been in existence since 1858, and there
were continual efforts to get the land laws repealed.

Whenever it was possible, Horace supported reforms, but in the
eyes of the peasants he belonged irrevocably to the Ascendancy, no
matter where his sympathies lay, and there were times when his

gentle soul despaired. He saw so much that was wrong, and he could do little to help.

* * *

In 1874, Mary Susanna proposed to her husband that they should add an "h" to the name of Townsend. Their hyphenated name was not, she felt, distinguished enough. Mary Susanna was now established in the best society which the south of Ireland afforded; she was on visiting terms with the Kingstons at Mitchelstown Castle, with the Earl of Bandon's family at Castle Bernard, and the less noble but socially important families in the Big Houses. There was an impressive record of Townshends on the wall of the church at Castletownshend. She was sure that Horace should have an "h" too; another branch of his family had adopted one long ago.

Mary Susanna intended to take her daughters travelling, and it was important to get the name business settled first. They were now very comfortably off. Several family legacies, together with Horace's flair for good investments, brought them in a very large annual sum, and Mary Susanna wanted to spend seasons in Dublin and London, and to travel on the Continent. First, however—the "h."

Horace disliked the idea, but his wife was determined on the change. Ever conscious of her own middle-class origins, and aware that she had married into "real gentry," she was more than usually set on this latest prop to her gentility. She brought out every weapon in her arsenal: insistent argument, raging temper, loud reproaches, tears, hysteria. When Horace shut himself up in his library there was a lull, but the routine was repeated every time Mary Susanna had a chance to talk to him.

The hysteria, the noisy scenes, were a source of terror to Charlotte. She was now seventeen, and as far back as she could remember she had been a witness of scenes like these; an unwilling and frightened witness, for though she had always tried to get away as far as possible from the sound of her mother's voice, strident echoes had reached up into whatever room she had sought for refuge. She had tried pushing her fingers hard into her ears, but still the high, shrill voice echoed through her head and made her nerves

twang like discordant harp strings. Sissy had never been affected in
the same way. When a quarrel blew up she grimaced and shrugged
her shoulders, her face growing as hard as her mother's. She detested
these scenes as much as Charlotte did, but she seemed to flick them
away, so that they should not touch her.

The scenes over the "h" jarred on Charlotte with extra force,
because she saw how distasteful and stupid the whole idea appeared to her father. Then she made a terrible discovery. The years
of nagging, of violent, one-sided quarrelling, had clawed into the
very essence of her being, and she realized with horror that she
hated her mother—really hated her. The word, which for long had
been a dark outline at the back of her consciousness and always
thrust back, had to be faced now. Charlotte could not comprehend
the depths of her own unhappiness, or formulate its cause in clear-
cut terms, but when she saw her father's sad face after a bout of
sustained railing from her mother, she was seized with a volcanic
rage which stirred up the dregs of her own long drawn-out
wretchedness. She marched into the drawing-room one day and
faced her mother.

"You have no right to speak so to my father," she said.

Mary Susanna, seated on a sofa, majestic in outspread crinoline
and small lace cap, was astounded.

"What is this?" she asked. "I do not understand you, Lottie."

Charlotte could only stammer out the same protest, repeated
rapidly, and when she found that no more words would come,
turned and ran out of the room, her eyes full of angry tears. Her
own desire had been to protect her father, but she did not know
from what. Her overmastering emotion as she fled to her own
room was a raging hatred of her mother, a wild desire to see the
woman fall down dead.

When the two sisters went in to say good night to Mary Susanna
that evening, she bade them sit down. She wished to speak to them
on a very serious subject, she said. Obedience: duty to one's parents: respectful, unquestioning obedience in everything. They
must never forget what children owed to their parents, they must
never, never forget their duty. According to Mary Susanna, that
duty was the first law of life, and she talked on the theme to her

silent hearers with her usual masterful authority. When she had at last finished, and they rose to go, she added a piece of information. There was an "h" added to their surname. They were henceforth to be the Misses Payne-Town*sh*end and though the "h" was not to be pronounced, they must be careful to add it when they wrote their names, and they must correct people who misspelt their surname.

The change meant nothing to the two girls. Sissy accepted it as she accepted every edict from her mother—without argument. Charlotte tried to stifle her contempt; her conscience was complicated by a genuine sense of duty. Mary Susanna's words had sunk in. She must try, oh, she must *really* try not to be rebellious, to bow to properly constituted authority, and to order her thoughts into proper channels. Her mother was right: children owed their parents respect, devotion and obedience. Charlotte resolved to keep a watch on her tongue, and to try to be grateful to Providence for giving her such a good home and the privileges of her position.

But she could not, in spite of all her efforts, succeed in identifying her mother with Providence, which was what Mary Susanna had intended in her homily.

3

GROWING UP

$\overbrace{\hspace{4cm}}$

(1 8 7 4 – 1 8 7 7)

Charlotte had always liked reading French books, and at the age of seventeen she discovered Théophile Gautier. Here was someone very different from Racine, Corneille and the established classics which wrapped everything up in elegant language; here was a writer who put into plain words all her own hidden thoughts and longings. She had been aware of these longings ever since she had been thirteen or fourteen, and had always been half-ashamed, half-enthralled, by the amazing tides of ecstasy which had shaken her from time to time. Ever wary of her mother, schooled to repress the slightest show of emotion as being "unladylike," Charlotte had had to control her tempestuous feelings as well as she could.

Now she had found someone who seemed to know all about her. The last French governess had left *Mademoiselle de Maupin* behind, and the book was a revelation to the girl. She copied extracts into her private notebooks—not the schoolbooks which her mother scrutinized at intervals, but the commonplace books which were an outlet for her repressed rages. Angry diatribes against

"authority" were jumbled in with fragments of poetry, quotations
from the Bible, notes on her dogs, examples of peasant humour:

> *Coachman.* Which is the way to town?
> *Gosshoon.* The straight road.
> *Coachman.* Is there no turn?
> *Gosshoon.* Sure the road'll turn with you.

There was an anecdote told by one of her relations, who said the
last time he was at Clonmel Fair he could get nothing weighed at
any of the shops "as all the weights had been expended the night
before in a *fracas* between the downtrodden natives and the brutal
soldiery."

The extracts from *Mademoiselle de Maupin* were a startling
contrast to the rest.

"*I have been loved* . . . and the feeling is wonderfully sweet!
Lying awake in the darkness of the night, to be able to say—rising
upon one's elbow: 'Someone is thinking or dreaming of me; there
is one interested in my well-being; a movement of my eyes or of
my mouth makes the joy or sorrow of another human being; the
word I let fall carelessly is caught up with eagerness, meditated
and speculated upon for hours . . . my eyes are a horizon, my mouth
a paradise more longed for than the real one . . . were I in danger,
there is one who would interpose between the sword point and my
breast, sacrifice themselves for me!—this is worth much,' I hardly
know what there is in the world that one should desire before it."

Charlotte had found an ideal of romantic love. Gautier also set
down clearly what she already thought of men.

"Women have very little taste for dreamers, and always fancy
men who can put their thoughts into action. Obliged by their
education and social position to be silent and to wait, women
naturally prefer those who will come to them and speak out."

And again the hidden dream . . . "I loved neither this one nor
that one, but one whom I had never seen, and who must exist
somewhere, and one whom I shall find some day if it pleases God.
I know her every feature by heart, and when I find her I shall
know her well." Then came a passage which Charlotte knew well

to have some application to her own mental state. Gautier talked
of living much by himself, "the smallest details making themselves
of great importance, in a life as monotonous as mine is. I listen to
myself living and thinking: I hear the pulsations of my arteries, the
beating of my heart. By constantly poring over them I disentangle
my most fugitive ideas from the haze in which they float and I give
them shape and form. If I led a more active life, all these small
things would pass unnoticed, and I should not have time to look
at myself through a microscope, as I do now."

Charlotte was often intensely conscious of living much by herself, but she was not, in fact, leading a monotonous life. Her father
had asked her to be his secretary for a scheme in which he was
very interested, and which was to have unexpectedly important
results for herself.

Horace had long thought that something should be done about
building a railway for the small farmers in the district, to enable
them to get their produce to Cork market more quickly than by
the roundabout railway route via Skibbereen, which made the
journey sixty-three miles from Cork, whereas a branch railway
from Rosscarbery would cut it down to forty-four miles. Cork was
now a thriving small port. The early repressive trading laws had
been lifted and there was a flourishing export of dairy produce to
Britain and the Continent, which brought shipping into the harbour and prosperity to the city. The smallholders and farmers over
a wide radius round Cork loaded their donkey carts at dawn on
market days to get their butter and pig-meat to the stalls before
the provisions buyers and the ships' victuallers came along to spend
largely and give orders for the next time. Horace reckoned that if
the farmers in his own area could get to Cork in a reasonable time,
they would be encouraged to enlarge their holdings, sell more
produce and share in the new prosperity.

The best way to bring this about was to construct a light railway
which would serve Rosscarbery, Leape, Grand Union and other
villages east of Skibbereen. The line would be eight miles long
and on a broad gauge, so as to connect with the Clonakilty branch
of the Cork, Bandon and South Coast Railway system. Besides
opening up the land for cultivation, it would give employment to

a large and poor population. Such a scheme had, in fact, been proposed by a group of farsighted businessmen in Cork, who estimated that it would cost about £45,000, part of which could be raised by baronial guarantee, the rest coming from a Treasury grant and private subscription. Local landowners like Lord Carbery and Sir George Colthurst of Blarney Castle agreed that it was an excellent scheme, and were prepared to support it. The directors of the Cork, Bandon and South Coast Railway naturally opposed it, showing violent hostility from the beginning. The country people, they declared, had been going to Cork via Skibbereen for years: they were used to it, they all had friends in Skibbereen and liked going that way. Why, then, this nonsensical talk of another line? It was unwanted and unnecessary, and was bound to lead to the bankruptcy of all concerned.

The promoters of the scheme ignored the opposition. The firm of T. R. Wright, solicitors and land agents, wrote to Horace, saying that Lord Bandon and some of the other landed proprietors, through whose land the railway line would pass, had signed agreements accepting shares to the value of the land so taken. They added: "As you have evinced an interest in the success of the undertaking, I have been instructed by the promoters to acquaint you with the present position of the project, to be called the Clonakilty Extension Railway Company."

Horace replied offering to buy £200 worth of shares, and urged them to engage contractors as early as possible, when the bulk of the money was secured, so that the work could be started. He also undertook to get what support he could from the county, and to collect subscriptions.

Charlotte entered into the scheme with eager interest, copying the letters which her father sent to all his friends in the district. The promoters of the railway were trying to get a Bill for the scheme, and the directors of the existing Bandon line were, of course, opposing it at every step. Horace and his friends worked hard for months, but the opposition was too strong, and the scheme had to be set aside. Charlotte was bitterly disappointed. She had associated herself with the idea; she felt she had been doing something worth while for once, and a return to her everyday existence brought acute frustration. There seemed absolutely nothing for her to do except read, ride, and pay social calls under the strict supervision of her mother. Even if her sister had been a companion in the real sense of the word, the frustration would still have been there. Charlotte knew that she needed a definite occupation, and that there was no chance of getting one. She was one of the daughters at home, and so she would have to remain, idle, useless, until she met a "suitable" young man who would marry her, and she could be settled for life.

Mary Susanna was tired of the Clonakilty Railway, of Derry, of the country. She took a house in Cork. That provincial city could not, of course, compare with Dublin, but it was not a bad place. There were plenty of good families living in Cork. Officers from ships which put in at the port were invited to the houses of the gentry, and it was time for Charlotte and Sissy to be seen in the best society that the south of Ireland could afford.

Sissy, pretty and vivacious, attracted plenty of attention at the balls, assemblies and parties which they attended. Charlotte was not what one could call pretty, but she looked striking and unusual with her beautiful green eyes and abundant light-brown hair; she moved gracefully, and she could wear clothes with style. Their mother was lavish with money where clothes were concerned, and both girls were always exceedingly well dressed.

They had been taken to Cork on many occasions, but staying there for several weeks at a time was different. They were charmed by the lively little port. Sissy liked shopping with her mother, and could not have enough of social life; she was excited by the admiration she evoked. At plays given in the eighteenth-century opera house, at balls in the long drawing-rooms of the Georgian mansions, foreign young men in tight trousers and high-collared uniform jackets bowed over her hand and murmured compliments, while the Cork beaux, equally silver-tongued, competed for her smiles.

Charlotte, too, enjoyed a great deal of attention, but she could not be satisfied with compliments. There never seemed to be anyone at these affairs to whom she could talk, though she soon realized that, though she was not good-looking in the accepted sense, like Sissy, she possessed something—she did not know what—which

made men admire her, though in a different way. She calmly
accepted the fact that she was attractive. Her dancing partners,
escorts and riding companions left her in no doubt of that, but
she was too naïve to know that young men at a ball or a party
wanted to flirt. Charlotte had no talent for that game. She always
hoped that she would meet interesting new acquaintances, who
liked reading as much as she did, and who would be able to discuss
novels, and plays, and poems, and books of travel.

She especially hoped to meet people who were as interested in
religion as she was. Charlotte read all that she could find about
religion and history; she filled her private notebooks with studies
of vast historical eras, summaries of Egyptian history ranging from
the ancient King Menes to the last of the Seventeenth Dynasty
(the Pharaoh to whom Joseph was prime minister, as she wrote in
the margin); the outlines of French history from Charlemagne to
the nineteenth century, with much detail; and German history
from the tenth century, through the Thirty Years' War, to the War
of the Spanish Succession. These were not the kind of schoolgirl
exercises she had written for her governess, but elaborately set out
tables and synopses, as if she felt compelled to master every known
fact of every historical era.

It was no wonder that she could not find any young people of
her own tastes. Cork society talked about hunting, and the races,
and the prospects for the next season's shooting. When Charlotte
brought the conversation round to unsocial subjects like history,
there was a smiling pause, and she was adroitly led back to the
ever-popular topic of hunting, which she loved. It got about that
the elder Miss Payne-Townshend was delightful, but just a little
eccentric in conversation.

The town itself was a pleasant place, with its river and many
waterways, the tall Georgian houses adding dignity to the hilly
streets, and Shandon Tower rising imposingly above them. The
waterfronts were full of bustle; fishermen spread and tarred their
nets on the quays and called out to passing friends in soft, lilting
voices. And on Sunday it was a grand sight to watch the women
swinging by in their best shawls and multitudinous petticoats.
Charlotte liked, best of all, to pass along the harbour or riverside on

her way from a party at night, and see the riding lights of the ships rising and falling, their blurred red and gold reflections shimmering deep in the water.

Horace stayed in Cork for several days at a time, but he was always glad of an excuse to get back to Derry. Then Mary Susanna filled him with consternation by declaring that she was taking a house in Dublin. She had, in fact, already rented 25, Merrion Square South. The girls were not getting a proper chance in Cork. In Dublin they would be invited to the Castle, and so meet a far wider—and more important—set of people. It was her duty as a mother to give them every opportunity in life, was it not?

Charlotte and Sissy found Dublin stimulating. They were soon settled in Merrion Square, and at once people left cards, and Mary Susanna returned the calls, and invitations began to arrive in satisfying numbers. The Payne-Townshends were accepted into Dublin society as a matter of course. There were no fine distinctions of caste: the small middle class that existed was accepted as belonging to the upper stratum—or, if ignored, it was for personal reasons. In a country with two races and two religions, there were the Gentry and the People. The Duke of Leinster and Provost Mahaffy of Trinity, and Charlotte and Sissy and the doctor's daughters, were all equally the Gentry.

Mary Susanna, having a large income at her disposal, spent it generously and, as in Cork, bought her daughters the most fashionable clothes at the best shops. The coachman was fitted for a new livery, the brougham spruced up. The wealthy Cork family with the two charming daughters were asked everywhere. Mary Susanna was almost happy; here, at last, she and her girls were being properly appreciated.

There began a round of balls and dinner parties, commands to attend the Vice-Regal court, calls on new acquaintances, entertaining at Merrion Square. Charlotte and Sissy had many beaux, whose manners were more elaborate than those of the Cork young men, and their conversation more worldly. Everyone seemed to travel abroad, or to stay for long periods in London or on their English estates. The young men were gay and amusing, gallant and deferential, and they paid court to the Misses Payne-Townshends until at least one of them felt that she was living in a giddy whirl of pleasure. Sissy was an even greater success than she had been in Cork, and this was Dublin, second only to London! Mary Susanna was pleased.

Charlotte, too, was enjoying herself, but in her own way. She attracted plenty of attention with her unusual eyes and beautiful hair, and danced and dined and rode and went to the races with an ever-changing string of escorts. She was meeting people who, she hoped, might become more than acquaintances, but no friendships resulted. Apart from Lady Kingston, in Dublin for the season and now a long-standing friend of the family, Charlotte found that Dublin society women regarded her with tolerant amusement. She was always talking about books, they remarked to each other. One naturally read the latest novels, but Tennyson's *Princess?* And Hobbes—who was Hobbes? It was gently intimated to her that if so forceful an ingredient as learning must necessarily enter into conversation, it should be concealed by humour and mother wit. One should touch lightly on every subject and never appear to be much in earnest.

Charlotte was not, unfortunately, gifted with either humour or the native wit which sparkled on an Irishwoman's tongue. She had inherited the seriousness and high sense of purpose which had for generations been characteristic of the Townsends; and she possessed in good measure Mary Susanna's obstinacy and tenacity. Added to these were sensitiveness in an extreme degree, and a constant awareness that much that she could not understand lay under the careless surface of life.

She turned to men, who seemed to be more receptive than women when she talked of the things that seemed important to her. She had access to good libraries in Dublin, and as she spent most of her mornings reading, she had plenty to talk about when she went out into society. It did not occur to Charlotte that her partners at Dublin Castle balls or her neighbours at hunt suppers were perfectly ready to claim acquaintance with Edwin Arnold's poems, or the Gautama, or anyone else when in conversation with an attractive, wealthy young lady. She was surprised and puzzled that these conversations occasionally led to a proposal of marriage.

The first was from a callow young official attached to the Castle staff, who promised to read any books she cared to suggest, and begged her to marry him though, as he said, he was not in a position to support her in the manner to which she had presumably been accustomed.

Charlotte prescribed a stiff course of reading, and was relieved when her mother announced that they were all going to London as soon as she could find a suitable house. She would have been less pleased if she had known that Mary Susanna had no intention of coming back to Ireland to live.

4

LONDON

(1877–1883)

Mary Susanna took a house in London—21, Queen's Gate—near Hyde Park. She was tired of exile in "that accursed country Ireland," she told her husband. They would keep Derry as their country house; after all, many people in England had estates in Ireland, and one could give house parties there in the hunting and shooting seasons. But they would have their permanent abode in London, and travel abroad. Willie Townshend, who also had an "h" to his name, one of Horace's kinsmen, was land agent for a number of estates in County Cork and would look after Derry. For her part, she was not going to live permanently in Ireland again.

Horace was really distressed, for he loved his home. He belonged to County Cork; his old friends were there, and all his close interests. It meant giving up his work on the Bench and his personal contacts with the tenants on his estate; it also meant that there would be no question of reopening the agitation for a branch railway line from Clonakilty, for he had, in the end, been the driving power behind the scheme. He tried to explain something of this to his wife, but Mary Susanna looked at him without comprehension. What did any of that matter? Willie was perfectly competent to manage the estate: they had a large fortune and two daughters to marry off. Horace must not be ridiculous.

A few months later Mary Susanna moved the family to London. The Queen's Gate house was not yet ready, and they stayed at Bailey's Hotel while it was being decorated and furnished. Mary Susanna had made many English acquaintances in Dublin, and by the time she moved into her own house, the name of Payne-Townshend was on the invitation lists of many prominent London hostesses. On March 21, 1878, Charlotte was presented at a Drawing Room by a friend of her mother's, Mrs. Adams.

She and Sissy rode in the Park every morning, accompanied their mother when she paid calls, went to dinner parties and the theatre, drove into the country, joined race-going friends for the Derby, helped to entertain at Queen's Gate. Charlotte also found herself acting as a buffer between her mother and the father who could not settle down in this alien atmosphere.

Horace had grown very quiet during the past few years. Unhappiness had shrivelled his gentleness into silence, with occasional outbursts of petulance, and he had developed a number of personal habits which were a constant irritation to his wife. He hummed below his breath; he drummed with his fingers on the arms of a chair. He was rather trying to live with—even Charlotte and Sissy found that, at times—because he had become slow and blundering about little things. And then his silences. Mary Susanna would rebuke him sharply for his dampening effect on the dinner table when they were entertaining guests. Horace had no small talk and was quite out of his depth, she said, when the conversation turned to anything but horses. She was quite wrong. Horace was a good judge of horseflesh and fond of all country pursuits, but he read widely and had a great many interests. As his wife never bothered to find out what he thought about anything, and snubbed him when he attempted to express any opinion contrary to her own, he had gradually ceased to take part in any kind of discussion when she was present.

Mary Susanna tried to goad him into "correct" manners, but

he simply withdrew into himself when he was surrounded by a crowd of chattering women and smooth-tongued men at his wife's At Homes. It was after one of these "days" that Mary Susanna said something which was to stay in Charlotte's memory, like a burr that she could not pluck out, for the rest of her life.

"Who could get into society dragging such an incubus as that?" Mary Susanna demanded of her daughters.

Sissy said nothing. Charlotte flamed into a violent fit of rage, which frightened her mother at first. There was a terrible scene, with Charlotte incoherent and Mary Susanna alternately storming at her and bursting into noisy tears. The scene went on and on; Sissy disappeared, leaving her sister white-faced and her mother red with astonished anger, both talking fast and furiously.

Charlotte could not afterwards remember all she said, but she had to face the desolate truth that there was no chance of her being able to leave home, to gain the freedom she craved. Even if it had not been for her father, she could not have gone. It was hopeless to be a girl. A son went out into the world; from his childhood he had the consolation of knowing that he would ultimately leave home and make a place for himself. But a girl was supposed to live at home until she married. And if she didn't marry? She would have to go on living at home always, and "make herself useful"— though she did not have the consolation and satisfaction of doing useful work. "Useful" in this sense meant being in constant attendance on her mother, of spending her entire life following the pattern set by "Society": the Season in London, autumn in the country, travelling abroad, travelling at home, meeting the same people, saying the same things with slight variations over and over again.

The prospect appalled her, but there was no way out of the situation. Her conscience, the sense of duty which had always been her bane, were as strong as ever. Parents were the natural guardians of their children. Charlotte was turned twenty, but in her mother's eyes, unmarried daughters were still children. Unless she married, she would not be able to get away from this dreadful existence.

She had, however, no intention of marrying. The very idea filled her with horror. She had not thought it out: she knew, quite simply, that she did not want to bind herself to live with anybody. Her father's life with her mother was a daily lesson in the miseries of that particular kind of bondage. No, she would not escape into marriage. She would have to wait. After all—people were not immortal.

It had certainly been a wise move to take a house in London, reflected Mary Susanna contentedly. How agreeable people were here, to be sure. It gave her all the pleasure in the world to see her girls making such a success in society; even Charlotte, with her tiresome cleverness, and her dance card filled up within minutes of her arrival at a ball. If only she did not spend her time reading so much during the day!

Then Charlotte, unpredictable as usual, decided, of all things, to learn First Aid. Mary Susanna became irritated almost beyond words. Why First Aid? A well-brought-up young lady learning about things like that! It was totally unnecessary to know more than one need about one's body. That was a doctor's business.

"Please don't be absurd, mother." Charlotte, too, could be irritated. "I should like to *be* a doctor, but as that is out of the question, I suppose, I will learn First Aid."

It was really difficult to know *what* to say to such foolishness. In the end, Mary Susanna found plenty to say, but Charlotte continued with the first-aid lessons.

They spent Christmas at Derry, entertaining a house party which included an exceedingly eligible young man of family, Lord Oranmore, whom they had met several times at country houses.

"*Saw much of Lord Oranmore,*" noted Charlotte coolly in her Annuary. His name did not appear again.

They returned to London, where Charlotte was bridesmaid at a friend's wedding, made Mrs. Cavendish Bentinck's acquaintance, attended her first large London ball, and took the St. John's Ambulance Certificate of First Aid Qualification on June 21, 1880.

It was a gay London season that year. Charlotte was presented at a Royal Drawing Room, and enjoyed the experience. Dressed in the latest modes, the two Miss Payne-Townshends went everywhere and met everyone in the fashionable world. Their mother kept a sharp eye on the men-about-town whom they inevitably danced with at balls—after all, they were heiresses—and realized with renewed chagrin that her elder daughter was quite capable of fending off fortune hunters on her own account. What was worse, she was obviously not in the least interested in matrimonially desirable young men. Even Sissy was behaving with extraordinary demureness, considering her good looks. Sissy, in fact, while enjoying herself to the full, had no intention of marrying anyone unless she fell in love, and was beloved in return.

They went to Ireland in July, visited the Bandons at Castle Bernard, and spent a short time at Derry. Horace tried to pick up the threads of his old life, but it was not easy. Willie Townshend was managing everything efficiently, and the tenants, while friendly and effusive, did not seem to miss Horace unduly. The Clonakilty railway scheme was moribund and likely to remain so. He felt that he did not belong anywhere.

Back in London, they were at once caught up in the social merry-go-round. Balls and parties were enlivened by quite a number of officers from Camberley and Aldershot, and a great many engagements were announced during the autumn. Sissy had a pleasantly amusing time fending off proposals. Charlotte, too, managed to avoid situations which might lead to declarations, but an officer named Black had a short-circuit technique. He wrote to her from his club in Upper Brook Street:

"Dear Miss Townshend,
        "Having determined to propose to you, I shall use as few words as I can. So, will you marry me? I shall only add for the present,

                                        "Sincerely yours,
                                            "J. S. Black"

Charlotte replied by return of post, refusing him as gently as possible but making her decision definite. He wrote again on December 24, 1880:

"My dear Miss Townshend,

"I cannot help replying to you only to say how very much I appreciate your very kind note. It only has shown me I have judged you rightly when I thought you were sincere and straight.

"Wishing you a merry Christmas and many happy New Years,
"I am,
"Yours most sincerely,
"J. S. Black"

The Payne-Townshends paid a round of visits in January, the girls going to a ball at Badminton and staying at Alderley. Meanwhile, Charlotte was turning a rejected lover into a friend. Late in February J. S. Black wrote:

"I'm going to take you at your word in being my most sincere friend, and in accordance with your wishes, I have prohibited myself to think myself any more. Your letter has convinced me of your sincerity and consideration. Owing to a variety of circumstances I am comparatively friendless, but I hope to secure a friend by explaining matters. Till within the last few years, I generally eschewed ladies' society. Until quite recently, I never thought of being anything but a bachelor. I chose the method of writing to you because I thought it better for you. I have £170,000, and my father and grandfather were manufacturers. I mention this to justify my not mentioning it before because I knew you had ample means of ascertaining it, so that practically I have kept nothing secret. Especially proud as I am of my father, whom I never saw—he died when I was three—I can reconcile it with a clear appreciation of his being a sufficient reason alone for rejection, and I admire your tact in the matter, although I do not shut my eyes to the fact that there may have been many other reasons. I had no means of ascertaining anything concerning you so far as I could use my eyes. There were lots of rumours in Dublin when I was there which were various. There was tolerable general agreement enough, however, that £30,000 each was tied down on you and your sister. It was quite unnecessary to seek after this information, it was so often volunteered.

"If I ever can be of any service to you, please let me know. . . ."

Charlotte wrote back at once, telling him that her refusal had nothing whatever to do with their respective fortunes, and added:

"I like and esteem you, but I would be doing myself, and especially you, a great wrong if I married you without feeling a much stronger personal attachment. Cannot we be friends? I value my friends greatly, and would be happy to count you among them."

He wrote again saying that she was very generous and he would be proud to be her friend. He asked if she had read Buckle's *History* and *The New Republic*, and if she had ever seen Sothern act David Garrick.

Mary Susanna was seized with a perfect fury of visiting and travelling that year. They went to Ireland, and after a driving tour to Bantry and Killarney ended in a visit to Charlotte's cousin, Edith Somerville (later to be known as the half of a famous writing partnership, Somerville and Ross). After returning to London for a few days, they went over to Paris for the French Exhibition, stayed for a short time, and then divided for more travelling, Mary Susanna and Sissy going on to Nice, and Charlotte and her father turning westwards for Bordeaux, Arcachon, Bayonne, Pau, Biarritz, San Sebastián and Madrid. After a further tour through Córdoba, Seville and Gibraltar, they rejoined the others at Cannes, where they spent Christmas, and moved on to Nice at the end of the year.

Charlotte and her father had not often been together for any length of time, and they would have enjoyed their tour if Horace had felt well. He was a prey to a succession of small ailments, suffered from rheumatism, and was inclined to be a little difficult. Charlotte, too, was unwell; she had developed an abscess in her ear, and though they both went sightseeing in the places they passed through, they were glad to get back to the South of France, where they could consult doctors whom they knew.

Back in London, Charlotte felt better, though her father was still a little ill. At the end of the month they were in Dublin, returned home in March, during which Charlotte and Sissy attended another Royal Drawing Room, went to balls, and left London again for Derry. They did not stay long, as Mary Susanna thought a tour of the north of the country would be agreeable. They returned to Derry, and as Mary Susanna appeared resigned to a stay of some

weeks, Horace thankfully took up his country life. By the end of
November she was restless, and the family went to Castle Bernard on
a prolonged visit. Charlotte and Sissy found this sojourn very pleasant, as there was ice on the ponds and the young party at the Castle
went out skating.

They were in London for Christmas, and at once Mary Susanna
began entertaining. She had made many acquaintances during the
past year, and she was a good hostess. Mrs. Cavendish Bentinck
was friendly, and obviously liked Charlotte, who went to her house
a great deal. Mary Susanna noted with satisfaction that both her
daughters were being invited by the kind of people she had long
wanted them to meet. She looked forward to the future with confidence.

In July, Horace astonished her with a suggestion on his own
account. He had always desired to see something of Scotland, and
he proposed making a tour there—with Lottie. He felt tolerably
well, and if Lottie cared to go, he would be pleased. Charlotte was
more than pleased. She saw little of her father nowadays, he kept
so much in the background, and this was an idea which greatly
appealed to her. Mary Susanna could hardly think of objections,
and they made their preparations as quickly as possible and set off
by train for Glasgow in August.

Charlotte kept a daily account of their journey. On the second
day she wrote from Glasgow:

"The most enthusiastic of its lovers, the most evident of its
friends, could never call Glasgow a nice place. The streets are
irregular and badly built, the houses patchy and tumbledown. . . .
Glasgow is so *dirty* . . . it is as if the smuts and smoke of long ages
had accumulated and formed a layer everywhere . . . had established
itself there for ever by right of custom. But . . . there is energy in
Glasgow and life and work of earnest purpose. It is only the work
and purpose of making money, I am sure, but still it is work and so
far ennobling. These great shipbuilding yards along the Clyde—
what wonderful places they are. Messrs. John Elder are building a
great steam yacht, a floating palace, for the Emperor of Russia. . . .
There are officers' rooms and rooms for the Grand Duke and the
Emperor's own rooms. There are dining saloons and reception

saloons . . . and the whole when it is finished is to cost a million and a half of money! A million and a half to enable a poor trembling monarch to get out of the reach of the sound of the voices of his beloved subjects who, it appears, are beginning to tell him too loudly and importunately for his nerves to stand it any longer, that they are tired of starving, that they have lain down long enough for him to walk over them, and that at last a great, patient, silent people is going to rise and shake itself free of the fetters that his ancestors and his class have cast around it. The Emperor does not like hearing this, so he is spending a million and a half of money to get out of reach of it for a bit. Marie Antoinette took the opposite course when she refused to take the famous diamond necklace. 'France wanted the money,' she said—but that did not save her neck from the scaffold, so perhaps the Emperor is right, 'quien sabe.'

"Pah! Let me get away from it all, the noise of the hammers, the snorting of the steam engines, the ring of the iron, the smell of the pitch."

They travelled out to Loch Katrine, and on their return to Glasgow saw bills announcing Mr. and Mrs. Kendal were to be seen in *The Lady of Lyons,* so they dined and took a hansom cab to the Gaiety Theatre. Charlotte had long been a theatre-goer, and she knew the play; she could appreciate all the finer points of the acting, though she feared Mr. Hare, the chief supporting player, was unsure of his part and was always on the verge of being prompted.

The following day they went by train and steamer to Wemyss Bay, "a pretty watering place with a large pier," touched at Rothesay, travelled on through the Kyles of Bute and on to Loch Fyne. Inverary pleased them, though the imposing pile of the castle was ruined for Charlotte by "monstrosities of towers at each corner."

The tour went on, full of happiness for them both. Horace felt well, and lost his glassy reserve, and was again the affectionate, charming companion of her girlhood. The change in him was extraordinary. There was no one to nag him, no prohibitions or objections to this or to that; they had, for a short space, a freedom which was something tangible, to be savoured and enjoyed. Loyalty forbade them discussing Mary Susanna: they never mentioned her, except when Horace said:

"I will write to your mother to tell her we are safe and well."

They travelled over the mountains, across the promontory to Loch Long, by the "Scotch coach"—not at all a comfortable vehicle. Four or five good-sized benches were set on top of a long wooden box on wheels; the box was for the luggage, the benches for the passengers. Charlotte had the box seat in a corner beside the driver, a gorgeous person in a scarlet coat and beaver hat. She wrote "I had to cling on by my eyelids." She noticed everything as the coach sped along: the mountain lochans, the houses with their fine gardens and plantations, the hills which were neither purple, nor mauve, nor lavender, nor blue, but just *heather* colour. On another day they went again to Loch Katrine, where they spent the day sitting in the heather reading *The Lady of the Lake*.

Charlotte noted the progress of their journey sedately enough in her journal, until she saw the mighty head of Ben Lomond towering high above his surroundings, and then she burst into rolling prose.

"Ben Lomond is a truly *Scotch* mountain, with a great broad crown and long, heaving, swelling sides, bare of trees except for a fringe round his base finishing it off neatly before it drops into the water which kisses his feet with bright gleams of rippling laughter. . . . And the clouds which are flying fast before the bright summer breeze throw dark passing shadows upon his broad breast and on the sides of the clefts where the winter torrents descend, the grass sparkles a vivid emerald green, softening itself again into a wilderness of fragrant heather on the heights where his rocky ribs are more sparsely covered. Stately Ben Lomond, I would that I might live in your shadow and gaze up at your solemn head, until some of your lofty dignity and calm, patient strength should pass into me also and remain with me for ever."

Horace would have understood the deep misery below the undisciplined emotionalism if he had been able to read these outpourings. But Charlotte told no one of the journal which she wrote secretly every night.

They went to Oban and Callander, found "Scotch rain and weather in general" very trying, travelled in a cockleshell of a steamer up Loch Etive and saw Glencoe on a wild day which seemed to Charlotte to be entirely suitable to the scene. Dunkeld, Blair Atholl, Inverness, where "the only thing of any interest is its cemetery, which is curious and picturesque in its own way." Next came Aberdeen, and Ballater, with a not-enthusiastic look at Balmoral Castle; Charlotte found the central tower out of keeping with the long, low wings.

After a journey south by Durham, Scarborough, York and Lincoln, Charlotte and Horace reached Cheltenham at the end of September, and joined Mary Susanna and Sissy, who were staying there. They heard that fever had broken out at Derry, and Horace at once insisted on going to Ireland. Mary Susanna naturally objected, but for once Horace had his way, and they crossed to Dublin a few days later. Mrs. Townshend firmly took her daughters to Mitchelstown, and Horace went to Derry. The fever in the neighbourhood had somewhat abated, and there was nothing much he could do for anyone, but it was good to be in his own home again, catch up with the news, discuss estate matters with Willie and see his neighbours.

He was not left long at Derry. Before the month was out, Mary Susanna required him to accompany her and the girls to France, and Horace returned to England; the others were already at Cheltenham and they would all meet in London. Horace was tired. He felt vaguely ill: he had been feeling like that for a long time. The long holiday in Scotland had been a wonderful tonic, but now he was back in a curious twilight world where nobody was ever at rest. They were not having an interesting tour, such as he and Lottie had enjoyed: they were simply not *still*. They could not remain in one place for more than a few weeks at a time. Horace had been caught up on this extraordinary moving-belt of existence, and he could not stop himself. He was tired. He was tired.

The family stayed for a brief space at their house in Queen's Gate, and went over to Paris at the end of November. Four days later they were in Nice, where they found friends who persuaded them to remain until the middle of the month. But Mary Susanna liked being on the move—whom might they not meet at the next place? They went on to Bordighera, and Genoa, and Florence. Mary Susanna learned that there was "quite a good set of people" newly arrived in Nice, and she decided to return there, but they did not get farther than Genoa, as Horace developed a sharp attack of rheumatism.

Mary Susanna was always unexpectedly kind when Horace was ill. She railed at him with unceasing vigour when he did something which displeased her, but she possessed a streak of tenderness which was brought out when those nearest to her were really laid low. She at once found a doctor, and stayed uncomplainingly in Genoa until Horace was pronounced well enough to travel. It was then too late to catch up with the good set of people, and they returned to England.

5

HEIRESS

(1883–1885)

The years settled down to a pattern which became one enormous, variegated treadmill. The Season—balls—the opera—more balls— country houses—Cork, a Drawing Room at Dublin Castle— Mitchelstown—Mount Henry—Cheltenham—the Continent. Back to London and a short stay at "home" in Queen's Gate, then the Continent again. Ireland, and a fleeting visit to Derry, a longer one to Cork City. Dublin—Mitchelstown—Mount Henry—Dublin —Cheltenham and London. The Continent: London: the Continent: London. And the Season again.

Sometimes Horace remained behind, or went to Derry, but usually he accompanied his wife and daughters on the treadmill. He now had a respectable number of ailments, but as they were small ones, Mary Susanna was not sympathetic. What he needed, she declared, was change. Change of air, change of scene, change of society. If only he would acquire a modicum of—she could never find the word to express exactly what she meant. He lacked polish. He lacked presence. He lacked so much of the top dressing which impressed Mrs. Payne-Townshend in her friends' husbands that she was constantly ashamed of him. Here they were, wealthy, well launched in the best circles, and her husband must remain a country squire, and Irish at that. It was maddening.

She did not trouble to hide her feelings when they were alone. Charlotte and Sissy did not, of course, count—and the scenes which had embittered their early years began again, though in a different form. Before, Mary Susanna had demanded changes in their way of life which Horace, however reluctantly, had been able to accomplish. Now, she was asking him to do something that was quite impossible to the gentle, weak man: she was demanding that he should change his nature. He could only stand and listen, his head averted, his innate courtesy preventing him from turning and walking out of the room.

Charlotte found it increasingly wearing to stand up to her mother herself. She and her sister thankfully grasped every chance to visit people: every invitation was accepted. The continual travel on the Continent was a relief, too. Their mother was always at her best when staying at a palatial foreign hotel, greeting people she knew or making desirable fresh acquaintances.

The two girls now had other interests, too. Sissy had met a soldier, Hugh Cecil Cholmondeley, who had made an impression on her. He was a captain in the Rifle Brigade, tall, moderately good-looking, with a relaxed manner and not much to say for himself. True, he had no title, nor the prospects of one, but he was an officer and a gentleman, and—well, Sissy liked him very much. The fact that he had managed to be in several country house gatherings at the same time as herself indicated that he was not unaware of her existence.

Charlotte had acquired quite a number of men friends. In 1884, at the age of twenty-seven, she was conducting a regular correspondence with several of them: a mixture of gossip, political comment, ideas about books and religion and anything else that came into their minds. They found her a great deal more intelligent than most of the women they met on the social round, and it was plain that she was not husband hunting—quite the contrary. She liked men, and she preferred men friends.

One whom she liked best was Arthur Smith Barry, a barrister

whom she had got to know at the time of the Clonakilty business,
as he had land which adjoined the proposed railway line. His Irish
home was Fota, near the city of Cork; he was a Member of Parliament and possessed more than one English country house in the
Shires. Smith Barry admired Charlotte's forthright character,
though he found her ideas on Irish politics foolishly revolutionary.
Charlotte knew quite well that he was very much on the side of
the landowners in the perpetual tug-of-war over the Land Acts, but
she hoped to convert him one day to her own point of view. A man
as influential as Smith Barry would be able to make an impression
on members of the Government, if he were so minded. But this was
not the main reason why she valued his regular letters. They were
both very fond of riding and hunting and she liked to be kept informed of hunting affairs when she was travelling so much. On
Smith Barry's side, he was married, and there was no fear of entanglements; their friendship was refreshingly platonic.

Then there was Count Frederik Wilhelm Sponnek, who was
Secretary to the Danish Legation in London. Charlotte had met
him at a diplomatic function, and they soon became friends.
Sponnek was a man of charming personality, and had had an
adventurous career. He was travelling in Germany when the
Franco-German War broke out, and his sympathies being with
France, managed to reach that country and join the French forces.
He fought in several battles and reached the rank of captain; then
he returned to Denmark and joined the Foreign Service, being
appointed in turn to Paris, Stockholm and London.

Charlotte was always attracted to men of action. She made no
secret of her admiration for the Dane's soldierly record, and accepted
his escort to balls, and the theatre, and excursions to the country.
Mary Susanna noted the friendship with approval. Something was
happening with Charlotte at last! And Sissy, too, was proceeding
with a very suitable friendship. Mary Susanna found Captain
Cholmondeley's position, prospects and person quite satisfactory.
Really, it was high time for a mother to be able to make an announcement; and *two* announcements would be better still. She
invited Cholmondeley and Count Sponnek to Queen's Gate as
often as the conventions allowed, and they always accepted.

Count Sponnek was an impressionable young man, and the elder Miss Payne-Townshend's unaffected pleasure in his company had the inevitable result. He fell in love with her. One day, in the drawing-room at Queen's Gate, he proposed to her. Charlotte was kindness itself. Her refusal was couched in gentle terms, and when he grew ardent and begged her to reconsider her decision, she said that it would be better if they did not meet again, and hoped that they would remain friends.

Count Sponnek rushed from the house in a highly emotional state. Charlotte was distressed. What a pity it was that she had decided not to marry. It was all rather sad. If anyone had told her that she found it all rather pleasant, too, she would have been shocked and indignant.

Charlotte got away to the Continent early that summer without her mother; Mrs. Payne-Townshend was remaining in London to chaperon her younger daughter, sure that there would be at least *one* announcement to make presently. Horace and Charlotte went to Paris, taking with them their kinswoman from Drishane, Edith Somerville. Edith was a highly individual creature, bluff and lively and a good companion. In Paris, she persuaded Charlotte to go with her to a palmist, M. Desbarolles, to have their hands read. Horace did not care for the idea, but Charlotte, who had always been interested in the occult, insisted on going, and she was given a written analysis of the lines of her hand:

Much to see in your hand, love art, sentiment, colour . . . memory for figures and languages—is not idle, likes travel. Causality—likes reasons for things . . . judges by impressions, is a little susceptible. A little passionate. Too much imagination, too much taste for occult sciences . . . very impressionable, always some little trouble and never quite happy. Little imaginary troubles, very nerveuse. . . .

Girdle of Venus gives ideality . . . and susceptibility to falling in love. Pains in her back . . . loves the sea . . . Marriage of love with a distinguished person, long life. Loves distinguished persons, and wide search for distinction in herself or husband. Exposed to much love . . .

It was, in fact, a remarkable reading of character together with power of prophecy, whether M. Desbarolles saw it all in her hand or not.

They went on to Dijon, Nice, Turin, Milan, Lugano and Bâle, returning to London by the late spring. Charlotte found letters from Arthur Smith Barry, written from Compton Verney, in Warwickshire.

"I am very much distressed to find that you have left the country and that I have thus lost the chance of seeing you again: no doubt you are enchanted at finding yourself in the Sunny South and basking among the palms and orange groves. . . . Hunting is nearly over, indeed this is the last week; foxes are getting scarce and the ground is becoming hard. . . . A beautiful place, a very pretty country, but a most dismal neighbourhood it always seems to me, the natives having no idea whatever beyond hunting, racing and pigeon and rabbit shooting. They are not extraordinarily good even at these pursuits: a friend of mine who used to come down here said that the whole intellect of Warwickshire had been exhausted in the production of one man, as since Shakespeare's day there had never been a native of the county who was not next door to an idiot; without going so far as my friend it has always struck me that there was a good deal of truth in his observation. . . . It seems as if one's head was full of nothing but hunting, Egyptian politics and the Liverpool steeplechase, all mixed up together; to correct this I have been reading Max Müller's Lectures on the Origin and Growth of Religion, which exercises a great charm over me as all M.M.'s writings do. I think he rides the dawn and storm-cloud hobby a little hard, but there is a catholicity about his views upon the great religious growths which to me commends them intensely."

Charlotte also heard a piece of news which caused her to sit down at once and write to Count Frederik Wilhelm Sponnek. He had been posted to St. Petersburg, and had given no indication that he intended to say good-bye to her. Surely there were no unkind feelings between them? Charlotte reproached him. A reply came.

"My dear Friend Charlotte,
      "You once allowed me to call you so. God bless you for your kind words. Why should there be any unkind feelings between us? Did we not both do our duty when we parted? Until now I have thought it better for us not to meet, but I, too, wish to say good-bye to you before I leave England, perhaps for ever."

He called the next day, made his adieux to Mrs. Payne-Townshend and her daughters with formal correctness, bowed again to Charlotte, and was gone. Mrs. Payne-Townshend made no comment, nor did she ever refer to him again. She turned with relief to the task of chaperoning her younger, less difficult daughter.

The family went to Ireland at the end of the Season, first to Derry, and later on to Mitchelstown, where Lady Kingston had a large house party which included Hugh Cholmondeley. Sissy became engaged to him there. Everyone was delighted. Sissy herself was radiant; it was clear to all eyes that here was a love match, and that the young people were set for true happiness. Charlotte was conscious of an extraordinary medley of sensations—relief that Sissy was "all right," together with a curious kind of envy of her sister who was getting away from home for good.

The round of visits continued. They stayed at Castle Bernard with the Bandons and went on to the Castletons; then Dublin for Vice-Regal balls, and a round of parties for Sissy and Hugh, returning to London for Christmas.

The New Year should have begun happily, for Mary Susanna was in excellent spirits and Sissy full of gaiety and excitement, preparing for her wedding. Charlotte filled her days riding in the Park, writing to distant friends and seeing others in London, reading for hours at a time, helping with all the paraphernalia attendant on a fashionable wedding. But there was a shadow on them all. Horace was ill. He could not tell what was the matter with him, and the doctors were unable to make a specific diagnosis beyond saying that it was internal trouble. Horace lay in bed, saying little, growing weaker every day. It was incredible to them all. It was as if he were fading and disappearing: ceasing to be.

Charlotte stayed in his room with the nurse, watching, waiting with a kind of stony sorrow for the end. Horace died at the beginning of February. Even Mary Susanna was stunned. He had often been ill, but apart from a few attacks of rheumatic trouble, never seriously so. She could not believe that a man in the prime of life could go out like—like a candle. It was incredible.

Her elder daughter did not find it incredible. She looked back along the procession of the years, and it seemed to her that her father had been slowly killed, little by little. Not the physical man, but the *essential* man. He had been separated from all his dearest interests, taken from the friends he knew, constantly snubbed and corrected. When he had gone back to Derry, it had been as a stranger—a guest; it was now Willie Townshend's home in all but name and title. Charlotte was too numb to feel anger, but her mind was very clear, and she knew that she had found the truth about her father's death. He had not wanted to live any more, and so he had died.

Horace was buried at Edstaston, Mary Susanna's old home in Shropshire, which she now owned. They returned to London to complete preparations for Sissy's wedding; it had been Horace's wish that this should not be postponed. Sissy and Hugh were married in March, and after a short honeymoon went to live at Aldershot. Charlotte visited them there the following month, before going off to the Continent with her mother and a cousin, Ethel Webb.

"Paris, Cannes, Nice, Genoa, Milan: over the Simplon Pass to Bex, on to Geneva, back in London in July. Off again to Edstaston, then to Ireland. Mount Henry and Mitchelstown."

Charlotte noted down the places, the dates, brief notes of the people she met. She had a bad fall while out hunting in November, and took some weeks to recover. Nothing seemed to matter: nothing was important. A letter came from St. Petersburg, from Count Sponnek; a long chatty missive in which he talked about life at the Russian court. He sounded very cheerful. Charlotte wrote back, saying how pleased she was to hear from him, and he soon wrote again.

"Have you seen my former Minister and his new wife since they married? He became . . . nervous and irritable in consequence of the great change in his life. Marry for money? Never, never, never! A married man's place is Number One. A man who accepts another number is not a man!"

Charlotte somehow felt pensive at these letters. He had really been a remarkably agreeable man. On an impulse she wrote to him once more, recalling to his mind some of the pleasant times they had had together. Count Sponnek replied to this letter some weeks later.

"My dear Miss Townshend,

"Do I remember? Certainly I do. Both Richmond and the Almack ball, and Howbery and the rest. But it is better not to stop too long among these shadows of the past. My dear Charlotte, when I left you that day in Queen's Gate, it required all a man's courage to keep me straight. . . ."

And then he told Charlotte that he was going to marry his little cousin, whom he was sure his dear friend would love. This lady was the Countess Anna Sophie Brockenhuus-Schack, an extremely suitable match from every point of view. He added: "It seems as if the sun were beginning to shine for me again after these long dark years of the past. Do let me hear a kind word from you. . . . I hope you will believe me to be in the future, as I was in the past, Most Sincerely yours, F. W. Sponnek."

Charlotte wrote him a short note of congratulation, and there the correspondence ended.

Horace's will was proved later in the year. He left rents on his lands to his wife, Mary Susanna Payne-Townsend, for life, and afterwards to his elder daughter, Charlotte Payne-Townsend and her sister Mary Stewart Payne-Townsend; shares in Imperial Continental Gas Association, the National Provincial Bank, General Steam Navigation Company, East London Water Works, North Eastern Railway. There were leases of lands at Derry and in other parts of Ireland, property in King Street in the City of London, shares in various companies, a freehold farm he had bought at Wem, in Shropshire: all of which went to Mary Susanna for life. After her death, his two daughters were to share equally in the estate.

The will was clear and, to some extent, illuminating. Horace had spelled his surname throughout the document without an "h."

6

SUITORS AND OTHERS

(1885–1887)

Heiresses, Mary Susanna averred, had always to be careful. Fortune hunters abounded in Society, and it needed constant vigilance to make sure that one's daughters did not meet them too often—unless, of course, they were titled. Mary Susanna was shrewd and realistic about the men who paid court to Charlotte, but she was also worried. Charlotte calmly admitted that she was carrying on correspondence with a number of men, all undoubtedly eligible, and that they were simply friends and nothing more. Why write, in that case? Mary Susanna could not understand it at all, and was unfailingly exasperated whenever the subject came up, especially as Charlotte never showed her any of the letters.

David Finch Hatton was one of Charlotte's most regular correspondents. She had met him at Irish country houses on several occasions, and they had become friends through their mutual love of horses. Finch Hatton was a good-looking, straightforward young man, and like many Irishmen of that time had decided to go to America to try his fortune. It was the period of the great cattle boom; the Union Pacific Railway had reached the mountains and the Indian wars had come to an end, though sporadic fighting still occurred. There were vast numbers of wild horses to be rounded up and broken in, and Irishmen—who understood horses better than anyone in Europe, except perhaps the Hungarians—went out to the American West for a few years, worked long and strenuously, and either settled there or returned home with money. They formed partnerships of three or four young men of their own kind, and it was one of these which David Finch Hatton joined.

He asked Charlotte to write to him. He was already in love with her, but he felt he could not declare himself until he had made some kind of fortune. Charlotte promised to send him regular letters telling him about their circle of friends, the races, hunting, and other subjects of interest to them both, and she kept her word. Finch Hatton sent her long, descriptive accounts of his new life. In 1883 he wrote to her:

"In the Chihuahua Mountains . . . I found that the Apache Indians were on the warpath and had killed no end of people . . . I came down to Texas and am going South . . . I am going to buy a herd of horses and run them up North to Nebraska. This is a lovely country. I could not have believed that any country could be so beautiful . . . if you could only see the flowers—verbenas, geraniums, lilies, roses of all kinds. . . . I sleep out of doors every night. We always have to go armed, and never think of going anywhere without a rifle and revolver. The traders down here are nearly all men who are outlaws from other States, and come down here where there is virtually no law. . . ."

He asked for Charlotte's photograph, which she sent him, with a long letter and copies of the *Spectator*. He next wrote from Colorado, where he was staying for a time after having driven 500 horses 2,000 miles from Texas, through country full of marauding Indians. He had had the terrifying experience of a night stampede, but had not lost a single horse, and had had the satisfaction of making a great deal of money. Would Miss Payne-Townshend continue to write to him? He thought of her all the time.

A few months later Charlotte received the skin of a bear which he had shot in Wyoming, and he also sent her twelve dressed beaver skins. Charlotte acknowledged them with graceful thanks,

and went on writing him lengthy, friendly letters, sending books
and newspapers at intervals. She spent much of her leisure writing
to her men friends; it was the only intellectual activity, besides
reading, which she had.

One of her most delightful correspondents was Herbert Oakley,
a barrister, who had contracted tuberculosis. He had been a constant visitor at Queen's Gate, and Charlotte had formed a real
affection for him. Herbert Oakley was one of the few people who
understood her very well; he was interested in what she thought
and read, and in what she was trying to find in life—instead of becoming bemused by her fine eyes, with the idea of her fortune ever
at the back of the relationship. When his growing malady obliged
him to give up his practice and live abroad, they kept in touch by
frequent letters.

"Scandal," Oakley wrote from Arcachon, "is very rife in this
Lazaretto, as is usual amongst people who are defective in health or
reputation. If the lungs are not out of repair, the reputation is, and
when we pass one another in the street our eyes plainly ask 'I wonder what the dickens that person's come for?' If it turns out that we
are not invalids, then it becomes everyone's business to unearth the
secret of the past: for we are all very sure that no one comes for
pleasure. . . . I am taking advantage of my superabundant leisure
to dip deeply into French novels by way of gaining greater fluency
of expression. Some are . . . of the class which George Eliot speaks
of when she expresses the hope that there was some adequate reason why such trash should have ever been foisted on the public
and suspected that empty writing was the result of an empty
stomach. . . ."

When the Townshends travelled in France, Herbert Oakley
always tried to call on them, even if it meant going a considerable
distance. It was clear that his lungs were getting worse. He wrote
to Charlotte from Davos the following year:

"In spite of favouring sunshine, illness has made great raids on
our community, and haemorrhages have been distressingly common. But the death-rate is low: it seems difficult to die in this
mountain air. . . . We are apt to set solemnly to work at getting
well . . . and in this search after material and hygienic welfare we

are very prone to ignore our 'plot culture'! The loss of the Kapunda, the colliery accident, the Reichstag speeches, Riviera earthquakes, Debate of Address and Closure, all these avail not to raise our eyebrows a fraction of an inch. Perhaps the war scare is the sole topic that stirs our imagination or appeals to our feelings to any marked degree. And even in this case, we judge the whole question from our own small point of view, i.e. the fittest moment for departure in case of a declaration of war. The prospect of a carnage of nations —of an additional £100,000,000 to our National Debt and the possible re-carving of the map of Europe—weigh very little with us. . . ."

He was a realist, and he kept this lightness of touch to the end. Charlotte grieved deeply when he died.

David Finch Hatton returned from America, and called on Mrs. Payne-Townshend as soon as he possibly could. Charlotte had written dozens of letters to him; he had amassed a fortune and was full of hope. Charlotte greeted him warmly, but he had no opportunity of speaking to her alone. He watched her as she moved through the crowded drawing-room—it was Mrs. Payne-Townshend's At Home day—and thought how attractive she looked, her masses of light-brown hair twisted into a loose knot at the back of her head, her pale face calm and somehow very distinguished.

He went down to stay with his family at Brighton, and wrote to her.

"You will probably be very much surprised at hearing from me and at what I am going to say. If only I could have had one single opportunity of speaking to you in London I would have done so, but that opportunity never came. I am writing to ask you if you will marry me. Do not be angry with me. I know full well that I am not worthy even to speak to you; my only excuse is that I love you so deeply, so truly, with all my heart and soul and strength. . . . All through the years that I was in America I have been just as true and loyal in my love for you as if you had been there with me. God knows how I have striven to bury my love for you, but it is utterly impossible. I swear to you that you are the only one that I have ever loved or cared for. There is no one in the world that can ever be to me what you are. Do not blame me, do not be angry with me . . . I will wait so patiently if you will only give me a little hope. . . . Whatever happens, think always of me as your true and faithful friend."

It was hard to answer his letter, but Charlotte knew she must do so immediately.

"I, too, will be your true and faithful friend," she wrote. "But I cannot marry you, or anyone. I do not wish to marry. Do you feel it all so deeply? I do not wish to hurt you . . ."

He sent her a reply at once.

"Forgive me for writing once more to you. I cannot bear to let a day go by without thanking you for all your kind and tender words to me. . . . Of course I feel it all, could I otherwise. God only knows how much, but you have decided for the best. . . ."

Charlotte was sorry the friendship must end; she was always sorry. It was with some relief that she turned to Arthur Smith Barry's more prosaic, angry outpourings on the state of Ireland, especially now that the Land Acts were being implemented.

"It is terrible to think of the number of landowners who must inevitably be ruined," he wrote. "My own impression is, that in 10 or 20 years' time, nine-tenths of the houses in this country will be deserted, and their owners disappeared, and the property passed into the hands of the tenants."

Charlotte regretted, for the sake of her landowning friends, that this was bound to happen, but, she felt, it was time. High time.

By the following year, the tone of their letters had subtly changed, had become more intimate. Smith Barry's wife had died and he was left lonely, with a young daughter. He took long trips abroad—to the Azores, to Algiers—and wrote very long letters to Charlotte wherever she was, in England or Ireland or travelling on the Continent, where his letters followed her. She wrote lengthy letters in reply, telling him where she had been and what she had seen, the people she had met and the books she had been reading. When he returned from abroad, she wrote to say she would be glad to see him again, and he took that up.

"Thanks for your kind expression of satisfaction at my return, especially as you profess to hold adverse political views. I want to

talk to you upon that matter, as I venture to cherish a doubt as to
your really entertaining the principles of our political opponents."

He did not know Miss Payne-Townshend as well as he thought,
or he would have cherished no doubts on the matter. Charlotte's
sympathies had been with the Irish peasantry ever since she could
remember anything, and no amount of "talking" upon the matter
was likely to change her views now.

Arthur Smith Barry became more and more friendly. He had a
house in Wilton Crescent, and whenever he was in London he saw
a lot of the Payne-Townshends. He came to dinner, took Charlotte
to the theatre, accepted invitations to make up parties to balls.
Charlotte asked his daughter, Geraldine, and her governess to tea.
Mrs. Payne-Townshend became hopeful. True, Arthur Smith
Barry was a widower and there would be a stepchild. But Charlotte
was herself approaching thirty, and if she was going to marry *anyone*
—and here the eternal question mark reared itself. *Was* Charlotte
going to marry anyone?

Charlotte, in sober fact, was beginning to bore Smith Barry a
little. She was sending him books which went "to the root of things."
They contained chapters on Immortality, and Reward after Death,
and the Law of Absolute Negation. Smith Barry wrote that he
would not leave the latter book in Geraldine's way, as the food contained in it seemed better suited for older and more robust mental
appetites.

They saw little of each other now and presently the letters
thinned considerably. Smith Barry spent his time between Fota,
the house in Wilton Crescent, and his houses in the Shires; he
also went abroad frequently. Charlotte was hardly in one place for
more than a week or two at a time, except during the Season in
London. They had not corresponded for many months when she
went one day to a public meeting on the Irish question. She was
so indignant afterwards that she wrote to Smith Barry, making a
strong attack on the Unionists. She softened this a little by saying
it was a long time since he had written, and she wondered whether
he intended to end their pleasant association. Smith Barry replied:

"You have written me many charming letters during the years
we have known each other, and I can think of no reason why our

correspondence should now be abandoned. . . . I can assure you that our friendship, which is not of yesterday, is on my side an increasing and not a decreasing quantity. What have I said or done to make you think otherwise? . . . So you want to hear Father McFadden: he is an able man but like most of the honest Nationalists holds views which in practice it would be impossible to work out. . . ."

He was certainly dyed-in-the-wool. The correspondence lapsed once more. The next letter Charlotte received from him was sent on to Yorkshire, where she was staying at a country house. It described a week he had spent shooting, mentioned various mutual friends, and added:

"And now I have something to tell you—something which will make a very great change in my life, but, I hope, none in our friendship. I am going to be married. The lady is a widow and an American—Mrs. Arthur Post. You probably know her sister, Mrs. Adair, whom she somewhat resembles. She is very handsome and very charming, and will I feel sure make me a good wife and Geraldine a good stepmother."

Charlotte was glad that Arthur Smith Barry's solitary life was to become normal again, with a real home and a mother for Geraldine, but she did not think she could keep up a friendship with one who was so hard-bitten an opponent of all the forces of progress. She wrote congratulating him on his approaching marriage, and she did not write again.

7

YOUNG WOMAN ALONE

(1887—1894)

Mary Susanna insisted on spending the early part of 1887 on the Continent. There was no need to go to Derry, and London was almost "empty."

Charlotte was quite willing to travel; it was, in fact, the only way to make her life supportable. Existence was far worse now that Sissy was no longer there to take up part of her mother's attention. Mary Susanna still made scenes, still nagged, still broke into fretful tears at the slightest hint of criticism, or into stormy fits of temper at any real opposition to her whims. Charlotte found these scenes so nerve-racking that she tried to avoid all argument. She protected herself as best she could by silence, but sometimes her mother goaded her into angry speech, and then Mary Susanna wept and declared that she had ungrateful children, that she had sacrificed herself for years in vain, and that Charlotte was an unnatural woman not to try to get a husband.

There were times when Charlotte asked herself if indeed she was not as other women. She now had such a fierce hatred of the very idea of marriage that she did not attempt to hide her feelings.

Would her mother please cease from looking at every unattached man as a possible son-in-law? She had no desire whatever to marry! It took all her self-control not to tell Mary Susanna that the recollections of her childhood had made her firmly resolve never to marry and be the mother of a child who might suffer as she had suffered.

It was a relief to go to Shropshire after their return, to visit Sissy and Hugh; they now had a baby daughter, Cecily. Charlotte found her brother-in-law kind and tolerant; he sometimes reminded her of her father. But she never stayed at Edstaston for long, and was soon off to another country house, crossing to Ireland for the Punchestown Races, or going for a week or so to Lady Kingston at her castle of Mitchelstown.

Later in the summer, Charlotte was invited by friends to attend the Review at Aldershot, and there she met two men who were to force her, in turn, to reconsider her views on marriage. They were both soldiers, General Clery, and Major Hutton. The General was a reserved type of man, with very intelligent eyes which betokened an unusual character. Major Hutton had a direct, uninhibited approach when his interest was aroused, and he was interested in Charlotte within five minutes of being introduced to her at the Review. They were soon out riding together. When the day came for Charlotte to return to London, Major Hutton begged to be allowed to visit her at Queen's Gate. Charlotte assented, and in due course he came up to London and called.

He was a man of action. He called again—and again. One day when he came, he found that Mrs. Payne-Townshend was not at home, but Miss Payne-Townshend would receive him. Charlotte began, as usual, to talk vivaciously of what was going on in London and what she had been reading, but Major Hutton had no time to waste. He asked if he might escort her to the Park for a walk—it was clear he did not wish her mother to interrupt them. When they reached a shady avenue running northwards from the Row, he took her hand and asked her to marry him.

For a few minutes, Charlotte was nonplussed, but her first instinct was to save his pride, and in the friendliest possible way she disengaged herself and said that, very regretfully, the answer had to be "No." They walked back to Queen's Gate, and Major Hutton took his leave.

It was by no means the end of the affair. He began to write to her. At first he said nothing of what had passed between them; he wrote about the political situation on the Continent, and of his promotion to be commandant of a new regiment of Mounted Infantry, with the rank of colonel. Charlotte sent him a short note of congratulation. Hutton now renewed his suit by letter.

". . . I have thought almost constantly of our last meeting at Queen's Gate. The recollection of that sad afternoon is ineffaceable, and all my life through I can never forget the agony of the half hour after I left you at the door of your home."

Charlotte wrote him a long letter. She tried to put down some of her innermost feelings, but she could not. How difficult to make anyone understand! The words came out at last, stiff and uncompromising.

"I have reluctantly arrived at the conclusion that we are not sufficiently suited to one another to make it wise that we should be more than friends."

She blamed herself for encouraging him, though she knew that she had not done so deliberately. Hutton wrote his last letter to her with strong feeling.

"You need, my dear Miss Payne-Townshend, accuse yourself of nothing as far as I am concerned. . . . It was the instinctive knowledge of your power and grasp of mind which fascinated me from the first. I felt that I had at last met the woman who could exert a lasting influence for good over my life . . . I have yearned for a woman to whom I could look for sympathy and help in the long continued battle of life—one who could fathom my thoughts and understand my ambitions. This is the phantom I have followed and have not secured. I know that I possess many qualities which cause men to succeed in life—an instinctive power over men, a strength of will which seems to make the impossible possible, an impetuosity which sees no difficulties, brooks no hindrance. Without a personal ambition, something (is it a phantom?) seems to beckon me forward. Can you wonder when thrown into your society I felt as if, like Edgar Poe's knight, I had found a kindred shadow . . ."

Early the following year, Mary Susanna fell ill with double pneumonia, and was in bed for some weeks, with nurses in attendance. Sissy and Hugh came down to visit her, and after they had gone, Charlotte made a determined attempt to overcome her intense dislike of her mother. It was a hatred which had never abated from her earliest years, and it frightened her. She possessed a sensitiveness about family relationships, inherited from her forebears, and though she longed to be free, she yet feared that her "bad thoughts" would have some evil psychic effects on the sick woman.

Mary Susanna recovered, and Charlotte took her over to Derry for convalescence. While she was there she found that there had been renewed interest in the Clonakilty railway. She had not forgotten her father's great desire to see the railway built; the scheme had been kept alive by some of his friends. Now that Charlotte was likely to be at Derry for some time, she determined to throw all her energies into rallying support for the proposed railway. She went to see Willie Townshend, and after some discussion, her cousin wrote a letter which was likely to carry weight:

"1 December 1890

"As a land agent in West Cork representing nine different landlords I am strongly in favour of the proposed line from Clonakilty to Glandore. In the first place, if begun at once, it would give plenty of employment during the coming winter. Then it would open up a large country as yet not within railway communications. It would afford a quicker market and better prices for the large quantities of fish brought into Glandore harbour. It would enable us . . . to undersell the Welsh slate in Cork and thereby encourage home manufacture. In fact if begun at once it would largely benefit the peace and prosperity of the country and I am convinced that if the Chief Secretary[1] had only come as far as West Cork on his travels he would at once order the line to be begun.

"William Tower Townshend"

Charlotte also wrote to George Colthurst, asking him to join a deputation to Dublin Castle. He replied that he was unable to go to Dublin, but he supported the scheme wholeheartedly.

[1] The Chief Secretary for Ireland was A. J. Balfour.

"You cannot too strongly dwell on the enormous advantages that accrue to any large agricultural district from the establishment of railway communications . . . enabling them by reducing the cost of feeding stuffs to embark in that branch of agriculture for which the mild and equable climate of the South West seaboard of Ireland is so peculiarly adapted, namely that of winter dairying and early vegetable raising. . . . I must instance the result of the opening of the Cork-Coachford Light Railway Co. In the district of Coachford and Peake alone in three years from the opening of the line, the number of dairies had increased by 20 per cent and the farmers resident in that district have much embarked in winter dairying, thereby growing more roots and crops for winter feeding. . . ."

The Rector of Kilmacabea—her grandfather's old parish—wrote in the strongest manner advocating the scheme, on account of the great distress in that neighbourhood, owing to the failure of the potato crop. Charlotte knew what a failed crop meant. The people found themselves held more closely in the clutch of the gombeen man, that mixture of public-house owner and money-lender found in every village, fattening on the distress of the poverty-stricken and encouraging them to mortgage their future. She redoubled her efforts, determined to take the scheme to the highest quarters.

Her mother was angry at such a wasteful manner of spending time which should be devoted to society life. She had not given up hope of Charlotte's marrying, even though her elder daughter was now thirty-three years old. Mary Susanna still could not understand the girl. Charlotte had always refused to discuss her men friends, and took no notice of hints, but Mrs. Townshend was sure her daughter had received more than one proposal of marriage. It was exasperating in the extreme to meet with such obstinacy, when all that Mary Susanna wished—the perfectly normal wish of any mother—was to see her daughter married. And now this Clonakilty business. What possible concern was it of theirs? It had kept Horace occupied, which had been a relief at the time, but—Charlotte! It was so unladylike to meddle in that kind of thing. She would speak to the girl.

It was, however, extremely difficult to "speak" to her daughter. At thirty-three Charlotte was a poised, self-collected, rather formidable young woman, with a mind of her own, and a private income which enabled her to do what she liked and go where she wished. She had no intention of discussing the Clonakilty railway with her mother. Mary Susanna had never shown the slightest sympathy with the country people, and it would be worse than useless, Charlotte well knew, to try to explain the strong impulse which was driving her to get the scheme put through. It was not only for her father's sake. Charlotte was subject to furious fits of rage when she came across injustice, and she was prepared to do anything to force the Cork and Bandon Railway Company to drop their opposition.

Thomas Wright, the solicitor and land agent in Clonakilty, was handling the legal and business side of the scheme and he wrote to Charlotte in December, 1890, to say that he was trying to see Mr. Balfour, who would be in Dublin the following week, and he would ask for government assistance. A few days later he wrote again, saying he had received a wire from Dublin that Mr. Balfour would see him in two days' time, and that he must be in a position to inform the Chief Secretary that the landlords would give the land free, that the local people would provide the necessary funds for an application to be made to a Grand Jury, and that the work would be started within a month.

Charlotte immediately sent off letters to her friends. Lord Carbery and others promised land, and a friend in Glandore wrote:

"My dear Lottie,
"The Dean will give £10—and I have got £2.12s. . . . Brien will give you I think £2. I asked him. Mr. Wright has sent a memorial to be signed by all the inhabitants, Glandore, Union Hall and Leape. I am getting it filled up. Father Fitzgerald will do all he can. The Dean says if you will work the Grand Jury through Mr. Pike and Sir G. Colthurst it will be done. . . . The distress is *very* great and Balfour's fund is of no use as there is no work for the men and no house where there is a man or boy able to work will get anything. Therefore work is an absolute necessity."

Towards the end of January, Charlotte heard from Mr. Wright that the Government proposed to grant special rates for money for relief works, and that if they could carry their application before the Grand Jury, they might get a reasonable guarantee that a portion of the relief money would be allocated to the Rosscarbery line. If they could get from the Grand Jury a guarantee for half the money, the Government might give them the other half.

Things were not going to be easy. Very large sums of money would be involved: £45,000–£50,000. The directors of the existing railway line were able to produce smallholders who said that in their opinion no other railway was necessary. Charlotte countered by calling on many of the small farmers and carefully collecting *their* opinions—all of which were enthusiastic for the project. Mr. Wright was cautious, and pointed out that the scheme might have to be dropped. Charlotte insisted that it must go on, at whatever cost, and the Bill be put before the Grand Jury. She also set down cogent reasons why government help should be forthcoming, making many pencilled notes before sending out further appeals for support. She thought it would be businesslike to be as objective as possible and to avoid emotional overtones.

"Reasons for thinking we ought to get our money.
1. We have done much for ourselves.
2. We proceeded when we might have been stopped.
3. We believe more money *must* be found for our railway. (Give reasons.)"

Besides Charlotte's advocacy of the scheme, she had the benefit of the advice of hard-headed businessmen who knew what she was up against. One of these was Mr. Shuldham, of Dunmanway, a commissioner of the peace:

"I . . . sympathise with you in your desire to get the railway you are interested in, but . . . I have had a good deal to do with railways and tramways in this country and endeavour, in forming a judgment in these matters, not to do so until I have heard everything connected with them fully discussed, as they are bound to be before the Grand Jury. There are often questions which require to be thoroughly threshed out, not only as regards the utility and paying prospects of a line, but as to whether people of a district (where a guarantee is expected) are for or against the line. . . . It would

strengthen the chances of your line being passed if influential people like Smith Barry and Bandon, who own large properties in the
district, would be examined in its favour, but . . . spare no pains to
have the line supported by the ratepayers."

Charlotte spared no pains. She again drove round the countryside, talking to the villagers and smallholders, pointing out the
benefits which would come with the new railway line. Her sincerity
and single-mindedness were obvious to all, and they promised to
back the petition to the Grand Jury as far as they could. Charlotte
reckoned that even if the opposition's bribes had some effect, she
would still be able to count on an appreciable number of farmers.
As to Mr. Shuldham's influential landowners, Arthur Smith Barry
would support her, she knew, in spite of her political opinions.
George Colthurst wrote in April, saying that if she raised the money
and got past the Privy Council, the Bandon company would "come
to terms re working the deal." The task before her was clear. She
worked ceaselessly, going to Dublin to talk to men she knew who
would have influence in the highest quarters, returning to Derry to
plan yet another round of the district, to keep the project in the
minds of the people who would benefit most by it. When she met
any of the opposition, she accused them in forthright terms of trying to thwart what they knew was a scheme to benefit the people.
She refused to recognize the fact that she lived in a hard economic
world, and that she could scarcely expect men who derived large
incomes from one railway line to be enthusiastic at the setting up of
a rival line.

Mary Susanna was glad to stay in Derry during the first two
months of 1891; she had recovered from her illness, but she felt
disinclined to travel far. Charlotte visited various friends, and returned home to help entertain a house party which included Lady
Bandon and the Colthursts. The solicitor from Cork also came, and
Mary Susanna thought it downright unnatural that her daughter
should spend so much time with George Colthurst and the solicitor,
working for hours each day on papers which would enable them to
put the fullest possible case before the Grand Jury in March. It
was no business for a lady! Mary Susanna had said it before, and

it was likely she would say it a good many times more before the
Grand Jury sat. Charlotte ignored her.

Mary Susanna was soon in her usual form, and social life went
on. They stayed at Castle Bernard and went up to Dublin for a
Drawing Room. Mrs. Payne-Townshend was popular in Dublin;
she was generous, hospitable to the right people, took an interest in
every fashionable topic of the day, and was well-travelled. It was
an anticlimax to return to Derry after the delights of Dublin, and
Mary Susanna said she was going to London. Charlotte insisted on
being at Derry until after the Grand Jury had sat, and her mother
returned to Queen's Gate without her.

In the second week of March, 1891, the Clonakilty-Rosscarbery
Railway application was put before the Grand Jury at Cork, and
nothing else was talked of. Some of the opposition evidence was
farcical, but Charlotte and her friends had prepared their case well,
and the Grand Jury declared in their favour.

Arthur Smith Barry sent her a note from London.

"I hear this morning that the Grand Jury have passed the
Clonakilty and Rosscarbery Railway. You have worked so hard at
it that I couldn't help writing you a line of congratulation. It is a
genuine proper scheme which will be of real benefit to the county."

So that had been well worth doing.

Charlotte went over to stay with Sissy and Hugh, who had taken
Keyham, a hunting box in Leicestershire which they rented while
Hugh was hunting with the Quorn and Cottesmore. Charlotte got
plenty of riding at Sissy's, and met many new people, but she soon
wanted to get away again. She was fond of Cecily, her niece, but
the child was looked after by a nurse and lived a circumscribed
existence quite apart from the adult world. Charlotte was also attached to Hugh, but, again, there seemed few points of contact.
Neither he nor Sissy was in the least interested in ideas of any
kind, beyond the obvious subjects suggested by the morning newspapers. Hugh was kind and considerate, Sissy—well, as she had always been. Charlotte went to London.

There was the usual spate of invitations to balls and parties await-
ing her. Charlotte accepted all she could. It was now almost impossible to spend an evening at home alone with her mother.

"You don't love me as you should." This was Mary Susanna's continual complaint. She talked of undutiful daughters, of the sacrifices she had made so that Lottie should have her "chances." Charlotte remained silent. The complaints continued. Now Mary Susanna dwelt on her health, which was in a low state: she never felt well. Yet she never faltered in *her* duty, to take her daughter out in Society. Had Lottie no gratitude? No sympathy? How could she be so hard and unfeeling! And here Mary Susanna took the opportunity of envying other people their daughters, who were sweet, and obedient—and, of course, married. Mrs. Payne-Townshend had a sense of failure at not getting *both* her girls "settled" well.

In July they went to Switzerland, Italy and Germany, travelling to Zurich, Davos, Maloja, Bellagio, Lugano, Lucerne, Bâle, Heidelberg, Mayence, Cologne, and back through Brussels—hardly staying anywhere for more than two days or seeing anything when they got to a place. Mary Susanna was fretful the entire time. Nothing pleased her: she grumbled at everything. She also declared that she was ill, demanding attention from her daughter at all hours of the day, and sometimes at night. Charlotte had been able to get away for a few hours at Maloja, where she walked alone up to a lake in the mountains, but the rest of the time was a nightmare. The hatred between them was almost a tangible thing, yet Mary Susanna could not bear to let her out of her sight: she had a compulsion to keep Charlotte always there.

They returned to London in August, and a few days later Mary Susanna was really taken ill. The doctor was at once called, but he could find nothing organically wrong, and talked about nerves. Less than a week later, on September 9, 1891, Mary Susanna died.

Charlotte had plenty to occupy her during the next months. There was a great deal of business to be attended to, and the training in business habits which she had had from her father came in useful. She let 21, Queen's Gate and moved into a house in Hamilton Place, near Hyde Park Corner. Derry was now hers, and once the transfer had taken place, she let it formally to

Willie Townshend, who had looked after it for years and was very fond of the house.

And now? Charlotte took stock of herself. She was thirty-four, with no pretensions to conventional good looks, a temperament she was certain had been warped, a passionate temper which no longer needed an iron discipline to enable her to face each day. And she was exceedingly wealthy. Other women were agitating for proper educational facilities, for the right to work and earn their own living. They demanded to be economically independent, so that they could be *free*. Charlotte was economically independent—but was she free? She no longer had to endure the tyranny of domination, but she could see no way of changing her way of life. Her education had given her certain accomplishments, such as her facility in languages, and her enormous appetite for reading had made her interested in esoteric thought, but she had an untrained brain and no special ability for anything whatsoever.

There seemed nothing to do but continue to see her friends, follow the Irish political news, and travel. She had a bout of influenza in January and went up to Keyham afterwards. General Clery, whom she had met at Aldershot and with whom she had carried on a desultory correspondence, wrote asking her to come for a visit to Camberley. He was at the Staff College, and had a house there run by efficient servants; he was sure she would get the rest and change she needed. His own duties kept him fairly occupied, but he would see to it that she was comfortable. Charlotte put Camberley on her list, and went there in April. General Clery's house was very sunny, and he was a keen gardener. She found both him and his home pleasant and restful. Clery was an unusual type for a soldier, she thought; he was interested in many things, and his comments on public affairs, especially on Ireland, were shrewd and wise. She decided he was a friend well worth having.

Winchester—London—Mitchelstown—Castle Bernard for the races, and a meet. Charlotte found political ferment as well as hunting, and she was so incensed by the mulish attitudes of her fellow guests that she sat down and dashed off a long, angry letter to General Clery. He replied:

"I was amused (most respectfully, of course) at your indignant outbreak on the subject of your outraged feelings with reference to the Emerald Isle. I always looked on you as English, with an amiable but quite gentle affection for what was not wholly objectionable in the Irish and their land. But I never hoped for anything more. However, I must be on my guard against stirring up that latent little volcano, or those wretched Unionists will get buried under a sea of lava. . . ."

He obviously had the right ideas about important matters. The correspondence gained momentum. They exchanged letters throughout her peregrinations to Blarney, to Derry, where she was joined by Sissy and small Cecily, and to Bray to stay with friends for the Dublin Horse Show. In September she went for a long tour with a woman friend: Lucerne, Milan, Venice, and then by sea to Corfu, Nauplia, Athens, Malta, Gibraltar. General Clery often wrote to her from camp, where he was on manoeuvres. On her return, he took her to dinner at the Savoy. Charlotte enjoyed his company immensely; for the first time, a man was treating her as an adult, without any "nonsense." She felt completely at ease with him, and it was a delightful sensation.

She went to Rome, to join some friends, and wrote regularly to Clery. Somehow, the bright interchange of opinions about books and plays modulated to a personal level. They began to talk on paper about themselves. Charlotte wrote that she had long been dissatisfied with her mode of life, and wanted to be of service to others. She also tried to explain her character to him. He replied:

"My dear Miss Payne-Townshend,

"I am now going to have a chat with you over your last letter received yesterday. . . . You ask if I think you would be good as a worker of charity if you took to it sincerely. Yes, I think you would do it well. But as a métier, I don't think it is yours. I think it would give you great and real *satisfaction,* but I don't think it would, in itself, be at all satisfying to your nature. But then, do I know your nature? This brings me to something else. You say that I don't know you in the least, and that there is a whole side of your character the core of which I have not guessed at. You are probably right. But is that strange? Though such old acquaintances, we have really not

seen much of each other. And is it not strange, rather than otherwise, that, in some ways, I know you so well . . . ? You are self-
contained . . . you can keep your own care, your own sorrow, your
own disappointment to yourself, and ask for neither solace nor
sympathy from outsiders. . . . You keep your heart too closely and
too constantly sealed up . . . I do not say your heart does not feel,
or does not open, but . . . may you not have taken too much care
to prevent it from showing that it felt. *What* it felt?"

This was getting too near sparking point, and Charlotte withdrew a little. She decided to join some friends in Delhi, and sailed
to India on November 25, 1892, arriving in Calcutta at the end of
the year.

*   *   *

India was an experience she was never to forget, though she did
nothing exceptional for one in her circumstances. She had letters
of introduction and was at once welcomed into the best society
in Calcutta. She attended a State ball, dinners and dances, went
with Bishop Barry to see native villages, was admitted into zenanas,
attended the Bengalee Theatre one day and the Consecration of the
Bishop of Lucknow the next—and there were nine bishops to dinner
that night. Then came journeys to Benares and Agra, where she
met the friends she had come out to visit. They went on to Delhi,
and there was another round of entertainments which included a
panther shoot. She visited temples in the jungle, rode and drove
through strange, marvellous country, was taken to places of unbelievable grandeur and passed by villages of unbelievable poverty.
    She saw that the life of these people was entirely governed by
religion. She would have liked to pause awhile, to stay and talk
to many Indians, to ask them questions: to see if they could help
her to find—what? She did not know. But she had to go on seeking,
and she knew with unshakeable certainty that this was a country
in which she might possibly find what she sought. But her friends
made it clear that it was unthinkable to talk to Indians on terms
of equality, let alone discuss intricate questions of religion with
them. Charlotte was passed from host to host, and was shown the

"sights" wherever she went. But for all she saw of the real life of
the country she might have stayed in London, or at Derry.

Letters from General Clery reached her at different places. He
hoped she was continuing to enjoy herself. As to deeper matters:

"It is very difficult to talk with any comfort or pleasure about
those things unless you have got a sympathetic listener. I mean
someone with an open mind on the subject, and how rarely you find
anyone of this kind. . . . There is no real harm in any form of
Christian belief—on the contrary a great deal of good, as there is
no finer or higher moral teaching in the world than that of Chris-
tianity. The fiddle-faddle crotchets of rival sects, Greek, Roman or
Protestant, are straws. The Protestants jeer at the Catholics for
believing in *tran*substantiation, and with the most charming inconsistency hug *con*substantiation and the Nicene Creed as the
pillars of their faith. Every church takes its stand for better or for
worse on its creed or dogmas. I myself always treat these with the
outer respect and forbearance that I treat the Throne and Constitution and other existing social institutions. But I don't accuse myself
in so doing of real hypocrisy. . . ."

Charlotte found that she was looking forward greatly to seeing
him again, and wrote to tell him when she expected to arrive back
in England. General Clery met her at the ship and escorted her to
London. They were in the stages of a happy relationship: the kind
of friendship Charlotte had always longed for. Sissy and Hugh were
in London, and Charlotte introduced General Clery to them; he
invited them all to visit him at Aldershot, where he was now
stationed.

The Queen's Gate house was let, and as she did not want to go
back to Hamilton Place, Charlotte took the lease of a flat early in
October, 1893, in Walsingham House, Piccadilly. It was rather
daring for a single woman to take a flat, but when one was as
rich and independent as Miss Payne-Townshend—and as in-
destructibly respectable—much could be allowed.

Ireland again, staying at Derry, Mitchelstown, Kingstown for
the Horse Show, Castle Bernard, back to Derry, Mitchelstown
again, then London. General Clery reminded Charlotte of her

promise to visit him, and she drove to Aldershot with Sissy and Hugh. The following day, Clery asked Charlotte to go for a walk with him, and they took a path across country, Charlotte talking about India. Clery was unusually silent. When Charlotte looked up and saw his expression, she also fell silent. Diffident, reserved as herself in many ways, he was open as a boy when moved by strong feeling, and it was clear that he was possessed by very strong feeling indeed. He told Charlotte that he was passionately in love with her, and he would do anything in the world if she would marry him.

Charlotte was shaken. She could not, with this man, let him down with kind words and say she hoped they would continue to be friends. For the first time in a familiar situation, she felt acutely unhappy. She longed to be *able* to love him, to feel for him what he felt for her. Charlotte had a curious perception where sincerity was concerned, and General Clery was completely, deeply sincere. Something responded in the heart she thought was cold and sealed up. Words began to stumble out: she tried to tell him how much she liked him. If it were possible for her to marry, he could easily have been the man. But it would not be fair to him, feeling as she did about the whole institution of marriage. General Clery naturally wanted to know—what was it she felt about the institution of marriage? Charlotte was unable to explain.

"I shall have to think," she said. "I cannot give you an answer. Not now."

He suddenly took her hands in his and bent his head. Charlotte raised her face, and he kissed her on the lips.

It was an era when a kiss between a bachelor and an unmarried woman meant something. After Charlotte had gone back to London, Clery wrote her a long letter, reiterating his great love for her and begging to know if she considered his uncontrollable impulse to kiss her wrong. Charlotte replied:

"I am going to Keyham tomorrow morning and cannot truly answer your letter quietly and thoughtfully as I should like to do—and will do later. I do not mean to entrench myself behind conventionalities. I only want to be quiet and think—exactly as I

told you. I do not think you realise how entirely unconventional
my views of life are now. . . . Write to me . . . anything you like—
whatever comes into your head, and do not be afraid of my misunderstanding. No, I do not think there was anything 'wrong' in
that incident. If I had thought it was wrong I should not have done
it. You know me well enough to believe that. Also I consider I have
nothing to 'forgive'—my feeling to you is of deep gratitude.

"Write to me at Keyham Hall, Leicester, and tell me where I
shall address a letter to you.

> "Yours most sincerely,
> "C. F. Payne-Townshend"

There followed an extraordinary correspondence, with both of
them saying a great deal about "understanding" and "misunderstanding" the other, commenting solemnly on the hollowness of
conventional life and the blankness of the future. Clery now realized
how he might possibly appear to Charlotte: a soldier dependent on
his pay, except for a very small private income, courting an exceedingly wealthy woman. He felt desperate, for he was fathoms
deep in love with her, and she appeared to like him greatly. She
kept telling him that he must try to understand her, and he did
indeed make every effort to gain some insight into her strange
character. He wrote:

"Perhaps from thinking over your peculiar position in the
world, for some time back I felt it must be a trying one when year
after year went on, and you did not choose to marry. I somehow
became impressed with the idea that you were not happy. . . . You
are never to think that you are quite alone, if one friend could ever
be of service to you."

He asked her to come again to Aldershot, so that they could have
a long, quiet talk. Charlotte by now was more than half in love
with him, but she dreaded going any further; her revulsion against
the final surrender, and all that it meant, was too strong. She tried
to tell him something of this in letters which she wrote practically
every day. Clery begged her not to allow her reason to crush the
dictates of her heart. If she would only come and stay for a few
days! They must be with each other, quietly, calmly, to talk over the
future. Mrs. Cholmondeley could come too, if Charlotte wished;

but Clery was as unconventional as Charlotte, and if she came alone it might be better.

Charlotte travelled to Aldershot. She sat under a shady tree in the garden of Clery's house while he was occupied with his duties during the day, and in the evening they sat and talked. Clery saw that Charlotte was in a state of tension, and he was tenderness itself, reading to her, encouraging her to rest and relax completely. But the quietness between them could not last long. One evening when they were walking in the garden, Clery took her hand in his and she allowed it to remain there. They came back to the lamplit drawing-room, not speaking. Clery drew her into his arms and kissed her as if he would never stop. Charlotte felt as if she were drowning, but she returned his kisses.

She returned to London next morning. Hardly had she reached home when she sat down and wrote to Clery. She hadn't meant anything; she hoped he would understand.

The ding-dong letters went on. Charlotte had developed an obsession about being "understood," though she expected people to understand her motives without giving them clues to the underlying causes of her actions. She told herself that Clery knew of her dread of marriage, but she wanted to be quite certain he realized what was holding her back. She wrote:

"My dear General Clery,

"You said in one of your letters 'You cannot surprise me and I cannot misunderstand you.' Now one of my axioms is . . . that everything is discussable, and that what one can do, one can talk about, quite simply and naturally. I, for one, think it would be a great misfortune if you and I misunderstood one another, especially just now . . . I feel that either the incident of our last meeting should have a sequel, or else that we should not meet again for a long time. If it has a sequel, that will be a serious matter to me—perhaps in a lesser degree to you, too. Now the serious things of one's life mustn't be done in a hurry, or on a mere impulse. If we had taken any irrevocable step that evening I might very likely have hated you afterwards. . . . One's reason ought to approve, and one ought to be quite certain one has made up one's mind . . . I don't want to discuss it now. Later on I will be able to talk to you quite simply and straight about everything. Will you wait for that?"

Clery wrote back, agreeing; he could do nothing else. He added:

"And may I say one thing . . . if I kissed you too passionately my kiss was as pure and sacred as your own . . . I never saw your eye so soft before. Will you, if you write, say you forgive whatever there may have been to be forgiven?"

Charlotte went on a long visit to Sissy and Hugh at Keyham, and tried to come to terms with herself. Now that she was away from Clery, she felt more able to see things in perspective. She cared for him a great deal, in a way. Was that enough on which to base a lifelong union? A life sentence. She thought of her father, who had loved her mother when they first met. It was a love which had led him into bondage. She watched Sissy and Hugh together, but could get no clue to their relationship. They were both perfectly satisfied with the life they led: hunting, shooting, visiting friends, having house parties. Their only child was being brought up to lead the same kind of existence as themselves.

Was this all life meant? Was there no other purpose in it except going round and round, meeting the same kind of people, making the same kind of conversation, observing the same sets of conventions? General Clery had often said that he understood her frustrations, but she wondered if he really did. She wrote to him, the first letter for some weeks, and put everything down that came into her mind. It was a very long, incoherent letter, and it was a measure of her complete trust in him that she was able to say things that she had never uttered to a living soul before.

She had to be free, she told him. Free—free—free. She had to make something of her life: she did not yet know what, but *something*. Marriage with him was not the answer. The fact that her feeling for him was not strong enough to affect the deepest urge of her nature, the urge towards personal freedom, must show him that it was not right for them to marry.

Clery wrote her two more letters. In the first he told her that he must accept her decision. In the second he said she must not think about these things so much. And she must not regret, or be conscience-stricken, about what had passed between them.

"You are free, as free as if that night had never been. The only one tied to that is *me*. Whatever step you may take, even if the saddest for me . . . I still remain your debtor for a debt nothing in this world could enable me to repay. I wouldn't for a moment offer you advice, but don't, in affection and what it leads to, neglect too much the dictates of your own true heart and true instinct; and don't trust too much to what reason alone may seem to justify. When heart and affection, and perhaps passion, are not involved, life must be cold though it may be logical, so don't try to shut them out too much."

8

AXEL MUNTHE

(1894—1895)

It was 1894, and Charlotte had reached her thirty-seventh year. She lived in her flat at Walsingham House with competent servants, she had many friends, Sissy and Hugh welcomed her at Edstaston whenever she wished to go, she was the mistress of a large fortune. To the outside world she was a self-possessed, cultivated woman without ties, who was in the fortunate position of being able to go where she liked and do what she liked. Her friends now took it for granted that she had no inclination towards marriage, and stopped their speculations; she must, they thought, be one of those curious beings who were sufficient unto themselves and did not need the security of a normal home life, with husband and children, for fulfilment.

Charlotte was, in fact, in a state of despair. She had put General Clery out of her mind, telling herself firmly that she had done the right thing to stop the affair before it got beyond her control. Now that she was no longer seeing him, she could think of the past two years calmly and clearly, and she was increasingly sure that it would have been wrong to marry him, as she could not have met the demands he would have been bound to make on her. She must take care not to become too friendly with any man in future, unless she could keep the relationship on a platonic level.

Meanwhile—there was the year to get through. She had not been at all well; after a visit to Derry before Christmas she had been taken ill with a low fever, and had not properly recovered. A trip to Egypt seemed a good idea, and Charlotte left London and sailed on the *Khedive* on January 5, 1894, leaving the steamer when they reached the Suez Canal, and travelling overland to Cairo. She knew a number of people who were wintering in Egypt, and was soon with friends. Lord and Lady Waterford invited her to stay with them on their yacht, she saw the usual sights, she was taken to have lunch with Kitchener. More sightseeing followed, and then Charlotte had to decide what to do next. There was nothing in London to take her back, and she decided to go on to Italy by sea.

The voyage to Naples was rough, and Charlotte did not remain there long; she went to Rome, where she knew several people in the English colony. Mrs. Edmund Gates, an old acquaintance, asked her to dine at the Grand Hotel, and when she arrived there she found another guest. His name was Axel Munthe, and he was a doctor.

*   *   *

Rome was a hotbed of gossip in Byron's time, and it had not changed by the last decade of the century. The English nobility and gentry, rich Americans and aristocratic Europeans who spent the winter and spring there, enjoyed the lavish social life, enlivened by occasional scandals and a constant flow of gossip. A new subject of conversation was a godsend—and in the early 1890's, Dr. Axel Munthe was being talked about with never-waning interest.

He was a Swede, a tall man with a personality so powerful that he seemed to bewitch even those who disliked him. He was to write a book, *The Story of San Michele*, which would make his name known throughout the world, but that day was in the far future. In 1894 he was a physician in Rome, and was rapidly putting every other fashionable doctor out of business. His career had been extraordinary enough already. Even as a medical student in Sweden he could make people do what he wished. He had gone to Paris to continue his studies, and had graduated in medicine in 1880, at the age of twenty-three. He married a nineteen-year-old girl, Ultima Hornberg, and took her to Capri; he had already travelled in Italy and loved the country. An epidemic of typhus broke out on the island, and Munthe quickly won the affection of the people by attending the poor villagers who had been stricken.

His next move was to Paris, where he and his wife were very popular in the English colony as well as with the Swedes resident there. Munthe became a nerve specialist, and was much influenced by Jean-Martin Charcot—part genius, part charlatan—who had a considerable following for his hypnotic treatment of hysteria at public sessions given at the hospital of the Salpêtrière. Most of Charcot's patients were women, whom he treated both at the hospital and at his consulting rooms; some had nervous maladies, others came with imaginary ailments, and the young Swede acquired a cynical outlook on idle women and their illnesses which was never to leave him.

Munthe's marriage lasted only eight years; his wife divorced him, and he went back to Capri for a time. One day he climbed up the seven hundred steps to the top of the cliff, and there he saw a little ruined chapel. Not far away was a house set about with vines. The old man who owned the house told him that the Emperor Tiberius had had a villa there and hundreds of fragments of columns and statues had had to be cleared away before the old man could plant his vines. Axel Munthe looked at the wonderful prospect over the Bay of Naples, then at the chapel. One day he would buy the old man's house, and the chapel, and join them together with avenues of cypresses and garlands of vines. He would live here, he resolved, and call his home San Michele.

He returned to Paris, hoping to make enough money to buy San Michele, but he found it difficult to save: it was easier to give money away. Impulsive, complicated, clever at sizing people up—and taking advantage of that faculty when it suited him—he was a centre of attraction wherever he stayed. He had an original mind but very little self-discipline, and a fantastic imagination which made it difficult for him always to distinguish fact from fancy.

His life often took unexpected turns. He went for a month's holiday to Swedish Lapland, and on the return journey read in a newspaper of a terrible outbreak of cholera in Naples. Munthe did not hesitate. He was a doctor, and doctors were desperately needed in Naples. With great courage he travelled to the stricken city instead of returning to Paris, and worked heroically among the cholera victims. When the epidemic was over he went to Paris, and before long built up a lucrative practice. Everybody wished to consult this extraordinary Swede, especially women. Munthe was brusque with the time-wasters—and they recommended him ec-statically to their friends. He despised them, but he treated them and took their money. He wanted to buy San Michele.

Munthe resumed his studies of hypnotism with Charcot, and made many acquaintances in the Parisian underworld—actresses, prostitutes, drug addicts. Guy de Maupassant became a friend; the novelist, like so many writers and artists living in Paris, had wrecked his life by loose living and was destroying what remained of his splendid mental powers by ether and other drugs.

The Swedish doctor, successful as he was, found his life in Paris sickening and frustrating. He believed that Charcot's methods were not without dangers, attracting, as subjects, many frauds and ex-hibitionists, and invalidating anything of real value which the doctors were trying to find in hypnotism as a treatment. Munthe also began to question Charcot's theories, which angered the Frenchman, who used an unfortunate experiment with a patient, in which Munthe was involved, as an excuse to forbid the Swede to come to the Salpêtrière again. Munthe was in despair.

He went to Capri. He had managed to save some money, and he took a room in a cottage near the house among the vines, determined somehow to realize his dream of building San Michele. One of his closest friends, the Swedish Minister in Paris, came to visit him. Munthe talked enthusiastically of his plans, but the Minister forced him to look at the future more realistically. How was the dream house to be built? With his own hands, said Munthe. It would cost half a million lire to build this imaginary San Michele, the Minister pointed out. And when it was built, what was Munthe going to live on? His savings would not last a month. He, the Minister, had actually made this journey to persuade Munthe to give up his present absurd existence and return to Paris, to his proper work as a doctor. He could then save really seriously.

Munthe was forced to see the wisdom of the argument, but he refused to return to Paris. Well, then, said the Minister, what about Rome? If Munthe worked hard, in less than five years he would have made enough money to finish San Michele and spend the rest of his life there.

After the Minister had left, Munthe spent an agitated night trying to make up his mind, and by morning he knew what he must do. A fortnight later he was in Rome, and from the very beginning he prospered. His first patient was the wife of an English banker, who had been lying on her back for three years after a fall from her horse while out hunting in the Campagna. All the foreign doctors had attended her in turn; now she was trying the newcomer, the Swede. Munthe thought that it was shock, not any permanent injury, which was keeping her prostrate, and he prescribed a treatment of massage which, with his method of blunt speaking about a patient's mental state, put the banker's wife on her feet within three months. Munthe's reputation was made.

*   *   *

This was the man whom Charlotte met at the Gateses' small dinner party. Axel Munthe had been in Rome a number of years; he lived in the house on the Piazza di Spagna where Keats had lodged, and his consulting rooms were always full of women who felt that no week was complete without a visit to the fascinating Swedish doctor. He was asked out everywhere; his work in the Naples epidemic had not been forgotten. He never spoke of his broken marriage; people did not know that he had ever been married. He was a romantic figure, with the added aura of royal patronage. The Crown Princess of Sweden had made him Physician-in-Ordinary, and when she came to Italy for her health, he was attached to her entourage. Mrs. Gates considered herself fortunate to have him as a guest to meet Miss Payne-Townshend, and took the opportunity privately to tell her so.

Charlotte was unimpressed by Dr. Munthe's fame, but she was much interested by the man himself. He had an excellent command of English, and he gave his hostess a picturesque description of the crowd of models, dressed in their brightly coloured regional costumes, who lounged on the steps of the Trinità dei Monti all day, waiting for artists to engage them. Munthe had an *ambulatòrio,* a surgery, in a poor quarter of Rome and he talked about that, too, and of the dogs and monkeys, as well as human beings, whom he treated for diseases. Charlotte found him a most unusual man.

Rome was at its best in early spring, and she decided to stay for a few weeks. She took rooms at the Hôtel de l'Europe, and as she was still not feeling well, consulted Dr. Munthe at the Piazza di Spagna. He prescribed valerian. She went again. He told her she must control her nerves: there was nothing really the matter with her. Perhaps a change of air? He suggested Venice. He himself would be going there shortly, as the Crown Princess, who had been visiting her parents at Baden, was travelling on to Venice, and required him to be in attendance. Munthe said that it would be exceedingly pleasant if Miss Payne-Townshend decided to visit Venice at the same time. He conveyed the impression that he was making the suggestion as a friend, not as her physician.

It did not occur to Charlotte to refuse. It did not even occur to her to think of the conventions. She was her own mistress, and was now used to making decisions without consulting anybody. It gave her a sense of warmth that this vital, much-admired man should want her to be in Venice at the same time as himself, and she did not hesitate. She had visited Venice before, and she went to some of the galleries and took familiar walks; but it was Axel Munthe who filled her mind. He called on her, and they talked. How he could talk! They were the same age, and that established some kind of equality between them. Munthe had been through the most amazing experiences—and his stories did not lose in the telling. Charlotte was a perfect listener, intelligent, genuinely interested. Munthe found her company delightful, and showed it.

They met several times. On two occasions Charlotte saw him out walking with the Crown Princess and several ladies and gentlemen in waiting, and he swept off his hat to her as they passed.

Charlotte found herself thinking of him very often. He called again, and once more they talked. By the time she was back in Rome, a fortnight later, a friendship had been established. She did not know it then, but she had fallen in love for the first time in her life. It took her some weeks to realize what had happened to her. She had thought that she had put love and marriage right behind her, and at first she could not bring herself to admit that the over-whelming desire which now absorbed her could indeed be love. It was not love as she had thought of it in the past—reasonable, sensible, based on a clear appraisal of the suitability of both parties from every point of view. Munthe had returned from Venice, and had come to dine with her at the hotel several times. Used as she had been all her life to controlling and hiding her feelings, she was painfully aware that he knew she was in a growing state of emotional upheaval.

He certainly did know. Axel Munthe was used to infatuated women. They stimulated him. And this conquest was a normally reserved, well-bred woman of taste. He exerted himself to be as devoted and attentive as he knew how to be—and when the Swedish doctor wished to have a woman at his feet he could be very fascinating indeed. He had to have admiration: it had become one of the most urgent needs of his nature. The silly society women who flattered him and crowded into his consulting room to flutter their eyes when he felt the pulse under their lace cuffs were the regular ministrants to his vanity, though he despised them. The Irishwoman intrigued him. He sent her cards by his servant:

"From Le Docteur Munthe, Piazza di Spagna, 26 Will you lunch today, 12.30 sharp."

"I will fetch you about 8—you are invited to dinner."

Charlotte lunched and dined with him; she could not help herself. She knew that people were talking, but she did not care; the affair had deprived her of all common sense. Her reason told her that Munthe had cast a spell over her—there was no other explanation of this terrifying emotion which held her in thrall—and she could do nothing but wait. For what? She did not know. Munthe did not make love to her; he reached the edge of tenderness—and went no further. Her health and her nerves were never mentioned now, though she often felt physically ill. The intimate little dinners at his house continued. They talked. Charlotte told him of her early life, of her despairing search for beliefs which would help her to live with some hope of contentment. Munthe was wonderfully understanding: he, too, had ideals, aspirations; Charlotte, listening to him, knew a happiness which she had never experienced before.

The Roman season was nearing its close, but there were still many At Homes and parties to which Charlotte was invited. She went to as few as she could without offending people. Her days were spent waiting in her room at the hotel, attempting to read, listening for a servant who might come with a card from Munthe. She no longer tried to think where all this was leading or what were Munthe's intentions; she did not think at all. For the first time in her adult life her actions were governed solely by emotions —powerful emotions over which she had no control whatever.

Then Munthe stopped sending her invitations. He did not write to her for over a week. Frightened—and ashamed of her fear—she decided to give a dinner party at her hotel, and sent a note to Munthe asking him to come. He replied:

"Thanks for your kind invitation to dinner. I am much too far gone for a table d'hôte dinner and know the people you are inviting—their inside and outside—since 10 years. But it might be good for you to lunch here any day you like. When I can manage to be at home—simple food. Tomorrow I shall be out of town and today no time for luncheon, but after tomorrow I shall be in if you like. No preparation whatever will be made for you except that I will try to appear myself."

She went, of course. Munthe was waiting for her, and in the best of spirits. Charlotte, too, was elated; she felt well, excited and happy, and she was attractive when she forgot her ailments and expressed opinions in her forthright way. Axel Munthe found her worth listening to when she talked vivaciously on subjects which interested her. He admired her independence and the quality of her mind. She was rich, but she was not idle; at least, she was constantly endeavouring to improve her knowledge and widen her experience by reading. And she had a real social conscience; not one that was assuaged by charitable deeds, but which was awakened by a sense of injustice on behalf of the poor.

Munthe, for all his exhibitionism and almost pathological vanity, possessed the same kind of conscience. True, he drove about Rome in a smart, red-wheeled victoria drawn by a pair of splendid Hungarian horses, his Lapp dog on his knee—nobody could miss Dr. Axel Munthe when he was out in his carriage. But he was still the same man who had fought for the lives of destitute Neapolitans in the cholera outbreak, and there was nothing exhibitionist about him when he was at work in his *ambulatòrio* in the slums of Rome.

The bond between him and the rich Irishwoman grew stronger. He took her to visit the Little Sisters of the Poor, who spent their dedicated lives among the unfortunate, and who could put every lira to good use. Charlotte gave generously. Munthe did not thank her; he was exceedingly open-handed himself, and took it for granted that her benefactions should be large.

The days passed. They were again meeting often, usually at Munthe's house. The moment they parted, Charlotte began to count the hours to the next time. Sometimes Munthe sent her a note to say he was too busy to see her, and then Charlotte knew the meaning of real misery. If she ever thought of Edward Hutton or General Clery at this time she must have understood what suffering could mean.

The weather was growing sultry, and Dr. Munthe's wealthy patients began to leave Rome. One day Charlotte heard a rumour that Munthe himself was going. Charlotte held herself back from doing something she knew was foolish—to write and ask him if it was true. He had not invited her to dine with him for some time, and the next time she met him was at the house of a mutual friend. Munthe escorted her back to her hotel. Charlotte could not stop herself asking the question: was it true that he was leaving Rome? Yes. Charlotte could hardly control her agonized feelings, and said that she would miss him. Munthe replied that he, too, would miss her, and asked in a light tone for her photograph, as he liked having mementoes of his friends.

Charlotte had no photograph of herself in Rome, but next day she went to see Giulio Aristide Sartorio, a well-known painter, and asked him to make a pastel portrait of her. After a few sittings, having satisfied herself that Sartorio had made a reasonable likeness, she left for England, directing that the portrait should be sent to the Piazza di Spagna, together with one of Kipling's books which she knew Munthe wanted to read. She enclosed a note, telling him she was returning to England, and gave him her address at Walsingham House. She added that she hoped they would see each other in England; Munthe had told her at their last meeting that he intended going there to visit friends, on his way to Sweden.

Charlotte had never had many women friends, but the few whom she found compatible always gave her a deep loyalty. She had got to know Louise Mock, a writer of plays and romances, while she was in Rome, and they had often discussed the "woman question" and the works of outspoken writers like Grant Allen, who defended a woman's right to live the way she wished. Louise had a bitter, cynical streak, but she also possessed many likeable qualities, and a generous, outgoing affection was one. Charlotte could always talk to Louise. Another bond was the fact that Louise was a source of information about Axel Munthe. Her sister Maud was married to a German and lived at Baden, where the Crown Princess of Sweden often visited her parents. Dr. Munthe, too, frequently came, and Maud sometimes mentioned him.

Back in London, Charlotte waited for a letter from Munthe acknowledging the portrait and book. None came. She wrote to Louise, who went out a great deal in Roman society. Charlotte did not attempt to hide her feelings: Louise knew how it was with her. Had Munthe left for England? Louise replied:

"17 June, 1895

"Dearest Charlotte,

"Though I lunched with Munthe today at the Barberini, I know nothing of when he goes to England or whether he will take Sweden first. I asked my sister—she couldn't tell me. I asked him in a roundabout way—he gave me no answer, only saying he was

obliged to go to England. . . . He came up from Capri last night
and is leaving again tomorrow morning for an 8 or 10 days' cruise
to Monte Cristo and Elba with Captain Fors. . . . Munthe is looking very well, browned by the sun, and was in good spirits at the
lunch, laughing and joking the whole time. He will spend a night
or so at the Barberini on his way through. Maud says it will depend
on the Crown Princess whether he goes first to Sweden or not. I
am so sorry I have no definite information to give you. Perhaps
Maud may mention what becomes of him later on. When he comes
back I presume she will know what his intentions are . . ."

There was a note inserted later the same evening, written at
7.30 p.m.

"I've just met Munthe at Waldo's studio. Talking of his big
dog he said he must take it to England as the poor beast couldn't
stand the heat of Capri. 'Will you take it to Sweden as well?' I
asked. 'Oh no,' he replied. 'Then you are going first to England?'
'Yes,' he said.

"One can never build on that sort of thing from him, but there
it is. . . . He told me he was much better, even sleeping slightly
better."

Charlotte went to Edstaston, where she was warmly welcomed
by Sissy and Hugh. They would have liked her to stay, but she
was on edge, and within a week she was arranging to go on to
friends at Birtles Old Hall in Cheshire. She wrote to Munthe,
asking if he had received the portrait and the book. Still no answer.
Another letter came from Louise in August:

"Maud . . . has received a letter written to her husband by
Munthe. He is staying at Cowes with the Duchess of Manchester,
who will not let him go, although he ought to be in Sweden by
now. She wants to keep him till the end of the month, but on the
16th he is obliged to set out to join the Crown Princess, who has
chartered a yacht and claims him. Till that date, he remains at
Cowes. On September 1st he returns to England and goes to
Scotland as Lord Dudley's guest. On the 20th he hopes to be back
at Capri. He is on the water constantly, either racing or cruising,
and seems in high spirits."

Charlotte had once told her friend that she had thought of visiting America, and Louise ended her letter with a strong plea to carry out this intention.

"I had hoped to hear you were about to start for America. Don't delay any longer. You need to be taken quite out of yourself . . . do cross the ocean as quickly as you can. . . ."

It was so easy to say! But Charlotte was bereft of will-power, of pride. She wrote to Munthe again, reminding him of his promise that they should see each other in England, and telling him that she had arranged to go over to Derry the following month, but would be willing to return to England if they could meet.

To Louise she wrote to say that she had decided not to go on the projected visit to America after all. She could not be away just now; she was sure Louise would understand. Louise replied from Switzerland, where she was making a short tour.

"I am disappointed at your change of plan. But you are the best judge where your innermost feelings are concerned."

At last there came a letter from Munthe, forwarded to Charlotte at Birtles Old Hall from Walsingham House.
"Dear Miss Payne,

"Thanks for your 2 letters and the book. I have been away sailing for 2 weeks as I found Sorrento full of patients and 'friends' who had all planned their programmes to pay a visit to Capri and myself. So I lolled on the blessed little boat, went to . . . Porto d'Anzio, from which place I went in to see Mrs. Field in Rome and slept there one night. I had been at the helm for 2 nights as we had rather rough weather. All my post mailed here as I knew nothing when I was going. I read Kipling's *lovely* book last night straight through; it does but confirm my opinion that he is the greatest writer living—not the greatest mind but the strongest writer. It was very kind of you to send it. As to your other present, Sartorio's picture, I have given orders to have it sent to your house in London. I cannot and will not accept it. If you do not want it, I shall make Sartorio take it back if you like. . . . I am off again for a cruise after tomorrow down to Calabria and probably Sicily. My further plans are very dim—you ask when I am coming to England. I wish I knew myself. I ought not to go there at all but to remain here till I go to Sweden, because the state of my finances is very seriously alarming now when I have time to think. However maybe I can manage it, if I turn up it will be in August. Of course I shall let you know in time."

Charlotte received his next letter when she was at Derry. It was sent from Sweden, and was written on paper embossed with a crown.

"I have now received a letter from you. Sorry you have not been well. You want to know when I am coming to London, and so would I. I have been staying here with the poor lady you saw in Venice since I came to Sweden. She is going abroad already next month and alas! I fear I shall have to see her parents (Baden) next month. I leave her today. . . . She will stay with the Queen some days. I hope she will let me off soon, but my experience from last year is not reassuring. She is very 'entétée,' but very kind to me."

He went on to say he had been asked to join friends in a yacht and sail back with them to England, and the temptation was difficult to resist, but he knew he ought not to go, as he was in a hurry to return to Italy. He was supposed to go to Scotland to some friends.

"What sort of life do you lead in Ireland? If it were not so far away I might come to see you although I am not very good in travelling. I wish I could charter a little cutter for a few days and sail down to Ireland but they cost a good deal too much. I shall write to you soon in England, as soon as I am free from an urgent medical visit I have to make first of all. Never think of leaving Ireland for my sake—we shall discuss it before—maybe I can go down for a few days. . . . I never knew before you told me that Musset was my favourite author and don't think the quotation true. *Beware of quotations.* It is bad for our individuality of thought, for our style. Hope you are better and enjoying your Ireland—here is so grey and cold—the Court life."

He wrote early in September from London.
"Dear Miss Payne-Townshend,
"I have been at your house and they would not give me your adresse but would forward the letter. They are looking after you well. I leave this horrid town—I have not slept at all since I

came—tomorrow to see some patients and a friend—drop me a
line at Levens Hall, Milnthorpe (Westmoreland), how you are
and when you intend to leave Ireland. From Levens I am supposed
to go to stay with Lady Cameron at Pixton Park, but feel not up
to it. Have been ill and miserable. And you? Where in Ireland
are you? If it were not so long to you, I could come to see you."

His next letter, written from the Savoy Hotel in London, was
forwarded to Charlotte at Mitchelstown.

"I wrote you yesterday to drop me a line at Levens Hall. I am
however first going to Lady Cameron and beg you to write to me
under adresse Pixton Park, Dulverton, Somersetshire. From there
I go to Levens I suppose. Tell me how long you shall remain in
Ireland.

"Your friend Munthe"

The next letter came from Inverchaolain Lodge in Argyllshire:

"Are you in London? I hope to be there in this week—have
unfortunately promised to see an old patient in Liverpool on my
way home. Will let you know as soon as I come to London. I am
not at all well, cannot sleep and feel more miserable than ever.

"Your friend Munthe"

They did not meet in London, and Munthe returned to Italy
and Capri. Charlotte wrote to him there, asking if he would like
her to send him *Trilby*. Apparently he did not wish to have it. In
a letter sent on October 9 he said:

"Thanks for your letter. I should have written anyhow. Since I
came back I have spent my days in the boat although the weather
has been horrid, and we should have gone to the bottom more than
once had not the boat been good and the helmsman watchful—
myself if you please. I sleep so badly and hear constantly that
ominous disturbance with the heart's action which will kill me
one day. Everything goes wrong. I told you about the house. Well,
I am losing all hope to secure it for me and this is a bad blow to
me. I sail tomorrow in the little craft—she is only 27 feet long—
and from there I start for Baden to the Crown Princess—shall be
back here anyhow before settling for the winter in Rome. I wish I
had not refused 'Trilby.' I have nothing to read here—lend it to
me if you have got it still, but I fear you must send it in two parcels

(book post) if it is big. I shall give it back to you in the Spring, or
send it back if it is light. . . . Write to me how you are—always to
Capri is best. Are you to remain in Ireland for long?

"Goodbye and God bless you.

"Yours, Axel Munthe"

Munthe's last letter, written on Schloss Karlsruhe paper, was
sent from Rome on November 9, 1895:

"I have received two letters from you and 'Trilby.' I cannot
give you a stronger proof of how busy I have been than that I have
not yet read the book, although I was so anxious to read it that I
telegraphed to a friend in London to send it to me and got it in its
volume state before I got yours. I shall read your copy, though,
when I begin to read the book. My journey to Baden was very
troublesome & a complete failure for me personally as notwithstand-
ing all my efforts to have her sent elsewhere & another doctor with
her the other 3 doctors agreed to send her to me again, and again I
shall have the entire responsibility and the whole bother for the
whole winter. Thanks for your enquiry about the house. A dear
friend of mine—from your country too—offered me to lend me some
money on conditions which I thought I could accept, and I shall
in all probability accept her offer, in which case I shall be able to
remain where I am even if I cannot get what I wanted. But now
I am at my Roman work and Capri must be out of my mind. I have
been round to see all my humble friends yesterday and today, and
more than ever I am struck by the terrible misery there, and by
my impossibility to help as I wanted to do and ought to do according to my unfortunate theories of life and its duty. When I see sights
like these I feel ashamed to keep a penny to myself. I do not *keep*
it but . . . I might eat less myself, although those few who now
and then share my meals say no. What I would like to do would
be to start a dispensary here. I could then have the feeling of being
useful to somebody which might restore the harmony of my mind
—always thinking of myself again. Up til now I have been able
to give away a good deal of medicine and money—all I have earned
in fact—but since a misfortune at home in Sweden last summer
this becomes more difficult. But alas! The realisation of my dispensary plan costs a good deal of money and I have not got it—you

must *give* the medicine, and a little money helps too now and then. If ever you decide to do good in grande style let me know and I shall put you on the right track. Did I tell you as one of my specialities that I never write letters? I love my only sister dearly and I never write to her more than 2 or 3 times a year—neither to anybody else except doctor's letters.

"Rome is quiet and serene now—a sort of laisser aller of the summer's rest still remains all over the place and no tourists are to be seen. But they will soon come.

"Yours,

"Axel Munthe"

Charlotte tried hard to pull herself together. She realized that Munthe was a very strange character, and that there was a great deal about him that she did not know. It was obvious that he was not going to ask her to marry him, and she knew that even if he did, there would be no real happiness for her. He had bewitched her, as he had done so many women, and she must break the enchantment.

Another woman friend, Augustine Henry, was a great help at this time. Augustine was an American whom Charlotte had met in Rome, a perceptive woman with a streak of practical common sense. She had grown very fond of Charlotte during their acquaintance in Italy, and when she was ready to return to her home in San Francisco, she came first to England, so as to say good-bye to her friend in person.

Charlotte was glad to see her again. Reserved as she was with people whom she did not know well, Charlotte responded with almost naïve frankness to genuine sympathy and understanding. Within an hour of their meeting, Charlotte was telling Augustine about Axel Munthe and the hopelessness which now threaded her existence. Nothing seemed to matter to her any more. She was rudderless: without direction. What could she turn to? Social work? She did not know where to begin. Here she was, a wealthy woman, with a terrible sense of guilt. She had been in the slums of Rome, but there were slums in London and other cities which were almost as bad. She had got to the point when every time she spent money on herself, she at once thought of the hungry and destitute. Should she give up her entire fortune to the poor? Was that the answer?

Augustine Henry listened, and gently changed the subject, trying to bring Charlotte's thoughts back to personal problems. Her English friend must forget Axel Munthe, but what about other men? Augustine tried to draw her out on the subject of love and marriage. Charlotte swerved away. She could not talk about Clery, the only man besides Munthe who had made an impression on her—if that was the word, compared to the tumultuous emotion she felt for the Swedish doctor. It was better to talk about the good her money might do among the poor.

The American woman had no advice to offer, and they parted affectionately, Augustine travelling to Liverpool, where she was to board her ship. Charlotte sent a note after her, to wish her Godspeed.

Augustine wrote a reply before she left.

"S.M.S. 'St. Louis'

"Dear Miss Townshend,

"Thank you very much for your 'Godspeed.' I have only a few minutes to write now, and I cannot say anything I want to say. I do think you want help and sympathy and I have thought much since I saw you in London how you could be helped. I am going very far away and for a very long time, and I'll presume on that to write to you.

". . . I'll tell you some facts that will help you. I very nearly did once (on a smaller scale) what you intend doing. I didn't though. You must be very wise to *do good*, and that is what you want to do. You want to be effectual and to do something real, not to have the credit or vanity of doing it. It is a mighty attainment to be real and true and noble to oneself. But it can be done. So go on . . . but be wise, be wise.

"I am glad you call me your friend. I am.

"Yours very truly,
"Augustine Henry"

She wrote again from San Francisco.

"I am compelled to write to you. . . . I do feel that you must be helped. Why should you give up all you care for in the world? Why do you think you ought to suffer as a protest against the existence of a degraded class of people? Do you understand the problem of good and evil? You perhaps fancy it is the fault of the rich that the poor are so miserable and degraded. It is not so, I think. . . . I do not advise you not to try to help people. But I do think you err in thinking of giving up the beautifying of your own life. Make yourself the brightest life, the best life possible; you will do more good that way than by throwing away cheerfulness and assuming that kind of Puritanism, or asceticism rather, which is actually in your idea of suffering as a protest.

"You could do as much good by remaining in your own rank and trying to show to some that you might influence that there is work to do in the world, that it is dull and stupid to live only for self. I am afraid I am not very convincing . . . I have met so many people, have heard so much, seen so much, I am so puzzled myself I cannot trust my own judgment . . . I plead with you to act slowly, and to get into the best mental condition. If you have friends, as you must have, whom you can trust, talk freely with them."

Louise Mock wrote asking Charlotte to come to Rome so that they could go on a tour together, and Charlotte went. Axel Munthe was in the city, but Charlotte did not meet him. She visited his *ambulatòrio* and gave a large sum of money to the Little Sisters of the Poor. Louise insisted on Charlotte's acting perfectly normally; she had always liked Rome, and she must not avoid her friends because of Munthe. Charlotte agreed. They went on excursions to Monte Cassino, Frosinone and Frascati, and Charlotte made an effort to enjoy sightseeing again. She left Rome early in June without seeing Axel Munthe, and sailed from Naples to Plymouth.

The shape of her social life was changing. She visited Keyham and Birtles Old Hall, but she also travelled to Ipswich for the British Association meeting that year. Her acquaintance had widened. There were many women in society who were very much interested in the "Woman Question," and who supported every scheme which might help them get rid of their legal disabilities. The various movements to secure the emancipation of women had been going on for most of the century, and there were now a number of groups which strongly supported the cause.

Charlotte met some of these progressives at the houses of her friends. One day, at a luncheon, two of her fellow guests were Mr. and Mrs. Sidney Webb. Charlotte found Mrs. Webb a little intimidating in manner, but she liked them both, and was exceedingly interested in their conversation and ideas. Beatrice Webb, for her part, thought Miss Payne-Townshend worth cultivating. She seemed to be a woman of means, and was apparently genuinely concerned with social problems. Her manner was so sympathetic that Mrs. Webb told her about the Fabian Society, a political society of a new kind founded some years before, which had as its chief aim the spreading of socialist ideas by non-revolutionary means: by reason and persuasion rather than by violence. Beatrice Webb also spoke with enthusiasm of the new School of Economics and Political Science, founded the previous year with part of a legacy left by Henry Hutchinson. The School had been started in John Street, in the Adelphi, but had now moved to 10, Adelphi Terrace, where there was more room.

Charlotte was interested. What were the objects of the School? The Webbs explained that the primary object was to train students to understand the economic structure of their own and other countries, and so understand the relation between economics and politics. Charlotte came away from the luncheon party excited and stimulated. This was the kind of idea she had often had herself, but Mrs. Webb, in her incisive way, had set out the problems with such clarity and authority that Charlotte saw them in a fresh light. She very much wanted to meet the Webbs again, and wrote asking them to dinner at Walsingham House.

Beatrice and Sidney Webb did not indulge in dinner parties which had no definite purpose, but Beatrice was pleased that a wealthy woman was interested in projects of great importance, and she accepted the invitation. In return, she asked Charlotte to luncheon at Grosvenor Road. They began to be friendly. Soon, Charlotte was meeting members of the Webbs' circle: people with exhilarating ideas, unconventional, new, *sensible*. They believed in the equality of women, and equality of opportunity for everybody, and a new outlook on education, especially education for girls. They believed in a new kind of social system altogether. It was wonderful.

Charlotte was at last finding a purpose in life.

PART TWO

Charlotte Frances Shaw

9

G. B. S.

(1896–1897)

On September 16, 1896, Beatrice Webb wrote in her Diary[1]:

"Last day of our stay in the Suffolk Rectory. Meanwhile a new friend has joined the 'Bo' family." ["Aunt Bo" was the Potter[2] children's nickname for their Aunt Beatrice.] "Charlotte Payne Townshend is a wealthy unmarried woman of about my own age. Bred up in a second-rate fashionable society without any education or habit of work, she found herself at about 33 years of age alone in the world, without ties, without any definite creed, and with a large income. For the last 4 years she has drifted about—in India, in Italy, in Egypt, in London, seeking occupation and fellow-spirits. In person she is attractive—a large graceful woman with masses of chocolate brown hair, pleasant grey eyes, matte complexion which sometimes looks muddy, at other times forms a picturesquely pale background to her brilliant hair and bright eyes. She dresses well—in her flowing white evening robe she approaches beauty. At moments she is plain. By temperament she is an an-

[1] Unpublished section of the Diaries.
[2] Potter was Beatrice Webb's maiden name.

archist—feeling any regulation or rule intolerable—a tendency which has been exaggerated by her irresponsible wealth. She is a romantic but thinks herself cynical. She is a socialist and radical, not because she understands the Collectivist standpoint, but because she is by nature a rebel. She has no snobbishness and no convention: she has 'swallowed all formulas' but has not worked out principles of her own. She is fond of men and impatient of most women—bitterly resents her own celibacy but thinks she could not tolerate the matter of fact side of marriage. Sweet-tempered, sympathetic and genuinely anxious to increase the world's enjoyment and diminish the world's pain.

"This is the woman who, for a short time or for good, entered the 'Bo' family. We, knowing she was wealthy, and hearing she was socialistic, interested her in the L S of E. She subscribed £1,000 to the Library. . . . It was on account of her generosity to our projects and 'for the good of the cause' that I first made friends with her."

Not only did Charlotte give £1,000 to the Library—under Mrs. Webb's skilful extraction—but she took rooms above the newly-formed School of Economics in Adelphi Terrace, paying £300 a year for rent and service. Charlotte, who had given up her flat, usually stayed at Bailey's Hotel when she was in London, and she was glad to have a place of her own. She had become very interested in the new School, and having her own rooms upstairs meant that she would be able to help on the social side and to take an active part in the venture when opportunities arose. It was the first time she had had the chance of being closely connected with a social experiment on any scale; this seemed to her a far more valuable idea than conventional charity giving, or coterie meetings of unpractical idealists with windy views. Mrs. Webb may have prided herself on getting a thousand pounds from a rich woman for her "cause," but she would not have got it if Charlotte had not examined the project in her methodical way, and decided that it was worth supporting. She also agreed to Beatrice Webb's suggestion that to bring her more directly into this new set of comrades they should take a house together in the country and entertain friends who were similarly interested in the new School, and in the Fabian Society.

Charlotte found the Webbs stimulating, and eagerly responded to this new friendship. Here were people who did more than talk of a progressive society; they were determined to lay the foundations on which it could be built. Their opinions on women's freedom, too, encouraged her to go on with an idea which had been long forming in her mind. She had for many years been interested in medicine, and now that there was at last a chance of women being admitted to the faculty, she wondered if she could train to be a doctor. In the event, she had no chance of admission anywhere, apart from the prejudice against women medical students, because she had been taught hardly any science in her schooldays. Nevertheless, she continued to try to find out all she could about the entrance examinations, and whether there were suitable tutors who could teach her sufficient for admission to the course.

She wrote in her Annuary for 1896:

"Returned to London 4 Jan. Went a good deal to School of Medicine and saw the Webbs now and then. Met G.B.S. first time at Webbs 29 Jan. School of Economics beginning."

On March 20, 1896, George Bernard Shaw made the following entry in his shorthand diary:

"Miss Payne Townshend 'At Home' to London School of Economics. Did not go."

This did not mean that he had no wish to go; his shorthand diary was a record of his engagements, and if he was unable to keep an appointment he added a note to that effect at the end of the day.

Charlotte went to Rome in March to join a number of her friends who had taken villas there or were staying at fashionable hotels. It was still the accepted thing for people in English society to spend the spring in Rome, and move to cooler regions for the Italian summer. They returned to London for the season in June, and went on to Ireland or Scotland for a sporting autumn. Winter was passed in the South of France, and spring found them in Rome again. It was amusing in Rome. One held a *salon* for English friends and one's acquaintances in Roman society; there was plenty of gaiety, continual animation as newcomers arrived bringing the latest gossip from home, not to mention the frou-frou of the latest Parisian fashions, for everybody stopped in Paris en route.

Rome was full when Charlotte arrived, and she entered at once into the social life of her set. She went to the opera, danced at balls, took her place in riding parties—where she always shone—walked in the squares and gardens with her friends, visited the galleries, conversed in the salons. Axel Munthe was not in Rome, and she determined to put him out of her mind. This was not easy, for there was always some talk about the Swedish doctor: of his continued popularity with the Swedish Crown Princess, his extraordinary mania for animals of all kinds, his courage in the cholera and small-pox epidemics, his fascination for women and his ruthless behaviour with them. He was building a curious habitation in Anacapri, it was said, and intended to become a hermit.

Charlotte listened but said nothing. The very mention of his name hurt her pride, remembering how she had betrayed her innermost feelings to him and made a fool of herself. She was certain that her feelings were no longer involved; but she went on listening to the gossip.

After a few weeks, the inevitable restlessness set in. She liked her friends and enjoyed their company, especially those whom she had known for a long time. But now she could not help criticizing them. She was tired of the empty round of their lives, of the smart *bons mots* which they laughed at so heartily and which she found silly. She disliked their preoccupation with trivialities, their side-long glances as they wondered in whispers who was attracted to whom, and why; and how this marriage was turning out; or what was at the back of the rumour that—and here voices were discreetly lowered. Charlotte grew more and more impatient. It was all so unimportant! She found herself thinking again of Munthe, missing him afresh because his conversation had always been worth listening to. He had had a certain flamboyance, yes, but he had had the most fascinating ideas and theories—of people's behaviour being related to pressures within their own natures, as well as by heredity and circumstances. Charlotte had not always been able to follow these flights, and when her emotions became entangled she had often listened to him without actually hearing a word he had been saying. Nevertheless, he had sparked off something in her mind, and she now found herself missing him with a feeling that had nothing whatever to do with blighted love.

The Roman light glowed into molten gold, and the air shimmered with a growing heat haze. Friends and acquaintances began to leave the city for villas and *palazze* in the northern hills. Charlotte did not accept any of the invitations which were pressed upon her to accompany them; she had had enough of trivialities, and decided to return to London. Beatrice Webb had rented the Rectory of Stratford St. Andrew, near Saxmundham in Suffolk, for a proposed Fabian house party, and Charlotte was to join them in August. She was looking forward to seeing the Webbs again. They attracted her because they had definite aims in life. Charlotte, with the Clonakilty Railway behind her, had known the satisfaction of having something to work for, and she hoped she would be of use to the Webbs and their circle.

August came, and Charlotte travelled to Saxmundham and Stratford St. Andrew. The party she now joined was very different from the society she had left in Rome. Besides the Webbs, there were two prominent members of the Fabian Society, Graham Wallas and George Bernard Shaw, as well as Charles Trevelyan, a Liberal, and a Miss Charlotte Perkins Stetson. The Rectory was a late Victorian house set in pretty grounds, and was not over-comfortable. The Webbs had never rated comfort as a necessity of life, and the insistence on plain living and high thinking proved to be too much for Miss Stetson, who made an excuse to return home and left the party. The others settled down to serious work; there was a great deal of planning to do for the new London School of Economics and the Library of Political Science, besides Fabian Society policy to discuss. The mornings were devoted to sessions of work, the afternoons to walks, or to bicycle rides in the surrounding countryside; after tea there was more work, and after the evening meal, general talk, with Bernard Shaw reading his latest play to them, or starting off an argument with a wild flight of fancy and insisting on pursuing it. Graham Wallas, six-foot-two and solemn, was the solid balance to the spritely Irishman.

Charlotte did not care much for Graham Wallas, but she liked Bernard Shaw. He was not as tall as the other man, though his lankiness gave him an appearance of greater height than his six feet, and his reddish beard showed up the pallor of a face which was nevertheless mischievously alive because of the extreme brightness of his blue eyes. He was dressed in curious clothes: a Jaeger suit which almost matched his beard, soft shirt and tie, sturdy boots. He was an unusual individual, and it was clear that he was aware of this fact.

The carefully-planned days passed according to schedule. Never in her life had Charlotte heard such concentrated talk. She did not say much herself when she did not know people well, but she was a good listener; and as her manners were impeccable and her company agreeable, Beatrice Webb considered the arrangement a success. It was useful having a wealthy woman sympathetic to their projects, which would require a great deal of money in the future.

Charles Trevelyan had to return to London, and Graham Wallas left later. Beatrice caught a chill which turned to rheumatism, and she was unable to take her accustomed exercise, so Charlotte and Bernard Shaw were left to go on their afternoon bicycle rides together—Sidney naturally remaining with his wife, so that they could go on working. Shaw enjoyed these rides à deux more and more. Miss Payne-Townshend was an Irish gentlewoman, obviously intelligent, and the way she regarded him with her fine green eyes made it plain that she had never met anyone quite like him before. This was the kind of encouragement which stimulated the brilliant Irishman to outrageous bursts of rhetoric and paradox; he sparkled, he set out to dazzle, he turned each facet of his personality until he had captured Charlotte's entire interest. This display of his intellectual plumage came as naturally to him as breathing. Charlotte found herself responding to his barefaced gallantries in spite of her usual caution. Before long, she was telling him about Derry, and her family—and even about Axel Munthe. He could be so sympathetic and understanding when he was not striking matches on his own wit.

Beatrice noted this turn of events without surprise; she was used to the way G.B.S. showed off. As the weeks passed, however, she began to grow a little uneasy. She wrote in her Diary:

"To me she [Charlotte] seemed a pleasant, well-dressed, well-intentioned woman—I thought she would do very well for Graham

Wallas! Now she turns out to be an 'original' with considerable
charm and certain volcanic tendencies. Graham Wallas bored her
with his morality and learning. In a few days she and Bernard
Shaw were constant companions. For the last fortnight—when the
party has been reduced to ourselves and Shaw and we have been
occupied with our work and each other, they have been scouring
the country together and sitting up late at night. To all seeming,
she is in love with the brilliant Philanderer and he is taken in his
cold sort of way with her. They are, I gather from him, on very
confidential terms and have 'explained' their relative positions.
Though interested I am somewhat uneasy. These warm-hearted unmarried women of a certain age are audacious and are almost child-
ishly reckless of consequences. I doubt whether Bernard Shaw
could be induced to marry: I doubt whether she will be happy
without it. It is harder for a woman to remain celibate than for
a man."

While Beatrice, who knew nothing whatever about Charlotte's
previous emotional life, was thus observing the new "comrade"
with clinical detachment, Charlotte was studying the Webb marriage. These two seemed to her to be perfectly matched. Their
intellectual gifts were exactly complementary, they had the same
tastes, the same basic interests, and, above all, they were deeply
in love. Charlotte, with her strongly-rooted antipathy to the married
state, was now seeing at close quarters what an idyllic marriage was
like. It seemed to her quite wonderful that there could be such a
real partnership between a man and a woman.

Meanwhile—there was her growing friendship with Bernard
Shaw. For twenty years she had been able to hold her relationships
with her men friends on a delicate seesaw, tipping the end away
from her when she wished. She had never done the tipping deliberately: it had always been an instinctive reaction away from
danger when she sensed a critical moment of avowal. She *had* to be
free. Axel Munthe had been the only man in her life to make her
feel helpless, no longer mistress of herself; and though, even now,
she could not think of him without pain, she knew she was glad
the affair had been cut short.

Bernard Shaw was the first man she had met since Munthe who

talked to her as a human being and not merely as a woman to be
flattered. Yet this was not wholly true. He made her doubly aware
of herself as a woman, even when he was talking political economy.
There was a challenge between them. He made her argue angrily
by his mocking dismissal of ideas which she cherished, and when,
on an inspiration, she found effective counter-arguments, he instantly evaded the issue and was off on something else. He annoyed
and irritated her: but he also intrigued her. She had never heard
anyone discuss love and politics with such candour; his talk flowed
on, provocative, beautifully phrased, in the soft cadences of Dublin
speech.

Charlotte could hardly have been aware that this tall, lean
Dubliner with the blue eyes and winning manner was calmly
weaving an emotional cat's-cradle for himself, or that when he sat
by the window answering his large correspondence, one of the
letters he was writing should be to Ellen Terry, in which he remarked:

"We have been joined by an Irish millionairess who has had
cleverness and character enough to decline the station of life—
'great catch for somebody'—to which it pleased God to call her,
and whom we have incorporated into our Fabian family with great
success. I am going to refresh my heart by falling in love with her.
I love falling in love—but mind, only with her, not with the million; so someone else must marry her if she can stand him after me."

In another letter, referring to his Irish lady with the light-green
eyes and the million of money, he told Ellen Terry that he had come
to like Charlotte so much that it would be superfluous to fall in
love with her. This was true. The liking was genuine. As for falling
in love, Bernard Shaw had not the smallest intention of falling in
love with anybody if he could possibly help it.

The six weeks came to an end: the holiday was over. As the
weather was warm and sunny, the quartet decided to make a short
bicycling tour of the journey home, and to take several days on the
road. It would make a pleasant ending to the house party.

They left Stratford St. Andrew on September 17 and rode by
way of Felixstowe, Harwich, Braintree, Hertford and St. Albans,

staying at small hotels for the night and arriving in London on September 21. Shaw rode gaily off to his rooms in Fitzroy Square, which he shared with his mother and sister, and Charlotte accompanied the Webbs to their home in Grosvenor Road, on the Embankment, accepting Beatrice's invitation to stay with them for a few weeks.

Bernard Shaw was set on following up this new friendship. Besides the association with Jenny Patterson, he had been involved in two love affairs, one with the actress, Florence Farr, and the other with Bertha Newcombe, a portrait painter of uncommon talent and a vulnerability to romantic passion. The Florence Farr affair was now finished, and he had been trying for some time to end his friendship with Miss Newcombe. Shaw knew that he was immensely attractive to women; it was beyond his powers to restrain himself from being charming to an interesting woman. If she responded, even slightly, he became extravagantly attentive; if she allowed her interest to quicken into something deeper, he began to draw back. Bertha Newcombe's devotion now bored him into irritation. They must part for good.

The advent of Charlotte Payne-Townshend into his life became an added incentive. Within a few days he was calling on Charlotte at Grosvenor Road, either in the morning or the afternoon. His work as drama critic on the *Saturday Review* filled most of his evenings, and he was doing a great deal of speaking at meetings for the Fabians and other socialist groups. He took it for granted that he would be welcome at Grosvenor Road while Miss Payne-Townshend was there, and that she would be extremely interested in everything he was doing, what people were saying about him, and the way his emotions were working.

Charlotte was amused, and she was certainly interested. Her life had become very full since she had got to know the Webbs; she had joined the Fabian Society, met many progressive people. And now there was G.B.S., who seemed to take it for granted that her life should now be dedicated to causes which he thought important. Charlotte, too, found the causes important, but she had no intention of cutting herself off from her old friends, however reactionary they might appear to the new ones. At the end of October she arranged to go over to Ireland and stay with the Kingstons at Mitchelstown, and to go on to Derry from there. She travelled up to Manchester with the Webbs, who were to attend a meeting in that city, and spent the night with them at the Grand Hotel. A letter-card from Shaw awaited her.

"I'm unspeakably hurried and worried—oh for ten minutes peace in the moonlight at Stratford! Keep me advised of your address; keep me deep in your heart, write me two lines whenever you love me; and be happy and blessed and out of pain for my sake.

"I'm glad you've gone: London and the cessation of our open air life and me bicycling were making you wretched. I had rather you were well and a thousand miles away than ill in my wretched arms.

"In haste—farewell,

"G.B.S."

Charlotte had forgotten that she had been slightly under the weather when she had last seen Shaw. She crossed from Holyhead to Dublin, stayed at the Shelbourne Hotel for the night, and travelled down to Mitchelstown. The welcome she received from Lady Kingston and the family warmed her heart; now that she was with old friends who knew her intimately and loved her, the kind of life she had been living lately in London seemed very remote. Here, a large income was not a source of guilt, but something to be enjoyed to the full. There were horses—hunting! In London, she missed riding more than anything else; it was not so easy to ride in the Row from Adelphi Terrace as it had been from the house in Queen's Gate. Charlotte felt happy and relaxed in this large, ugly, pseudo-Gothic castle; the familiar atmosphere of easy Irish relationships made her feel at home in a way she never experienced in London. And it was rather a relief not to be surrounded the whole time by "clever" people.

A letter-card arrived from Shaw.

"How much longer do you intend to stay away? It is about three weeks since I heard anything of you. Having accordingly totally forgotten you, I was reminded of Derry today by finding a description of it . . . in that number of 'Cosmopolis' in which my article appeared.

"I write dozens of love-letters now by using up all the things that came into my head to say to you at Stratford. Unfortunately this, though an enormous success with all the others, is not available for letters to you. I have been up until 3 every morning for a fortnight, and am a miserable spectacle in consequence—can't *feel* and therefore can't write as I want to write to you.

"I'm going to Bradford tomorrow to speak for Keir Hardie. If I don't get a letter from you to read in the train I shall blight the election.

"G.B.S."

On the following day he wrote a long letter in pencil on pages torn from the exercise book on which he habitually made his notes, while travelling in the train to Bradford.

". . . I really begin to doubt whether England *is* a beautiful country. Today it looks simply cold and dull . . . I have no idea what to say on behalf of Keir Hardie. Oh, if only I could talk to you without writing—without forming sentences—without setting that fatigued machinery going! Why do you choose this time of all others to desert me—just now when you are most wanted? Imagine the condition of a man who feels like this before 11 a.m. . . . Only for Ellen Terry, who is quite angelically consolatory, and Nelly Heath, who is painting my portrait, and Lottie Fairchild, who makes me read my plays to her, and Ailsa Craig, who chaperones Lottie, I should be utterly lonely without you. Janet [Achurch] carries out your worst theories of maternity. . . . The other day she got hold of Bertha and simply tortured her—telling her that we (you and I) were engaged, and that it was an excellent thing for me, and that she would much rather see me married to you than any other woman &c. &c. &c., whereupon the distracted Bertha wrote me such a letter that I confirmed the news, gave her the date and full particulars as to the huge sums of money you were settling on me, our arrangements, the house we had taken and the deuce knows what else. Whereupon Bertha came and bullied me personally; declaimed against the perfidy of Janet and Beatrice; said that it was so disgusting that I, of all persons, should stoop to think about money & so on. All this, mind, though she knew it was all nonsense. It irritates me, as if you were a house, or a sinecure. . . . They don't understand that I have come into the fortune you have brought me already—£50,000 a week for 6 weeks at Stratford. . . ."

Charlotte replied with cool friendliness to this outpouring, and described Mitchelstown in detail. Then she allowed other feelings to break through: an indignation which had been growing during the past few days. After her first flush of pleasure at being with her friends, she had begun to enquire about the progress of the land reforms, and had found that they were being obstructed in every way possible by the landed interests—not least by many of the people she knew. It was heart-rending. It was true that in some circumstances the peasants were being allowed to buy the holdings on which they had worked for some time, but the poverty and hardship everywhere were still lamentable. Charlotte poured all this out to G.B.S. in her letter. He replied by return of post.

"Now, was there ever so sentimental a woman as this! You quote Lefanu on the miseries of your country and then send me photographs of the palatial splendours in which you weep. This, too, is the way you care for me—an imaginative luxury. No matter: I wish I were with you among those hills: there are two laps in which I could rest this fagged head of mine—Nature's and yours. I would show you then with great eloquence that all Ireland's failures have been due to her incapacity for believing in success or happiness— for talking like Lefanu while Irishmen are going out into all lands & putting them on as a shepherd putteth on his garment. As long as Ireland produces men who have the sense to leave her, she does not exist in vain. The address of *my* Ireland is 10, Adelphi Terrace. . . .

"I shall go to Paris for 'Peer Gynt' . . . if I can manage it I shall try to put off going until I have seen you. Not that it matters—it is my instinct to put off my delights—but still! I wish—but this is all nonsense. I want to tell you lies face to face—close.

"Imagine! past forty and still going on like this. I hope when I am past sixty I shall be going on like it, and for you, even though you shall have been a thousand times faithless and have forgotten me with a nice husband in a first rate position in the county. But you may pretend as you please: you will find him very stupid after me.

"G.B.S."

Charlotte drove to Derry where her cousin, Willie Townshend, entertained her. She still loved her old home dearly; she visited the tenants and the estate servants, eager to hear all their news and pick up the threads again. But it was difficult, in spite of their pleasure at seeing her. She rode with Willie, paid calls on neighbours, walked in the demesne, went into Rosscarbery. The shopkeepers greeted her kindly; many stopped her and asked after her health and the young lady, her sister, now gone to live in England with a husband, God save her soul. Charlotte, to her own astonishment, felt a stranger among them. She kept reminding herself that her home was in this place, where the mountains folded themselves against the horizon and the wide curve of the bay stretched out to the sea she had known since childhood. She *belonged* here. But she also knew she could not come back to Derry to live. She had grown away from this place far more completely than when she had gone off travelling in earlier days. The centre of her real world had moved to Adelphi Terrace, in London.

She had tried to write something of this in her latest letter to Bernard Shaw. She had also said that she missed him—and was now regretting the remark. A letter arrived from him, saying he was still waiting to go over to Paris for *Peer Gynt*. Then, abruptly:

"No: you don't love me one little bit. All that is nature, instinct, sex: it proves nothing beyond itself. Don't fall in love: be your own, not mine or anyone else's. From the moment that you can't do without me, you're lost, like Bertha.[3] Never fear: if we want one another we shall find it out. All I know is that you made the autumn very happy, and that I shall always be fond of you for that. About the future I do not concern myself; let us do what lies to our hands and wait for events. My dearest!

"G.B.S."

Charlotte was angry with herself, realizing that she had said something in her previous letter which she had not intended, and which she now could not quite remember. She did not know the state of her own feelings. Bernard Shaw attracted her greatly, but she was not in love with him. So she reassured herself. Yet, when he wrote to her like this, he set up a ferment within her which sent

[3] See page 105.

her into a rage and made her idiotically happy at the same time.
She determined not to reply to his letter—and found herself writing a short note, telling him when she would be back in Adelphi
Terrace. Shaw replied at once, declaring that directly she returned
to London he must see her, at all hazards.

"I *must*: and that *'must'* . . . TERRIFIES me. If it were possible to
run away—if it would do any good—I'd do it; so mortally afraid am
I that my trifling and lying and ingrained treachery and levity with
women are going to make you miserable when my whole desire is
to make you hap- I mean strong and self-possessed and tranquil.
However, we must talk about it. Webb gave me a tremendous lecture about it on Sunday. . . . My one hope is that you are as treacherous as I am. No matter: let's meet, meet, meet, meet, meet: bless
me! how I should like to see you again for pure liking: for there is
something between us aside and apart from my villainy. . . .

"I've had my hair clipped as short as a horse's, so prepare for
a shock.

"I'll call after lunch—between 3 & 4, probably. If you are out
I'll call again in the evening after my last meal. Or no, stop . . . I
forgot that there is a Fabian publishing meeting at 4.30 . . . As to
the afternoon, don't let me hamper you in any way. So long as I
can come in the evening & have you all to myself, with all the work
over and done, until bedtime, I don't care how you disappoint
me in the daytime. Oh lies, lies, lies, lies, flattery & luxury & longing: can any good come of it? If only you will keep tight hold of
yourself & be to yourself the centre of the universe—if only you
will. Stratford was so happy: better a million times leave it as it is
than spoil it. Unless you have the nerve to use me for your own
development without losing yourself.

"Well, well, well, well: we will talk it over most wisely—tomorrow, tomorrow, tomorrow.

"G.B.S."

There is no record of the wise conversation which was to take
place tomorrow, tomorrow, tomorrow; it is probable that it turned
out to be a monologue, a bundle of firework sparklers. Shaw continued to call at 10, Adelphi Terrace, spending most of his evenings there.

G.B.S. was not unmindful of his friends where Miss Payne-Townshend was concerned. Elizabeth Robins, the actress, was raising funds in order to put on a production of *Little Eyolf,* in which she was to play Asta and Janet Achurch, Rita. If this was successful she intended to put on other Ibsen plays, and as Bernard Shaw was an enthusiastic Ibsenite, he supported the scheme whole-heartedly. He sent a note to Miss Robins.

"Miss Payne-Townshend . . . ought to receive circulars. She is a rich, unencumbered, and public spirited Irish lady, and a great admirer of 'The Quintessence of Ibsenism.' "

He was taking quite a lot for granted in relation to the rich, un-encumbered Irish lady.

On November 4, G.B.S. wrote to Ellen Terry:

"Well, shall I marry my Irish millionairess? She . . . believes in freedom, and not in marriage: but I think I could prevail on her; and then I shall have ever so many hundreds a month for nothing. Would you ever in your secret soul forgive me, even though I am really fond of her and she of me? No you wouldn't. . . ."

Ellen chided him for being like a girl who was more thoughtless than wicked, and accused him of giving Charlotte pain. G.B.S. wrote a confused reply to this, asking what kind of a swindler and fortune hunter she took him for? He ignored the fact that if he deliberately presented himself as a fortune hunter and cad, Ellen might take him seriously and reply accordingly.

In December he wrote again to Ellen, saying he was bringing Miss Payne-Townshend to see her play *Imogen,* and when Ellen suggested that he might bring his friend round to see her after-wards, he answered in a series of verbal flourishes.

". . . you won't see Miss Townshend unless she shews herself to you. She is, normally, a ladylike person at whom nobody would ever look twice, so perfectly does she fit into her place. Age certainly not less than 37. . . . Perfectly placid and proper and pleasant. Does not condescend to be anything more. And takes it all off like a mask when she selects you for that intimacy which she does in the most cold-blooded way. She is not cheap enough to be brought round to your room and *shewn* to you. She isnt an appendage, this green-eyed one, but an individual. No prejudices—has too much

respect for *you* to put up with anything less *from* you. In a dressing
room interview you can do nothing effective except by playing the
charming woman of experience and talent receiving with affectionate interest, condescension and a lovable artless childishness of delight, a young creature just venturing into the life you are queen of.
You'd feel instantly with her that the dressing-room was the wrong
scene for the right *line* . . ."

Charlotte had begun to learn typewriting, so that she could help
G.B.S. with the work which was continually piling up on his desk
at Fitzroy Square. He very rarely spoke of his "home," or of his
mother, with whom he shared the upper part of a house, 29, Fitzroy
Square, between Tottenham Court Road and Great Portland Street.
Lucinda Elizabeth Shaw had left her drunken, feckless husband
some years before, and had come from Dublin to London with her
two daughters, whom she supported by giving music lessons; she
was a fine teacher of singing. Bernard Shaw had remained in Dublin to live with his father, but he, too, decided to leave Ireland
and seek his fortune in London. He arrived in April, 1876, and
went to live with his mother and sister Lucy in a house they had
taken in the Fulham district. The other sister, Agnes, had recently
died.

It was a queer ménage. Mrs. Shaw, a cold, unemotional woman,
had one great passion in life: the system of singing she had been
taught by Vandaleur Lee, who had lived with the Shaws in Dublin.
She accepted her son into the Fulham household with neither
pleasure nor resentment: she simply accepted him. His sister Lucy,
on the other hand, disliked him and did not hesitate to show it.
She had ambitions to become an opera singer, and she angrily demanded that her mother should turn him out unless he was prepared to earn his living. She did not allude to the fact that she
herself was earning nothing: and Lucinda Elizabeth said little about
a legacy of £4,000 left to the children by a maternal great-grand-
father, money over which she had a power of attorney on their
behalf. When G.B.S. stated in later life, as he often did, with an
air of bravado that he had sponged on his mother while teaching
himself the craft of writing, he knew quite well that he was talking
nonsense; the money his mother spent on him was his own.

Lucinda Elizabeth was no housekeeper. She disliked cooking and housework, and employed a cheap servant to look after them. G.B.S. never knew what it was to have a properly prepared meal or a tidy room, either in the Fulham house or later in Fitzroy Square. Lucy had now gone off to find fame and fortune on the operatic stage, by way of an unfortunate marriage, and G.B.S. and his mother shared the rooms between them, though they lived entirely separate lives. Apart from the squalor which Lucinda Elizabeth did not seem to mind, and G.B.S. after a time ceased to notice, they had no point of contact in the ordinary human relationship which normally exists between mother and son. G.B.S. was to pour his unhappiness and resentments against Lucinda Elizabeth into the mouth of Adrian Herbert, in his unsuccessful novel, *Love Among the Artists*. Talking of his mother, Adrian Herbert says:

"Can you not understand that a mother and son can be so different in their dispositions that neither can sympathise with the other? It is my misfortune to be such a son. I have found sympathetic friendship, encouragement, respect, faith in my abilities, and love . . . from strangers. . . . In my mother, I found none of them. . . . She did not know how much her indifference tortured me, because she had no idea of any keener sensitiveness than her own. Everybody commits folly from youth and want of experience; and I hope most people humour and spare such follies as tenderly as they can. My mother did not even laugh at them. She saw through them and stamped them out with open contempt. She taught me to do without her consideration; and I learned my lesson. My friends will tell you that I am a bad son—never that she is a bad mother, or rather no mother. She has the power of bringing out everything that is hasty and disagreeable in my nature by her presence alone. That is why I wish I were wholly an orphan."

It was a bitter cry, and it may not be fanciful to believe that it came from George Bernard Shaw's heart. It was undoubtedly the cause of the mocking-cynical façade which he took pains to flaunt before the world where deep feeling was concerned—a grinning, dehumanized mask. Behind the mask there was always the thwarted child, hungering for affection and eager to give it.

Charlotte did not know the whole story then; Shaw was hardly the kind of man to disclose his innermost self, even to the attractive millionairess who was beginning, to his dismay, to take up rather more of his thoughts than he wished. He brought notes to Adelphi Terrace for Charlotte to type, dictated to her, argued with her, paid her fantastic compliments and bullied her delicately in the next breath. Charlotte made him welcome in her straightforward way, and asked no questions. She understood a great deal more about him and his background than he gave her credit for: she understood that particular brand of unhappiness very well.

10

TAMING THE PHILANDERER

(1 8 9 7 – 1 8 9 8)

Charlotte saw a great deal of Shaw during that winter of 1896–97. She went up to Keyham early in January to spend a few days with Sissy and Hugh and Cecily, but she was back by the middle of the month, as G.B.S. had arranged to take her to the matinée of a pantomime. She had written to him from Keyham to say she had had an attack of neuralgia, and he promptly sent her a letter-card saying he was glad the pain had gone:

"It lifts a weight of 90,000,000,000,000,000,000,000 tons from my heart."

Later in the month he wrote saying he had two stalls for the Lyceum, where Ellen was taking the name part in *Olivia*.

"Can you come? If not, let me know as soon as possible. But I decline to entertain the idea of your not coming."

He brought Charlotte more work to type, though he already had a regular secretary, Mrs. Salt, the wife of Henry Salt, one of the Fabians. Shaw admired Mrs. Salt because of her efficiency, but he did not otherwise care for her. He suspected that she had once been in love with him—nay, she was still the slave of a hopeless infatuation. If she was, it showed itself in sharpness of manner and tartness of speech. G.B.S. wrote to Charlotte:

"Mrs. Salt announces that she is going to Limpsfield and won't be back until Tuesday. She complains of my temper and wants to know whether I would dare to speak to you like that."

Meanwhile, Beatrice Webb was being drawn into the affair in a way that annoyed her. She had had a letter from Bertha New-combe asking if she would call and see her. Beatrice had always met the painter in the company of Bernard Shaw, and now that they had parted, she knew she would encounter a sad, lonely woman. She felt uncomfortable as she entered Miss Newcombe's house and went upstairs to the dark, wainscotted studio. Beatrice described the encounter in her Diary:

"She is petite and dark—about forty years old but looks more like a wizened girl than a fully developed woman. Her jet black hair heavily fringed, half smart, half artistic clothes, pinched aquiline features and thin lips—give you a somewhat unpleasant impression tho' not wholly inartistic . . . many people would call her 'lady-like' but she is insignificant and undistinguished. 'I want to talk to you, Mrs. Webb,' she said, when I had seated myself. And then followed, told with the dignity of devoted feeling, the story of her relationship to Bernard Shaw, her five years devoted love, his cold philandering, her hopes aroused by my repeated advice to him (which he, it appears, had repeated much exaggerated) to marry her—and then her feeling of dismay and resentment against me when she discovered that I was encouraging him 'to marry Miss Townshend.' Finally he had written a month ago to break it off entirely. . . . And I had to explain to her with perfect frankness that so long as there seemed a chance for her I had been willing to act as chaperone—that she had never been a personal friend of mine, or Sidney's, that I had regarded her only as Shaw's friend, and that as far as I was concerned I should have welcomed her as his wife. But directly I saw that he meant nothing I backed out of the affair. She took it all quietly—her little face seemed to shrink up. . . . 'You are well out of it, Miss Newcombe,' I said gently. 'If you had married Shaw he would not have remained faithful to you. You know my opinion of him—as a friend and a colleague, as a critic and literary worker, there are few men for whom I have so warm a liking—but in his relations with women he is vulgar—if not worse—it is a vulgarity which includes cruelty and springs from vanity.

"As I uttered these words my eyes caught her portrait of Shaw—full-length, with his red-gold hair and laughing blue eyes and his mouth slightly open as if scoffing at us both—a powerful picture in which the love of the woman had given genius to the artist. Her little face turned to follow my eyes and she felt also the expression of the man—the mockery at her deep-rooted affection.

" 'It is horribly lonely,' she muttered. 'I daresay it is more peaceful than being kept on the rack—but it is like the peace of death.'

"There seemed nothing more to be said. I rose with a perfunctory 'Come and see me—someday,' kissed her on the forehead and escaped down the stairs. And then I thought of that other woman with her loving, easy-going nature and anarchic luxurious ways—her well-bred manners and well-made clothes—her leisure, wealth and knowledge of the world. Would she succeed in taming the philanderer?"

Many years later, Bertha Newcombe was to write about this period of her life to Ashley Dukes, who wanted to edit and publish the Shaw-Janet Achurch correspondence. Shaw originally agreed to this proposal, but later withdrew his permission—probably because he did not want to upset Charlotte, who had always disliked Janet Achurch. Miss Newcombe wrote:

". . . I think it only just that I should be allowed to state what seems to me after nearly 40 years to be a fairly true account of our friendship.

"Shaw was, I should imagine, by preference a passionless man. He had passed through experiences, and he seemed to have no wish for and even to fear passion though he admitted its power and pleasure. The sight of a woman deeply in love with him annoyed him. He was not in love with me, in the usual sense, or at any rate as he said only for a very short time, and he found I think those times the pleasantest when I was the appreciative listener. Unfortunately there was on my side a deep feeling most injudiciously displayed and from this distance I realize how exasperating it must have been to him. He had decided I think on a line of honourable conduct—honourable to his thinking. He kept strictly to the letter of it while allowing himself every opportunity of transgressing the spirit. Frequent talking, talking, talking of the pros and cons of marriage, even to my prospects of money or the want of it, his dislike of the sexual relation and so on, would create an atmosphere of lovemaking without any need for caresses or endearments. . . .

"Lovemaking would have been very delightful, doubtless, but I wanted, besides, a wider companionship, and as I was inadequately equipped for that, except as a painter of some intelligence, he refused to give more than amusement. Shaw has not a gift of sympathetic penetration into a woman's nature. He employs his clever detective power on weaknesses and faults which confirm his preconceived ideas. He imagines he understands. I objected to my emotions being divided into compartments and still retain my opinion that the emotion of love can be a fusion of body, spirit and mind.

"Nevertheless I acknowledge now that the hand of Providence with Shaw's consent and guidance intervened with good results on his behalf in warding off any possibility of a marriage with me."

Towards the end of March, Charlotte had a blazing quarrel with Shaw. They had disagreed on many occasions, and Charlotte's temper had often flared at him, but this time it was serious. The cause was a well-intentioned suggestion from Charlotte that the Phillimores should not be expected to pay an equal share of the expenses of the house she and the Webbs proposed to take in the country for the usual Fabian house party, which was to include Robert Phillimore and his wife, Lion.

Beatrice Webb in the Diaries describes Lion Phillimore as "a bright talented Irishwoman—(reputed a drunken Belfast carpenter's daughter who worked her way up as a district visitor to Lady Henry Somerset's secretaryship, from that to a seat on the St. Pancras Vestry, and thence to a marriage with her fellow Vestryman—the socialistic, philanthropic and eccentric son of Sir Walter Phillimore)—a good deal older than her young husband."

The Phillimores attended Vestry meetings and committees, and were preparing to write a textbook on London Government, a subject in which the Webbs were closely interested. They lived in a cottage on Sir Walter Phillimore's estate, and were determined to be progressive in every way. This did not prevent them from accepting an adequate income from Phillimore *père,* and G.B.S. was enraged at Charlotte's suggestion that they would not be able to pay their way if they joined the house party. The quarrel ended in an explosion which threatened to break up everything between them. On March 30, G.B.S. was writing:

"Somehow, I am beginning to feel like my old self again. After all, it is magnificent to be alone, with the ivy stripped off. As I walk round the park at night, looking at the other stars, I no longer feel 42. The hopples are off; my soul is disentangled from Martha's[1] parlourmaid's uniform; I am natural once more. You count that I have lost only one Charlotte; but I have lost two, and one of the losses is a prodigious relief. I may miss 'die schone grunen Augen' occasionally, though the very privation throws me back, brutally great, to my natural dreamland; but then think of the other Charlotte, the terrible Charlotte, the lier-in-wait, the soul hypochondriac, always watching and dragging me into bondage, always planning nice sensible, comfortable, selfish destruction for me, wincing at every accent of freedom in my voice, so that at last I get the trick of hiding myself from her, hating me and longing for me with the absorbing passion of the spider for the fly. Now that she is gone, I realize for the first time the infernal tyranny of the past year, which left me the licence of the rebel, not the freedom of the man who stands alone. I will have no more of it: if you hate women who pull flowers, what do you think of women who cut down trees? *That's* the Charlotte I want to see married. The Charlotte of Iken Heath is another matter, yet I have her in my dreamland, and sometimes doubt whether the other devil ever had anything to do with her.

". . . I never heard such vulgar Irish rubbish in my life as your meaning that the Phillimores should pay nothing . . . Drivel— simple drivel! Why shouldn't they pay what they can afford? Why

[1] Martha was one of Charlotte's maids at Adelphi Terrace; the other was Mary Farmer.

shouldn't I pay? Are we to be Lady Bountifulled across our heads in
this fashion? . . .

"It is close to midnight: I must stalk off into the path round the
park to embrace my true mistress the Night. I hope this letter will
make the other Charlotte YELL with anguish—little enough to
expiate my centuries of slavery and misery.

"Wrrrrrrrrrrrrrrrrrrrrrrrrrrrrrrr!

"G.B.S."

Charlotte was not in the habit of yelling, and she was now used
to Shaw's exaggerations and flights of fancy. A house was rented
in Surrey, and Shaw took it for granted that he would be one of
the party, as usual. The Phillimores decided not to join them, after
all. G.B.S. arranged to come up to town for his lectures and other
engagements, and he was soon writing to Ellen Terry:

"I am in a ridiculous difficulty with Miss P.T. She insists on
coming to my lectures in all sorts of holes and corners—dock gates
next Sunday morning. I have noticed that the experience makes
her very unhappy. At first I thought she was bored and tired and
incommoded simply, but now it appears that my demagogic denun-
ciation of the idle rich—my demands for taxation of unearned
income—lacerated her conscience, for she has great possessions.
What am I to do: she won't stay away; and I can't talk Primrose
League. Was there ever such a situation?"

The situation was entirely of Shaw's making. Charlotte did not
insist on going to his lectures; he teased her into going, time after
time, taking advantage of her genuine social conscience over the
condition of the poor to force her to go and see for herself what
poverty really looked like at the dock gates in the East End. Charlotte shrank instinctively from the roughness and the foul language
of the dockers, but she showed nothing of her feelings: she listened
to Shaw's crisp speeches and to the raucous laughter which greeted
his sallies, and knew that an ardent flame burned in this man.

Shaw also got her interested in the newly-formed Stage Society,
which had grown out of the efforts of Elizabeth Robins to put on
productions of Ibsen's plays. The venture of the preceding autumn
had not been successful, but Miss Robins was trying again. There
were no theatres in London where the "new" plays would be ac-

cepted; it was the era of the fashionable drawing-room comedy and Irving's full-blooded theatrical interpretations of melodrama at the Lyceum. No playwright who attempted to portray contemporary life as it actually existed, or which presented grave social problems, had a chance of being produced.

The theatre progressives had formed a society which they called the Stage Society, and it soon had many supporters. The first committee included Elizabeth Robins, William Archer, the drama critic, H. W. Massingham, a noted journalist, Alfred Sutro, the dramatist, and Charles Charrington, husband of the actress Janet Achurch. Charlotte agreed to sit on the reading and advisory committee.

Shaw's play, *You Never Can Tell*, was performed at the Royalty Theatre in Soho, under the aegis of the Stage Society. It had been previously put into rehearsal by Cyril Maude, but had been turned down because the actors could not understand what it was about. The performance at the Royalty, with a more perceptive cast, was a great success and established the Stage Society as an important factor in the theatrical life of London.

The country house party at Dorking was bringing out Beatrice Webb's usual reaction where Charlotte Payne-Townshend and Bernard Shaw were concerned. She wrote in her Diary:

"I am watching with concern and curiosity the development of the Shaw-Townshend friendship. All this winter they have been lovers—of a philandering and harmless kind—always together when Shaw was free. Charlotte insisted on taking a house with us in order that he might be here constantly; and it is obvious that she is deeply attached to him. But I see no sign on his side of the growth of any genuine and steadfast affection. He finds it pleasant to be with her in her luxuriant surroundings, he has been studying her and all her little ways and amusing himself by dissecting the rich woman brought up without training and drifting about at the beck of any impulse. I think he has now exhausted the study—observed all that there is to observe. He has been flattered by her devotion and absorption in him; he is kindly and has a cat-like pref-- erence for those persons to whom he is accustomed. But there are

ominous signs that he is tired of watching the effect of little words
of gallantry and personal interest with which he plied her in the
first months of the friendship. And he is annoyed at her lack of
purpose and utter incapacity for work. If she would set to and do
even the smallest and least considerable task of intellectual work, I
believe she could retain his interest and perhaps develop his feeling for her. Otherwise he will drift away; for Shaw is too high-
minded and too conventionally honourable to marry her for the
life of leisure and luxury he could gain for himself as her husband."

Beatrice Webb's eyes were searching, but she could only base
her judgments on what she saw. She did not in the least realize
that Charlotte was being very strongly influenced by her own marriage, or that Charlotte's eyes were equally sharp when she watched
Sidney and Beatrice working together, or engaged in their "incorrigible spooning."

Every time Charlotte stayed with the Webbs, she was conscious
of the great happiness which was like a radiance in their life together. It had a marked effect on her own feelings and ideas about
marriage: she was not so sure of herself now. Shaw disturbed her.
She did not want their friendship to go any further, and yet—and
yet—Beatrice and Sidney Webb had achieved something which
she had once thought impossible. Could it not happen again?
Charlotte knew perfectly well that her own intellectual capacity
was far below that of Bernard Shaw; this was where they differed
from the Webbs, who were so well matched in mind. But Charlotte
was by nature an admirer of brains and character, and she was
more than eager to use what talents and capacity she possessed in
the service of some worth-while cause. She did not deny to herself
that Shaw attracted her as a man, but that was only a part of it. The
hero-worshipping element in her nature—which had almost been
her undoing in the past, more than once—was asserting itself
again. She reverenced men of intellect, men with the driving
power to push ahead and do something great in the world. Whenever she met people like that, she had an overpowering urge to
stand by their side, to identify herself with their genius. In a muddled, chaotic fashion Charlotte knew that this was an irrational

instinct, one which warred with the clear common sense which
was one of her characteristics. But the conflict went on, and she
could only hope that a sudden impulse would not sweep her into
doing something she would regret later.

Beatrice Webb was thoroughly angry with Bernard Shaw. He was
spoiling these beautiful sunny days at Dorking, creating an atmosphere which was different from any she had known before, though
heaven knew she had seen enough of his stupidities in the past.
She wrote in her Diary on May 8, 1897:

"Silly these philanderings of Shaw's. He imagines that he gets
to know women by making them fall in love with him. Just the
contrary. His stupid gallantries bar out from him the friendship of
women who are either too sensible, too puritanical, or too much
'otherwise engaged' to care to bandy personal flatteries with him.
One large section of women comprising some, at any rate, of the
finest types, remain hidden from him. With women with whom
he has *bonne fortune* he also fails in his object—or rather in his
avowed object—vivisection. He idealises them for a few days,
weeks or years—imagines them to be something utterly different
from their true selves—then has a revulsion of feeling and discovers them to be unutterably vulgar, second-rate, rapscallion, or
insipidly well-bred. He never fathoms their real worth, nor rightly
sees their limitations. But in fact it is not the end he cares for. It
is the *process*. His sensuality has all drifted into sexual vanity—
delight in being the candle to the moths—with a dash of intellectual curiosity to give flavour to his tickled vanity. And he is
mistaken if he thinks that it does not affect his artistic work. His
incompleteness as a thinker, his shallow and vulgar view of many
human relationships—and lack of the sterner kind of humour
which would show him the dreariness of his farce and the total
absence of proportion, and inadequateness in some of his ideas—all
these defects come largely from the flippant and worthless self-
complacency brought about by the worship of rather second-rate
women. For all that, he is a good-natured agreeable sprite of a
man—an intellectual cricket on the hearth, always chirping brilliant paradox, sharp-witted observation and friendly comments.

Whether I like him, admire him, or despise him most I do not
know. Just at present I feel annoyed and contemptuous. For the
dancing light has gone out of Charlotte's eyes—there is at times a
blank haggard look—a look that I myself felt in my own eyes for
long years. But throughout all my misery, I had the habit of hard
work and an almost religious sense of my intellectual mission. . . .
Charlotte has nowhere to turn. She can only wander listless
through the world, with no reason for turning one way rather than
another. What a comfort to be a fanatic. It is Bernard Shaw's
fanaticism to turn everything inside out and see whether the other
side won't do just as well, if not better; it is this fanaticism which
gives him genuine charm underneath his vanity—will she touch
that?"

A fortnight later she was writing in her Diary again:

"Glorious summer days. In excellent working form. Long mornings spent in work; re-casting some of the chapters, filling up cre-
vasses and thinking out the last chapter and fore-shadowing the
preface. Sidney sits at one table and I at another: the sun streams
in through the dancing leaves. . . . Charlotte sits upstairs typewriting Shaw's plays—Shaw wanders about the garden with writing
book and pencil, writing the 'Saturday' article, correcting his plays
for press, or reading through one of our chapters. With extraordinary good nature he will spend days over some part of our work,
and an astute reader will quickly divine those chapters which Shaw
has corrected and those which he has not—there is a conciseness
and crispness in the parts subjected to his pruning knife lacking
elsewhere."

Back in London, Shaw's letters to Charlotte continued. What
did she think of them? It is difficult to conjecture. She had had
dozens of love-letters in her life, many of them pedestrian but
sincere. General Clery's had moved and disturbed her, the others
had had an effect, even though her feelings had never been really
touched. These letters from G.B.S., coming almost daily, were
fantastically different. She replied to some of them, but even to
herself her answers seemed hopelessly inadequate.

She could not know that G.B.S. was engaging in useful literary

exercises—not deliberately, but because he could not help dramatizing everything he put down on paper. St. John Ervine, in his
book *Bernard Shaw, His Life, Work and Friends,* discussing one of
Shaw's letters to an early love, Alice Lockett, comments:

"The letter is incoherent, as a love-letter ought to be, for what
man can be coherent in a passion for a girl, but it is also curiously
calculating. Its writer knows how to make an apprehensive young
woman, accustomed only to formal addresses, feel that informality
in wooing is delightful, even if it is alarming."

Charlotte was not in the least alarmed. If she had been a young
girl, the letters would still not have been disconcerting; she would
simply have thought the man odd. Now, knowing G.B.S., she
took them as individual to him. Whether she thought he meant
any or all of what he wrote is not known. His letter of July 13 was
very characteristic:

"I have an iron ring round my chest which tightens and grips
my heart when I remember that you are still tormented. Loosen
it, oh ever dear to me, by a word to say that you slept well and have
never been better than today. Or else lend me my fare to Australia,
to Siberia, to the mountains of the moon, to any place where I can
torment nobody but myself. I am sorry—not vainly sorry, for I
have done a good morning's work, but painfully, wistfully, affectionately sorry that you were hurt; but if you had seen my mind
you would not have been hurt. I am so certain of that that I am in
violently, brutally high spirits in spite of that iron ring. Write me
something happy, but only a few words; and don't sit down to *think*
over them. What you think is all wrong.

"G.B.S.

"P.S. I am going out to lunch and to Grant Richards's shop. If you
send a line between, say 4 & 5.30 (after which I think I will go
off for a thousand leagues on the bike) I shall be here to receive
it. Oh, the ring, the ring: hasten to ease it a little: it clutched me
bitterly just then."

Beatrice Webb took a house called the Argoed for August and
September at Penallt, Monmouth, where she and Sidney intended
to work on their book on Trade Unionism. Shaw was with them,
revising his plays for publication, and Charlotte was there in the

capacity of his unpaid secretary. G.B.S. wrote to Ellen Terry:

". . . There is some question of my going over to Leamington with Miss P.T. . . . What are you wondering about me? She is getting used to me now, I think. Down at Dorking there was a sort of earthquake because she had been cherishing a charming project of at last making me a very generous and romantic proposal—saving it up as a sort of climax to the proofs she was giving me every day of her regard for me. When I received that golden moment with shuddering horror and wildly asked the fare to Australia she was inexpressibly taken aback, and her pride, which is considerable, much startled."

There is no record of what Ellen made of this fabrication. G.B.S. saw no inconsistency in stressing Charlotte's pride and at the same time dramatizing the situation in these extravagant terms. Charlotte was undoubtedly in a state of strain, however. Beatrice Webb wrote:

"Shaw and Charlotte's relationship is disturbing. Shaw goes on untroubled, working hard at his plays and then going for long rides with Charlotte on a tandem. But Charlotte is always restless and unhappy—too anxious to be with him. He is sometimes bored, but he is getting to feel her a necessary part of his 'entourage,' and would, I think, object to her breaking away from the relationship. He persuades himself that by keeping her occupied he is doing her good. If it were not for the fact that he were Shaw I should say he was dishonourable. But as he has always advertised his views on marriage and philandering from the housetops, every woman ought to be prepared for his logical carrying out of these principles."

G.B.S. came back to reality with an indignant comment to Ellen on the sins of Janet Achurch, who had borrowed £50 from Charlotte.

"Just imagine this £50 business. Can you imagine a more morally *thriftless* thing to do than to take advantage of a rich woman being fond of me and a play of mine being in the repertory to extract money, knowing all the time what she must think of the transaction and what I must feel about it . . ."

Charlotte went up to Keyham in October, and G.B.S. sent her

the first batch of notices of *The Devil's Disciple*, which had been
produced by Richard Mansfield in New York. The following day
he was writing to Charlotte that the play was wanted for a first-
class production in London, and that as he had to read *You Never
Can Tell* to Hawtrey the following day, he thought it best to make
a desperate attempt to get his voice into order, so he had descended
on his mother, and sang, mostly fortissimo . . . "all the Messiah . . .
an album of German songs, and an almost exhaustive selection
from Das Rheingold. I now feel equal to four acts.

"It is most inconvenient having Adelphi Terrace shut up. I have
nowhere to go, nobody to talk to . . .

"Fahr' wohl, mein treues Herz: zu tausend gute Nacht (quotation from Leider album).

"I ought to be correcting Widowers' Houses instead of writing
this."

Charlotte was now living a strange double life. At Keyham,
there were riding and hunting, dinner parties, drives in the carriage to return calls on Sissy's friends in the Big Houses of the
neighbourhood. When she told her sister about the School of
Economics and the interesting new people she had been meeting,
Sissy was not enthusiastic. Lottie's new "set" sounded distinctly
unconventional. To Hugh, they appeared to be dangerously radical.
Charlotte found it better not to talk about them.

She wrote at length to Augustine Henry in San Francisco;
Augustine had been sending regular letters to Charlotte, asking
what she was doing about her future. Charlotte replied:

"You asked if I am going to study the position of the depressed
and degraded from 'within or from without.'

"See here. If you were going to be a doctor, would you go to a
hospital ward or the scene of a railway accident and say 'You poor
souls, I am going to be a doctor and help you. Now, some of you
have fever, so I will bleed you and reduce it: some of you have
cankering sores, so I will close them up and patch them over; some
of you have broken legs, so I will support you and carry you because you cannot walk.' Is that what you would do? Or would you
go to a college and get books and listen to lectures and see demon-
strations and for years painfully and slowly acquire knowledge of

the causes and symptoms of the evils you wanted to remove, and of the best manner of treating them, and of all that has been found out by others on the subject before you even looked at a patient? I think you would do the last.

"Now it has occurred to me that those who try to remedy the terrible evils we see around us by healing individual wounds, and patching individual sores, by philanthropy, in fact, are like the doctor who tries to cure his patients by rule of thumb. It is a whole occupation—philanthropy—and I reverence those who are engaged in it, but I think their position says more for their hearts than their heads. (Note: the social evil has gone too deep for mere surface palliation. We must have something else. Something more virile and more radical.) Is what is wanted a new science? Something like the science of medicine applied collectively, and which will consist of the study of these social horrors we are talking of from the point of view of recent discovery: the study, in fact, of sociology. This is probably what you mean by going at these things 'from without' and, one might add, from *above*. It is a study which has barely been attempted yet, which has only just been rendered possible by the advance of modern thought, and in which nearly everything remains to do, the very methods of conducting the enquiry having still to be discovered. (Note: and what I hope to do is this: with all my power, physical, financial and intellectual, to study sociology as I describe it and to help and encourage others cleverer than myself to study it.) If I only make the way one little bit easier for the students who are with me and come after me, or if by my failures and mistakes I only show them what to avoid— that will be reason enough for me devoting my life to it."

Augustine Henry replied to this exposition with such lack of understanding that Charlotte wrote again.

"I have not made my position at all clear to you yet, I see. . . . You say: 'I am so glad you are not going in for so-called philanthropy —I hate it.' And yet you write as though you thought I was going to constantly visit and personally talk to the 'unhappy and degraded'—now, what is that but philanthropy? It is terrible to say, and sometimes I am afraid when the thought comes to me, but I know that in my heart I believe that there is *no* hope for the degraded, the oppressed, the poor under existing social conditions, that it is no use trying to help them directly. You may snatch a few brands from the burning, but the point is to put out the fire . . . the disease, not the symptom, must be cured. What are the lines along which the proposed alterations must run . . . ownership of property, the commercial system . . . and *above all* the marriage question and the raising of women physically and intellectually. There are questions sometimes better not discussed in letters, but I will say this much, that if you understand my feelings on this last, the marriage and the woman question, to go as far and be as extreme as it is possible for them to go and be, you will be near the mark. . . .

"Now I will tell you, as examples of my ideas (called so by courtesy!) of two ways in which I have already made small beginnings. I go, several times a week, to the London School of Medicine for Women. I have taken up Anatomy and Physiology, but not only because I am deeply interested in those subjects. My principal object is to get to know the students and teachers there and all the people connected with the School. I think medicine the finest of all professions and I would like to help women to get into it, and to be a credit to it when they do get in. The School here is still struggling: it has as much as it can do to make both ends meet and most of the young women who attend are very poor, and barely keep body and soul together, and pay the fees while they are going through their course. Some of them have failed to pass their examinations because they could not afford to buy the necessary books or have private instruction. I propose to watch and notice and get to know the School and its inhabitants well, and thus, if it seems desirable, to found a scholarship there which would help at least one woman every year to get along. I have also thought about helping them with the building fund of the new college they hope to start soon, and then there is a question. I think men and women ought to be educated together. So that is a problem for the future.

"Now about the second thing. (More difficult to explain.) Some friends of mine lately started a school of 'Economics and Political Science.' The idea in doing so was this. There is practically no in-

struction in political and economic science to be obtained in Great
Britain now. In the first place, what *is* political economy? A system
called by that name was taught by Adam Smith and his followers,
but modern research seems to have changed the whole of the data
upon which he based his arguments and conclusions—in fact has
altered the face of the world. The average educated person knows
nothing of the financial system under which he lives. He sees that
certain persons are millionaires and others are paupers, but ask
him 'why,' he does not know. . . . We must know something of all
these things before we can begin to think about answering the
question why the poor are so poor and the rich are so rich. My
friends have started their School to try and teach anybody and
everybody who is interested to learn any or all of these things. The
School is not committed to any political opinions. The lectures are
all given by men of standing and reputation: some of these men
are conservatives, some liberals, some socialists. . . . So I hope to
learn in this School and to help it on. It is only a small beginning
as yet. Soon we hope to take a house where we shall have lecture
rooms and classrooms, and where we shall start a library.'"

Augustine wrote by return of post, asking a great many questions.
She was genuinely troubled on Charlotte's account; she wondered
where all this was going to lead her friend. Charlotte replied with
equal promptitude.

"I am in the rather unusual position of being perfectly free. I have
no near relations. I am independent financially. I am unconventional by nature. The personal happiness which everyone puts
first and which I had within my grasp was lost to me, greatly by
my own fault and partly by circumstances over which I had no control, and my life is a wreck; so I am free from the ordinary individual hopes, fears and despairs which are so apt to become chains.
Under these circumstances there is nothing to prevent my doing
exactly as I choose. I have asked myself seriously the question
'What do you choose to do?' I love brightness, sunshine, art. So
does everyone else. My first inclination, of course, was to go to a
sunny land and brighten my life with all the resources of art and
intellect. But then comes another thought. I am able to do this,
but what about the thousands of my fellow country-men and

women who cannot follow my example. . . . An accident of birth
and social position has put me in a position of money and education.
. . . If I take advantage of the accident to use to the full my good
fortune in gratifying myself and beautifying and expanding my
own life . . . do you think I shall be doing a very noble and worthy
thing?

"Now supposing . . . as a matter of conscience, a person situated
as I am ought to give her time and her money to trying to make
things more even between the 'Haves' and the 'Have nots,' the next
questions of course are Can one do anything? and How is one
to begin?"

Beatrice and Sidney Webb had helped Charlotte to make a
beginning, and Bernard Shaw was continuing the process of educat-
ing her in the practical politics of effecting social changes. The
fact that he was mixing this up with ardent literary love-making had
amused her at first. Now she wondered whether it was not time to
stop him. She knew him well enough to recognize that he had set
out to fascinate her, as he tried to fascinate every woman worth the
charming. What worried and sometimes angered her was the fact
that he was succeeding.

His letters came almost every day.

"A curious thing happened to me last night. In the afternoon
I got a telegram from some old friends asking me to dine with them
at the Metropole, or at least see them afterwards, as they were starting for India in the morning. I couldn't dine, as my work kept me
until half-past ten here, Fitzroy Square. It was 10.45 when I
reached the Turkish Bath clock in Northumberland Avenue. I
willed to cross the street to the Metropole; but to my astonishment
my legs suddenly walked off with me through the railway arches
to Adelphi Terrace. The big staircase light was blazing Eddyston-
ianly through the night; but all the rooms were dark except two
bedrooms at the top, one of them yours. So I returned to the
Metropole. . . ."

At the beginning of November Charlotte went to Paris with
some friends, and G.B.S. sent her a card:

"Oh, what a Sunday! . . . I wish you could stay in Paris and that

I could get there in a quarter of an hour. I feel that you are much better and brighter there; but it is damnably inconvenient to have you out of my reach. Why don't you get introduced to Coquelin and tell him that Mansfield of New York plays a superb Coquelin part in a play called 'Arms and the Man'—this is a spartan life—but no matter.

"(Signed) G.B.S."[2]

On her return Charlotte stayed with the Phillimores at Radlett, in Hertfordshire. G.B.S. wrote to her there on November 14: "Ever Dearest,

"I had a toss on the big hill on the way home; but I was not hurt except for a black eye and a cut face; so do not be alarmed by the blood-curdling account I am sending to Mrs. Phillimore. A woman got into my way when I was going fast down the hill. I managed to twist the bike round her safely, but . . . literally wiped the road with my left cheek. I am a ludicrous spectacle—like a badly defeated prizefighter. I rode on gaily to Edgware, called a doctor there, got stitched up, and rode home. Visits were, of course, out of the question . . . I am too hideous to be looked at. I am glad I got just enough hurt to make you tender to me."

Charlotte sent him a note of sympathy, taking care not to make it too tender, went on enjoying her visit to the Phillimores, and returned to London at the end of November. She was to have gone to a theatre to meet Shaw for a matinée performance, but was delayed elsewhere. The next day there was a letter from him.

"As I did not see you at the theatre today I became possessed with a notion that the sudden sharp cold had given you neuralgia. The performance lasted until just six; and I had to rush away with Grant Richards after it. At 9, I called at the Terrace and was confronted by Farmer[3] and Martha, who informed me that you had been out all the afternoon, which at least disposed of the disablement-by-neuralgia theory.

"I shall not intrude on my secretary tomorrow. If she decides to resume her duties, doubtless she will come to me.

[2] When G.B.S. wanted to show his displeasure to Charlotte his signature was preceded by "(Signed)."
[3] Charlotte's second servant.

"You shall not be worried into any more headaches. I am now a perfect gentleman, and, under further notice, am

"Yours respectfully,

"(Signed) G.B.S."

Lion Phillimore, who had not been well and wanted some sea air, suggested to Charlotte that they should go over to Dieppe at the beginning of December. Her husband was unable to accompany them, and Charlotte wrote a note to Shaw, saying that a few days' rest would do him good. His reaction was sharp.

"Certainly the proposed treat is a real one. I am to embark in a piercing wind, with lifeboats capsizing and ships foundering in all directions, to go to a watering place in the depths of winter with nothing to do and nowhere to go; I am to be chaperoned by two women, each determined that the other shall seduce me and each determined that I shall not seduce her; I am to sleep in a foreign hotel with the window open and no bedclothes—perhaps without even a lock on the door to protect me; and next day I am to embark again for four hours more of seasickness. No, thank you. I am comfortable as I am: j'y suis et j'y reste. If you go alone, you will be company for the invalid. If I went alone, she would be company for me. But I bar the seaside à trois. . . .

"No use in looking for human sympathy from me. I have turned the switch, and am your very good friend, but as hard as nails.

"G.B.S."

Charlotte wrote to say she would be going with Lion, nevertheless. A card came by return of post:

"Secretary required tomorrow, not later than eleven."

She did not answer the summons. Two days later:

"What do you mean by this inconceivable conduct? Do you forsake *all* your duties—even those of secretary? Is it not enough that I have returned without a complaint to my stark and joyless life? Must I also go back to writing my own articles, and wasting half hours between the sentences with long trains of reflection? Not a word: not a sign! I send you instructions to arrive at eleven; and *wait* for you instead of beginning by myself, so perfect is my faith in your arrival. I get your shawl, your footwarmer: I sweep the hearth to make the fire look nice for you, and am openly grinned

at by the domestic for my pains! Is Dieppe China (assuming that
you are there)? Are there no stamps? Has the post been abolished?
Have all the channel steamers foundered?

"Go then, ungrateful wretch: have your heart's desire: find a
Master—one who will spend your money, and rule in your house,
and order your servants about, and forbid you to ride in hansoms
because it's unladylike, and remind you that the honor of his name
is in your keeping, and decline in your name any further acquaintance with me, and consummate his marriage in the church lest the
housemaid should regard his proceedings as clandestine. Protect
yourself for ever from freedom, independence, love, unfettered
communion with the choice spirits of your day, a lofty path on
which to go your own way and keep your own counsel, and all the
other blessings which 999 women cry for and the thousandth cries
to get away from. But at least tell me when you're *not* coming; and
say whether I am to get a new secretary or not.

"(Signed) G.B.S."

Shaw was having quite a lot of practice in writing love-letters.
He and Ellen Terry were at this time carrying on their correspondence with barely a week's cessation. They were fairy-gold love-
letters, giving each an outlet for the irresistible sprite within: the
girl and the boy who could never grow up. There was an unbreak-
able bond between these two, charmer and genius, which would
probably not have survived everyday life had they ever lived together. Pen in hand, they could reveal themselves with untroubled
candour.

Shaw gave Ellen Terry reports on his progress with Miss Payne-
Townshend, who was "a restful person, plain, green-eyed, very
lady-like, completely demoralised by contact with my ideas, forty,
with nice rooms on a solid basis of £4,000 a year, independent and
unencumbered, and not so plain either when you are in her confidence. So whenever you want to run away and hide, probably the
last place you will be sought for is in the London School of Economics and Political Science."

The trip to Dieppe freshened Charlotte up. She returned to London for Christmas, refusing invitations to go to the Kingstons at
Mitchelstown, or to Sissy at Edstaston. She was in a curious state of

nervous tension, and neuralgia was making her miserable with frequent attacks. G.B.S. was a gay and delightful companion at times, but he was not easy to work for. He could write with intense concentration for hours, then ask her to type from his dictation and expect her to work at the same pitch. This meant that when they did both relax, Charlotte was on edge. In March, 1898, he was writing her an irritated card from Fitzroy Square:

"The plays for the copywriting performance have arrived. They require endless cutting and folding and stapling into brown paper covers. If you can spare a little time tomorrow, come along and bring some long staples (⅝ths of an inch will do) with you—50, if you have them. . . .

"My nerves are shattered by the scenes of which I have been made the innocent victim. I wonder if you are at all ashamed of yourself. I have allied myself to a fountain of tears.

                                                    "G.B.S."

In March, Charlotte went again to the Continent with Lion Phillimore; they planned to travel through France to Italy, and remain for some time in Rome. Charlotte was still in an unhappy frame of mind, and her attacks of neuralgia were growing frequent. She had not been attending lectures at the School of Medicine for some time; it was clear that she would not get very far in medical studies, and now that G.B.S. was taking up so much of her time, she could not attend lectures regularly. She had achieved one of her objects, to meet young women who were trying to qualify as doctors while being harassed by financial difficulties as well as by the contemptuous prejudices of most of the profession. It was a satisfaction to be able to give unobtrusive financial help. Social attitudes could not be dealt with so easily. They made Charlotte very angry, but she realized that anger was not enough. She must do everything in her power to assist the societies which were trying to achieve the emancipation of women.

The trip abroad with Lion Phillimore came at the right time. Not only had Charlotte been unwell, but she could never think clearly with G.B.S. there. She was not in love with him, and she did not want to be in love with him: one devastating experience had been enough. Now she found herself unable to imagine her life apart from him. That made her feel insecure. She admired him with all her heart; she recognized the driving social purpose behind the sometimes tiresome behaviour, and she longed to be associated with it. But—how? G.B.S. made it clear that he had no intention of being committed to a lasting relationship, in spite of the extravagant nonsense of his letters. When she was away from him, Charlotte was equally sure that she must retain her independence at any cost. But when she was with him, she was not always so sure.

G.B.S. demanded addresses to which he could write. He had bought a tear-off engagement calendar, and he sent a leaf every day, covered with his tiny, neat handwriting, telling Charlotte all he had been doing. The first mesage was short:

"12 March 1898

"Charlotte deserts me at 11. Divide the rest of the day between tears and answering letters.

"Digestion wholly ceases.

"Try to sing 'Egypt was glad when they departed,' by Handel. Failure. No exercise today."

On March 14:

"Censor writes refusing to expurgate Mrs. Warren . . . says I can do it myself if I want to and offers to consider any licensable play submitted to him, obliterating the other from his mind. This means another two guineas—blackmail. Thirst for his blood. . . . Before going to bed make new version of 'Mrs. Warren,' omitting the second act, and making Mrs. W. a pickpocket who trains young girls to steal. Dispatch it with a cheque for £2.2.0 and my curse. Quite desperate for lack of exercise. Before retiring have to correct Miss Penfield's interview. A tissue of inaccuracies from end to end— the mildest a statement that Janet Achurch gave imitations of Mansfield, like Cissie Loftus. Relieve my feelings by abusive letter. Bed."

Two days later he was writing:

"Unexpected appearance during breakfast of Mrs. Salt . . . wants to know what about the secretaryship. I am cross and incommoded to the last degree by having to adapt myself to changed circumstances, but finally I set her to finish the article from my dictation. . . . For three sentences I am resentful, uncomfortable and quite put out. At the fourth the switch operates, and I am on the new line as if I had never dictated to anybody else. Such is manly fidelity. In the absence of sentimental interruptions we get along famously, and when we part at the restaurant I enjoin her strictly to come tomorrow."

On March 18:

"This is indeed a secretary . . . she eats her bananas between the sentences and sits here until five, copying out the letters fairly, so that they are ready for me to sign when I return . . . there is clearly no future for you as a secretary. You must get your own work, your own, own, own work. Do you hear?"

The Webbs were on the point of going off on a nine months' world tour to study social conditions in America and other countries. G.B.S. went with several other Fabians to see them off at Euston. He would not miss them unduly, as his days were full of work; writing tracts, preparing lectures, attending plays for the *Saturday*, making countless notes for future plays of his own. He wrote every detail to Charlotte, sending her the names of the cast for *The Devil's Disciple*, which Herbert Waring was to produce:

Richard—Waring	Judith—Lena Ashwell
Anderson—Macklin	Essie—Hilda Hanbury
(Charrington's suggestion)	Burgoyne—Bouchier
Mrs. Dudgeon—Mrs. Crowe	Sergeant—Playfair (L. A.'s
Christy—Duncan Tovery	husband)
Swindon & Stage Manager—Foss	

Charlotte wrote to him from various stops on her journey, describing places, asking questions about mutual friends, commenting on his various items of news. She said nothing about her own thoughts or feelings, or about their relationship, such as it was. She tried to keep things on a comradely level. At times she indulged in the lush prose which had filled her notebooks when she was a girl, and Shaw did not allow these to pass uncommented upon.

"I have almost made up my mind to give up the Sat Rev, if not now, certainly at the end of the season, unless the result of publishing the plays should be altogether terrifying. Another long wrangle . . . at the Exec. . . . When I get home your letter comes. My ferocity has subsided—want to hug you not to batter you and stalk off to commune proudly with the stars. Some of your resolutely good passages are so hypocritical that they almost set me off again; but on the whole I am amiable. 'The Irrational Knot' [which Charlotte had said she was reading] must have been a lacerating experience. But it was a magnificent thing to write that book at 24, out of appalling depths of ignorance and seedy indigence. Think of my circumstances and prospects getting worse and worse until they culminated in smallpox next year (81) when I forced 'Love Among the Artists' out of myself sentence by sentence! Have you yet read *that* masterpiece?"

On July 4 he wrote:

"Do you realize from 'The Irrational Knot' how far I've come— eighteen years from that time, when I wrote five books like that and, without turning a hair, listened in vain for the faintest response to them. When they first showed me the last scene in 'A Doll's House,' I said, 'Oh, I did that long ago,' and they laughed. Do you wonder at my being as hard as nails . . .

"Curse this cycling and the country air: it revives my brute strength and brings unrest. I want a woman and sound sleep. I am never happy except when I am worked to desperation in London & I can eat only a little. I may be frantic, desperate, piteous with arrears and burdens: but I am never unhappy. What people call health—appetite, weight, beefiness—is a mistake. Fragility is the only endurable condition.

"(Signed) G.B.S."

The following day, Shaw went to the cremation of Eleanor Marx, who had committed suicide. He was angry and upset, knowing Eleanor Marx's[4] story; she had been let down badly by a faithless lover, Aveling. G.B.S. wrote to Charlotte:

"Massingham wants me to write about her. *I* want to write about Aveling; so conclude to hold my tongue."

The following day:

"Wrote article. No secretary. Really at the end. Slamming the typewriter is furious nervous work. No exercise. No digestion. All my body is active preservation below the waistband and above the diaphragm; but the intermediate weak and won't digest, won't carry

[4] Eleanor Marx and Edward Aveling were socialist propagandists.

me about. Neuralgic still rather. Lonely—no, by God, never—*not* lonely, but detestably deserted."

Charlotte had reached Rome with Lion Phillimore, and had not written to Shaw for several days. He was hurt.

"All this time no letter from Rome. Some Italian doctor, no doubt, at the bottom of it. Well, I shall not be for ever snivelling to be pitied. In this grim solitude I shall recuperate: the steel armor will harden again, with a fresh deposit of adamant all over it.

"Hope you are not ill, by the way. But no: you would write to say it was my fault if you were."

He had had acute toothache and been to the dentist.

"Tooth sacrificed in vain. Not toothache—neuralgia. As I go crawling round the park on the bike I can intensify the pain— which is not of any consequence, by the way (I am not subject to the vulgarly cruel pangs of undivine mortals)—by simply putting on the pace. I will keep resolutely pottering over easy work tomorrow and next day and get restored."

On April 12, G.B.S. went to see *The Belle of New York* at the Shaftesbury Theatre. He was evidently missing Charlotte very much; he wrote to her in the small hours of the next morning:

"Gigantic recuperation from the tooth. Attacked Saturday article with violence. Attacked everything. Plenty of business in view of approaching publication of plays Plays Pleasant and Unpleasant. Worked like mad until midnight. Reached that hour in a parlous condition. No word from vindictive Irishwoman in Rome. Neuralgia warning me loudly. Nobody comforts me but my faithful Ellen. She writes me the tenderest letters; and when I write her savage and furious ones, blesses me with tears for softening her, making her feel, giving her the happiness of thinking and crying. Adorable Ellen."

Lion Phillimore returned to England, and Charlotte decided to stay in Rome for a time. Before she had left London, G.B.S. had teased her into declaring that she would do a serious sociological study, probably a survey of the municipal services of Rome. She decided that she would show him that she could apply herself to work if she tried, and she did, in fact, make scores of notes during

her stay in the city. The Webbs had often said that information
of this kind, accurately noted and properly collated, was of great
value, and Charlotte spent several hours a day writing short reports
after she had been taken to see the various services run by the
municipality.

She went to the *ambulatòrio*, but avoided seeing Axel Munthe.
If he knew that she was in the city—and someone would be sure
to tell him—he made no attempt to meet her, either. Charlotte
stayed at her old hotel, and was out most evenings visiting friends,
English and Italian. She heard that Sartorio wanted to have an
exhibition in London, and made enquiries about the pastel portrait
he had done of her: Munthe had said that he would either return
it to the painter or send it to London to her house. He had not sent
it. Charlotte wrote about it to G.B.S., angrily conjecturing that it
was probably somewhere in a corner, dirty and discoloured.

The usual calendar leaf arrived from Shaw, closely written. Mrs.
Phillimore had arrived home and had asked him down to Radlett
as he looked so exhausted and overworked.

"I can make no headway against the Phillimores, who bully me
for hours about you and my character and my age and my foolishness and selfishness and devil knows what . . . I have a headache
now . . ."

G.B.S. suffered a great deal from migraine headaches, just as
Charlotte was a martyr to recurrent attacks of neuralgia. They were
always sure of the other's sympathy when they were laid low with
these maladies. Charlotte wrote at once, saying how sorry she was
about the headache, and added that she was thinking of starting
for home soon. G.B.S.'s calendar leaf for April 14 arrived from
Radlett.

"Headache in full force. Lounge about reading Kipling. Take
the inevitable stroll to Wallas's cottage. Sit on stile talking to Lion.
She coolly ascribes my prostration to years of debauchery. My ashes
glow into mighty coals at the insult. The headache dwindles and
my spirits rise: my strength returns." He went to the theatre that
evening. "When I return I triumph; the vindictive Irishwoman has
written at last. Ha! ha! If only I had her in these arms: all her ribs
would crack."

Shaw kept in touch with Beatrice and Sidney Webb, sending
them letters to selected points on their world trip. On April 11 he
wrote:

"There is no news. I live the life of a dog. Haven't spoken to a
soul except my mother and the vestry since you left. The change to
Spring has struck me down with peevishness and weakness. I
have not gone anywhere for Easter, the theatres being too active.
. . . Whilst the cold weather lasted I so brutally exulted in my
loneliness and freedom, not to mention my taking on Mrs. Salt as
amanuensis . . . that Charlotte has given up writing to me. Ellen
alone remains faithful; she showers endearments on me by post."

He went on to say that he had invested £1,000 in New Zealand
stock. This had been made possible by the success of *The Devil's
Disciple,* the royalties being well into the third thousand from performances abroad, the play not having yet been put on in England.
Arms and the Man had made more than £800 for him, so he felt
comparatively affluent.

Shaw spent the week-end at Radlett, and wrote to Charlotte:

". . . I burst upon them like an equinoctial gale: yell with derision
over my supposed exhaustion by sexual excess . . . amaze them by
my resurrection. Unfortunately, I mention that I have heard from
you; and my recuperation is instantly put to your credit with shrieks
of laughter."

On April 18 he was writing to tell her that his foot was swollen
and apparently gouty.

". . . don't understand it. Seems to be positively putrefying. Air
full of reviews of plays etc. Why ain't you back: you'd enjoy it and
I'd enjoy *you.*"

And on the following day:

". . . Exasperating condition of things as to Rome. Thoughtless
woman there will not give me the faintest clue to her movements.
Leaves me with a definite statement that she leaves tomorrow and
yet evidently from the tone of her letters, hasn't the slightest intention of doing anything of the sort. In the evening I ride off to
Ealing to the Beattys. . . . I find my left foot unaccountably sore
and have to take off my shoe. Not easy to get it on again. Ride
home. On taking off the shoe again, my foot expands to the size

of a leg of mutton. Don't understand it, as there is nothing to account for it but the fact that a week or so ago I laced my shoe too tight and pinched my instep a little."

G.B.S. had a very full week, with lectures and committee meetings, and his foot began to bother him badly. He tried bathing it in hot water, but it got worse, and he was unable to walk without pain. Charlotte did not hear from him for several days, then she received four calendar leaves together; G.B.S. had held them over so as to give her the latest news of his foot. He had nearly telegraphed to know whether she was still in Rome, he said.

On April 21 he had to cancel an appointment but could not put off going to see *Lord and Lady Algy* at the Comedy Theatre because of his *Saturday* notice:

"Locomotion now very excruciating. Can it be gout? Looks awful. Have to lunch at home and not stir until the theatre in the evening. Spite of cabs the theatre makes it decidedly worse. Foot now as large as the Albert Hall. . . . Am a fearful wreck."

On April 22, G.B.S. went to a vegetarian banquet at the Holborn Restaurant, and on to a Fabian business meeting. He gave Charlotte an account of his day, though he was not sure if she would receive it, as she was due back in London:

"No further difficulty about locomotion, as I now simply hop, my left foot being no longer of any use. . . . Don't suffer so much from want of exercise as might be expected, as the hopping up and down stairs is very arduous and violent, and shakes up my liver with salutary vehemence. . . . Hopped down stairs and into cab in the evening. Hop from cab along passage from Fleet Street to Cliffords Inn, to the amazement of the populace . . . cab home, and hop upstairs. Hot water treatment repeated. Various theories by sympathetic friends—vegetarian gout popular because funny— Lucy [his sister] insists that I have dislocated a toe. This being just possible, I make up my mind to get Salisbury Sharpe to look at it tomorrow, on the chance of its being a bone setter's business.

"By the way, you have been elected to the Fabian Executive. . . . I half expected to see you at the meeting tonight: you missed the insane spectacle of my entrance on one leg."

On April 23:

"Mrs. Salt collapses with a sick headache and retires to bed after being dictated to. Snatch up my notebook and make a start at least on 'Caesar and Cleopatra.' . . . This enforced inaction is going to save my life. . . . After post hour the doctor comes. My medical skill is completely vindicated. I have been doing exactly the right thing. He opines that the long bicycle ride after a long period of inaction and the tight shoe made the two toe joints slip over one another and inflame. Remedy, hot water and minimum of use for the foot. He suggests three hours hot water in the morning and 1½ hours in the evening. Thank you—amputation sooner; but I will do my best."

He wrote on the following day:

"Hot water operations and 'Gotterdammerung' and 'Cleopatra.' . . . You had better ask Sartorio what has happened to the pastel. Not only will it be information, but he *ought* to know about it, as it is not fair to him either to leave him under the impression that he has left to posterity work which is, in fact, spoiled, or to show in London a blemished picture which he could possibly either restore or point out a way of restoring."

Charlotte had had neuralgia again and had mentioned the fact in one of her letters.

"Neuralgia—ill in Italy!" wrote G.B.S. "This is a knock down blow: I thought you were recuperating and that the balmy Pincian airs were beating Adelphi Terrace all to fits. . . . Come back then: *I* know what your nerves need."

G.B.S. was working steadily on *Caesar and Cleopatra* in spite of his foot. Charlotte had told him when she was starting for home, and he wrote that he would not be sending her many more calendar leaves.

". . . Finished whole scene of Cleopatra—Sc. 2 of the first act— quintessence of everything that has most revolted the chivalrous critics. Ha! ha! Julius Caesar as the psychological woman tamer. Ho! ho!

". . . I will try to find out when your train is due on Sunday night; and if the hour is not absolutely scandalous I shall present myself at the Terrace and crush in all your ribs into an embrace that has been accumulating for two months."

On April 27, G.B.S. had a special Vestry meeting, followed by a play at the Avenue Theatre he had to review.

". . . Fearful trials at vestry. . . . Particularly fearful business over resolution to stop free accommodation for women in sanitary conveniences. I moved amendment. Dixon, a pillar of the Church, arises in saintly majesty and says my remarks are disgusting. Then says Mrs. Phillimore [also a member of St. Pancras Vestry] has behaved indecently in seconding me. Chairman, much ashamed, rebukes him and he collapses. Lion indifferent to the personality, but furious and frantic about the resolution. I am too lame to take anything excitedly. . . .

"In the evening—theatre. Play with a baby in it. Might have been written by one."

Charlotte left Rome at the end of April and was due to arrive in London on May 1. Shaw's last calendar leaf was sent to Adelphi Terrace, late at night.

"At last. Charlotte due at 19½ at Victoria. . . . After lunch I strike work and take up a novel entitled Sunlight and Limelight, by one Gribble, all about the love affairs of an actress. They are not at all unlike mine. I finish the book at a sitting, as I don't want to be weary brained when Charlotte comes.

"After 20 I limp down to Tottenham Court Road, my troubles all over at last. I descend at Charing Cross and limp slowly, slowly, slowly to Adelphi Terrace. With a long gasp of relief, I lay my two months' burden down and ring the bell. Martha's footstep on the stairs.

"WELL I AM DAMNED!

"Wretch, devil, fiend!

"The train has arrived; and you are not on it! Stopped in Paris to see Cyrano again, perhaps. No: Satan's own daughter would have telegraphed.

"Let me be polite to Martha at least. I suppose train has missed its connection, and you will not arrive until midnight. 12.30 Martha says, tacitly putting it to me whether, as a gentleman, I can wait. Clearly I cannot. I limp back to my bus, and here I am."

Charlotte had travelled from Naples by sea, and arrived very late that night. She wrote a note on the back of G.B.S.'s letter which she had found waiting for her:

"Well, here I am anyway now! Yes, I *might* have telegraphed: it was horrid of me. I am a wreck, mental and physical. Such a journey as it was! I don't believe I shall ever get over it.

"My dear—and your foot? Shall I go up to you or will you come here and when? Only tell me what you would prefer. Of course I am quite free.

"Charlotte"

She sent the note off next morning and G.B.S. replied:

"I cannot get about very well today, as I must save up my foot for the Officers' Committee at 5. Until I leave for that I shall be here; so come when it is most convenient to you. Or, if you prefer it, come *after* the Committee, it will probably be over before 6, as there is nothing important on. Or come both times. It is as you like, the sooner the better (for the first moment, at least).

"G.B.S."

Charlotte went to 29, Fitzroy Square the following afternoon. Glad as she was to see G.B.S., she could not repress her surprised horror at his surroundings. She had long known that Shaw's mother was completely uninterested in housekeeping: in his "devil of a childhood," of which he had told her a little, he had had his meals in the kitchen with a slatternly servant, who fed him mostly on stewed beef and badly cooked potatoes, washed down by strong tea. His reaction in later years was to become a vegetarian, but he was never greatly interested in food, and the unappetizing meals which his mother's servant at Fitzroy Square—another slattern— slapped down for him were eaten or not, as he felt hungry. Hesketh Pearson, in his life of Shaw, gives a description of his "home" surroundings at this time:

"He worked in a very small room which was in a perpetual state of dirt and disorder. He kept the window wide open, day and night, winter and summer, and the dust and smuts that entered thereby settled on books, furniture and papers, being scattered over a wider area whenever attempts were made to remove them. The mass of matter on the table was chaotic: heaps of letters, pages of manuscripts, books, envelopes, writing-paper, pens . . . butter, sugar, apples, knives, forks, spoons, sometimes a cup of cocoa or a half-finished plate of porridge, a saucepan, and a dozen other things, were mixed up indiscriminately, and all undusted, as his papers must not be touched. The table, the typewriter and the wooden-railed chair in which he sat filled the room, forcing anyone who entered it to move sideways like a crab. Occasionally he would have a general clean-up, a job that took two full days' hard work."

As G.B.S. read books while he was dressing and undressing, and deposited them, open, on the table without bothering to shut them, there was a fair state of chaos. His mother never came into the room, and they did not have their meals together. They were on good terms, but Lucinda Elizabeth still lived her separate life, giving music lessons and going her self-sufficient way. When her son was to be in for a meal, the servant brought in a plateful of cooked eggs and put them down on the nearest pile of books or papers.

There is no record of Shaw's being nursed by his mother when his foot became unusable; it is probable that he said nothing to her about it, and if she noticed it during their infrequent meetings in the house, she did not mention it, either. Charlotte was used to difficult personal relationships, but she had never come across anything so callous as this; the neglect of G.B.S. by his mother began a dislike of Lucinda Elizabeth which was to last. She was appalled by the way he lived, and determined that he must somehow be made to uproot himself and find apartments or a flat where he could have proper attention.

Shaw was meanwhile keeping the Webbs up to date with his latest news. He wrote to Beatrice on May 7:

"Your letter dated 26th. April has just arrived. . . . Your departure has had the most disastrous consequences for me. Cut off at once from domesticity and gallantry I had nothing to do but work, when I collapsed so pitiably that the Phillimores bore me off to Radlett in the condition of a mouse in the abject shape of delirium tremens. Having got me down there they promptly proceeded to lecture me for my folly in not marrying Charlotte; to explain the delights of married life (chief among them being the escape from the pre-nuptial obligation to be constantly paying amorous attentions to one another) and to point out to me the numerous grave defects of my own character.

Charlotte Frances Payne-Townshend on the lake at Derry

Charlotte and Sissy at Derry

Derry

Cottage in the Derry Demesne

Mitchelstown Castle (now destroyed)

Horace Payne-Townshend, Charlotte, and Hugh Cholmondeley

Horace Payne-Townshend in Morocco

Mary Stewart Cholmondeley (Sissy), Charlotte, Mrs. Payne-Town-shend (Mary Susanna), with Hugh Cholmondeley

Beatrice Webb—*Photo Pictorial Press Ltd*

G.B.S. at the time of his marriage

Charlotte in 1900

G.B.S. and Charlotte
at home, 1899

Garden group (Charlotte on left), 1897, taken by G.B.S.

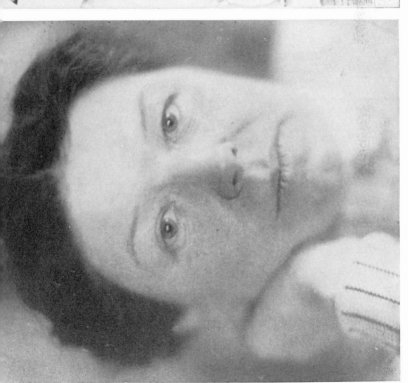

G.B.S. on holiday, taken by Charlotte

Charlotte aged forty-three

G.B.S. "at sea," 1898

The patient model,
taken by G.B.S.

T. E. Lawrence

Axel Munthe:
as Charlotte knew him

Octogenarian

"Now something still more awful has happened. I pinched my left foot a little in a tight shoe. About a week after I went for a bicycle ride. Next day my foot swelled to the size of your largest cat at Grosvenor Road; and since then (three weeks ago) I have been practically confined to the house and hopping up and down steps on one leg. . . . All this anguish would have been averted if you had stayed at home to take care of your family. . . .

"Charlotte came back five days ago with a gigantic collection of documents concerning the Roman municipality. She found her position as secretary usurped by Mrs. Salt, who suits me very well, as I can bully her unlimitedly because she has no idea how effective she is. Charlotte demanded her post back again. I insisted on her setting to work at once on the Roman report. She declined. So Mrs. Salt went off to Kew Gardens for a holiday; and Charlotte had one delirious day of being dictated to. Then, as usual, Reason resumed her sway. Mrs. Salt came back; and the Roman book is supposed to be under weigh. The only question is, what form should it take. Her lady-like instincts strongly urge her to a dry official report for the use of students at the School. I, on the other hand, insist on a thrilling memoir giving the whole history of a lady of quality suffering from a broken heart (with full particulars) and being rescued from herself by the call of public work. The extent to which the call was reinforced by the renewed activity of the mended heart is to be described, and the whole is to conclude with the voyage to Italy, the adventures there among the old romantic associations, and, incidentally, a complete view, by glimpses, of the municipal honours of Rome. Charlotte sees dimly that the accomplishment of such a *magnum opus* would be indeed the conquest of a profession for herself, and consequent salvation; but she has got no further at present than arranging her material."

Charlotte, in fact, had not got so far. The municipal honours of Rome did not at this distance seem very important, with G.B.S. in his present condition. He had had to have an operation on the foot, and was quite evidently in considerable pain most of the time.

Ellen Terry sent G.B.S. two stalls for May 5, now that Miss Payne-Townshend was home, and Charlotte called for him in a

cab to take him to the Lyceum. G.B.S. tried to banter, but she saw
that in spite of his unquenchable spirit and blarneying tongue, he
was under great strain. He was trying to carry out his commitments
and engagements using crutches, and he looked haggard and ill.
If something was not done soon, there might be serious consequences.

The following day she called for him again, and brought him to
Adelphi Terrace for a talk. Matters could not go on like this any
longer, she said. He must be properly looked after. What he needed
was complete rest and country air: he *must* get away from London.
Charlotte intended to take a house in the country and herself look
after him there, with nurses.

At first Shaw demurred. He could not leave London: there
were his *Saturday Review* job, his committees, the Vestry, his
writing. Charlotte quietly disposed of the objections. He could take
his books and papers and do his writing anywhere; he had done
so in the past, and he could do so now. The other things could wait.
If he did not try to get well, if he were not looked after *now*, he
might become a permanent invalid. He had to face the facts.

They talked for a long time. All that they said has not been
recorded by either party, but the conversation came to a climax
with Bernard Shaw asking Charlotte to marry him.

It had always been G.B.S.'s way to hide the deeply emotional
events in his life by highly romanticized, often clownish descriptions of these happenings. It was one of his least admirable traits.
He was to put it about that Charlotte took a house for him to
convalesce in, and that in order to save her reputation he sent her
out for a marriage licence and a ring. The last item was, in literal
and practical fact, true, as he was hardly in a physical condition to
go out and get them himself. The rest was false.

Charlotte proposed to take a country house staffed by proper
servants, with two nurses in attendance on Shaw. She could,
with the greatest of ease, have asked any of her own friends, or
some of the Fabians, to come for a visit during the period of Shaw's
recuperation. Everyone knew that they were friends. He had been
in the habit of coming frequently to Adelphi Terrace, with two

servants as the only chaperons. They often went out together. They were both known as persons of moral integrity, in spite of their unconventional opinions. Charlotte's reputation was in no danger.

The legend which grew later, that she had come rushing back from the Continent in order to carry off a helpless Shaw to her country house, where he chivalrously offered to marry her to avoid a scandal, is ludicrously wide of the facts. We have seen from his daily letters how much he missed her, and how he tried continually to get her to return as the weeks went by. It is probable that Shaw, during that long conversation, realized that a decisive moment had come. He was not physically in love with Charlotte Payne-Townshend to the extent he had been with Jenny Patterson and the others, where the sexual impulse and practically nothing else had been the basis of the relationship. He had come to have a very deep affection for Charlotte, and though this, too, contained a physical element, it was interwoven with a great need for the companionship, sympathy and understanding which she had given him during the past two years. In a characteristic letter to Beatrice Webb written soon afterwards, a hint of this real feeling is apparent in the camouflage. He had told Beatrice with a certain amount of relish that his foot had had to be operated upon, and described the post-operative treatment—the hole in his foot being packed every day afresh with iodiform gauze and treated with boracic fomentation. He went on:

"It was planned I must go away to the country the moment I could be moved, and that somebody must seriously take in hand the job of looking after me. Equally plain, of course, that Charlotte was the inevitable and predestined agent, appointed by Destiny. To have let her do this in any other character than that of my wife would (in the absence of your chaperonage) have involved our whole circle and its interests in a scandal. You may wonder why I did not find that out long ago, instead of exploiting the chaperonage with complete selfishness. I can only say that I did not know—that the situation was changed by a change in my own consciousness. I found that my own objection to my own marriage had ceased with my objection to my own death. This was the main change: there were of course many other considerations which we shall probably discuss at some future time. Possibly one of them was that the relation between us had never until then completely lost its inevitable preliminary character of a love affair.

"She had at last got beyond that corrupt personal interest in me, just as the 'Devil's Disciple' had relieved me of the appearance of a pecuniary interest (more than was reasonable) in her. The thing being cleared thus of all such illusions as love interest, happiness interest, and all the rest of the vulgarities of marriage, I changed right about face on the subject and hopped down to the Registrar, who married me to her on one leg, after beginning the ceremony with Wallas, who had a new coat on. The papers noticed the event as eagerly as the death of Gladstone. Mrs. Chumley (I forget the full length spelling) wrote to Charlotte, 'Don't ask me to meet this man: and as a last kindness to me, and for my sake, I ask you to secure your money.'"

G.B.S. made the most of the occasion, writing variations on the theme of his marriage to various friends. On May 23, he wrote to Grant Richards, apologizing for not completing the pamphlet on Wagner which he had promised the publisher, adding:

"I have written a lot of it, but the operation stopped me dead: I was forced to lie there and feed myself back to life. As it is, I cannot do much until I can be moved to the country . . .

"What on earth do you want to get married for, at your age? As a matter of fact I am going to get married myself as soon as I can get round to the workhouse (where the registrar officiates); but then I am 42. Keep this dark until I have done it. I only tell you to keep you in countenance."

On June 1, he wrote to Lena Ashwell from Fitzroy Square: "Dear Miss Lena Ashwell,

"This morning I hopped into a registrar's office and got married, and then hopped back again and found your letter. If it had only come a post earlier, I think I should have waited on the chance of something fatal happening to Mr. Playfair[5] in the course of the next forty years or so.

"I have given up writing about the theatre because I have said all that I have to say about it."

[5] Lena Ashwell's first husband.

And so on, discussing *The Devil's Disciple* and other matters of theatrical interest, and ending:

"I am completely tired out and run down; but I shall break out again presently in some direction or other as soon as I have had a few months in the country. Thank you for the kind expressions in your letter, and believe me, dear Miss Ashwell,

"Yours sincerely,

"G. Bernard Shaw"

He also sent a notice of the wedding, unsigned, to the *Star* newspaper, where it appeared on June 2.

"As a lady and gentleman were out driving in Henrietta-st., Covent-garden yesterday, a heavy shower drove them to take shelter in the office of the Superintendent Registrar there, and in the confusion of the moment he married them. The lady was an Irish lady named Miss Payne Townshend, and the gentleman was George Bernard Shaw.

"Mr. Graham Wallas and Mr. H. S. Salt were also driven by stress of weather into the registrar's, and the latter being secretary of the Humanitarian League would naturally have remonstrated against the proceedings had there been time, but there wasn't. Mr. Bernard Shaw means to go off to the country next week to recuperate, and this is the second operation he has undergone lately, the first being conducted, not by a registrar, but by a surgeon.

"Startling as was the liberty undertaken by the Henrietta-st. official, it turns out well. Miss Payne Townshend is an Irish lady with an income many times the volume of that which 'Corno di Bassetto' used to earn, but to that happy man, being a vegetarian, the circumstance is of no moment. The lady is deeply interested in the London School of Economics, and that is the common ground on which the brilliant couple met. Years of married bliss to them."

One of the subjects that Charlotte and G.B.S. had discussed during their long talk was money. Both of them were completely realistic on that topic. G.B.S. had often mentioned the "green-eyed one's riches" in his letters to Ellen Terry and others, but he was sensitive about being thought a fortune hunter. He was earning what was to him an adequate income, enough to contribute substantially to the household expenses at Fitzroy Square and to meet his own modest needs. The success of *The Devil's Disciple* had brought in good royalties, sufficient to invest. But he was not making enough money to support Charlotte in the style in which she was accustomed to live. And if he left Fitzroy Square, his mother would not be able to manage on the fees she earned from teaching music, which amounted to little enough.

The answer was sensible and simple. Charlotte would settle an annuity on Lucinda Elizabeth for life. As to the rest, they would not pool their resources, but would each pay a proportion of the joint expenses of the household. G.B.S. was not extravagant: Charlotte had many expensive tastes, especially in clothes. She liked good hotels and large country houses. She possessed the money to pay for these, so why should they not benefit from her large income?

Shaw agreed: he usually responded to practical good sense. They made arrangements for the wedding ceremony, which was to be as quiet as possible. When G.B.S., back in Fitzroy Square, broke the news to his mother, she made no comment beyond saying that it was not unexpected. She supposed that she must call Miss Payne-Townshend Charlotte now, though "Carlotta" was rather more descriptive: she *looked* a "Carlotta." Lucinda Elizabeth had lately taken to ouija boards and séances, and she had ideas on the unseen forces beyond the material world and their influences on people. Names were important. Her daughter-in-law became Carlotta in Lucinda's mind and in private conversation. Beyond that, she had little interest in the marriage.

Charlotte went to Fitzroy Square and packed up Shaw's papers and books under his supervision, her fastidious soul outraged anew by the dirt and general disorder of the place. It was a relief to get back to Adelphi Terrace, where a room had been prepared for G.B.S., and the faithful Martha instructed to cook extra-nourishing meals from now on.

George Bernard Shaw and Charlotte were married at the Register Office in the district of the Strand on June 1, 1898. Shaw was 42, described as a bachelor, journalist, of 29, Fitzroy Square, London; and Charlotte Payne-Townshend, 41, spinster of 10, Adelphi Terrace. The witnesses were Graham Wallas and Henry Stephen Salt.

Charlotte looked for a house in Surrey, and after going to see a number of possibles, chose a pleasant country house, Pitfold, situated between Haslemere and Hindhead. She rented it for four months, and they travelled down to Surrey in sunny weather, glad to leave London behind.

It is perhaps time, at this point, to attempt to deal with the question which seems to have fascinated so many people: were they man and wife in the accepted sense?

The short answer to that is simple. No one knows, and no one has ever been in a position to know. Charlotte was an extremely reserved person where intimate details of her life were concerned. She could talk and write of her emotions, and of the religious beliefs which meant so much to her, to trusted, sympathetic friends; it is impossible to imagine her discussing her marital relations.

Shaw had no such inhibitions, but there is no trustworthy record of his having stated *explicitly* that his marriage was platonic from beginning to end. He said, at various times, that Charlotte was afraid to have children at her age, and that she disliked physical contact and so he was bound to respect her wishes in that matter. But in his letters to her before marriage he made frequent allusions to embraces in the recent past, and the love-making which awaited her when he saw her again. They were quite obviously on terms of physical affection right up to the time of their marriage, and it is difficult to believe that she died a "vestal virgin," as one of their friends has asserted. They must have discussed the question at length before their marriage. With Shaw ill and on crutches, a normal honeymoon could hardly have been expected, but there is no evidence at all that they eschewed the more natural relation, at any rate in the very early days of their marriage. Shaw was capable of great sensitiveness and tenderness, and could understand Charlotte's complicated attitude to sex far better than even Clery had done, but he was perfectly normal as a man, and he knew that behind her "principles" Charlotte was perfectly normal, too.

It is probable that after Shaw was well again, they enjoyed as normal an intimate life as other married couples do; but they were not young. Living in a state of intellectual ferment, with Shaw's energies almost completely absorbed by the creative power of his extraordinary brain, such physical passion as may have existed between them could well have turned into the "higher" relationship of affectionate respect which G.B.S. undoubtedly felt for his wife. When he talked in later years of wishing that he had "insisted" on marital relations, he may well have forgotten a great deal about the early Charlotte. She did not want children, but she was not averse from love.

In October of that year, G.B.S. wrote to Beatrice Webb from Pitfold:

"At last, after much searching, we secured this house, on the south slope of Hindhead, until October. I came down on crutches. The air was so fine that our troubles seemed to be over: but they had only just begun. The moment I began to get strong I recklessly returned to work on a Quintessence of Wagner which I had begun earlier; and in a few days I was at it as savagely as ever. Sharpe wrote vehemently commanding me not to tempt the gods. Before his letter arrived I found out, after dictating Wagner criticism one morning for half an hour, that I was myself conscious that all the strain was on again. I called a halt and went upstairs on crutches (a foolish feat) to get something from my bedroom. Coming down, the crutches got planted behind my centre of gravity and shot me into the air. I snatched at a bannister on the landing above, and caught it in my right hand, but it snapped like an Argoed tree, and I was precipitated 50 fathoms or thereabouts into the hall, with my left arm doubled up in ruin under me . . . imagine poor Charlotte's feelings! She got a pair of butter pats and made splints of them. The local doctor, who did not come for half an hour, during which I lay in the hall with all the strain gone, perfectly relieved and happy, was fortunately a capable man, and the setting was a success. But fancy my condition *now* (this happened four days ago). I am helpless—the nurse has to wash and dress and all but feed me. I have a wheeled chair, which I cannot wheel, since when worked with one hand it simply spins round and round. Heaven knows what will happen to Charlotte when the anxiety about me is over. Last night a cat, shut up accidentally in the pantry, simulated a burglar so successfully that I sallied out, walking recklessly on the bad foot, at three in the morning, and thereby did myself as much harm as possible. I no longer feel any confidence in my ultimate recovery: it seems certain to me that I shall presently break all my other limbs as well.

"I am sitting in my wheeled chair on the lawn looking over the hills through a gap in the trees to a bit of heather which reminds me of the Argoed, and of all my previous honeymoons, with respect to which I may now, as a correctly married man, speak to you, dear Beatrice, with frank sentiment. Not until you left me a widower was I driven to be unfaithful to your fireside.

"G. Bernard Shaw"

"P.S. Tell Webb that I note his instructions about Ashley, and will keep Miss Townshend (ha! ha!) in mind of them."

Beatrice and Sidney Webb returned from their world tour soon after Christmas. Beatrice wrote in her Diary:

"With regard to our friends and relations, we found three persons whose lives have been completely changed during our absence— our two friends George Bernard Shaw and Charlotte have married each other. Shaw has become a chronic invalid, Charlotte a devoted nurse. They live in an attractive house up at Hindhead. He still writes, but his work seems to be getting unreal: he leads a hot-house life, he cannot walk or get among his equals. He is as witty and as cheery as of old. But now and again a flash of fatigue or a sign of brain irritation passes over him. Charlotte, under pressure of anxiety for the man she loves, has broadened out into a motherly woman and lost her anarchic determination to live with her momentary desires. These are some compensations for the sudden cutting off of his activities."

The third person whose life had been radically changed during the Webbs' absence was Graham Wallas, whom Beatrice had once, in her practical, logical way, thought a suitable husband for Charlotte. He had married Ada Radford:

". . . a woman of 40 or thereabouts, and one of a cultivated, public-spirited, somewhat aesthetic middle-class family. She was educated at Girton—became assistant mistress of High School, then Secretary to Working Women's College, then writer for the Yellow Book. A woman of a certain originality of life, and with a pretty little literary gift for writing short stories. I do not take to her. She is obviously a good woman—sweet-natured (Graham says she is humorous) with decision and capacity. Her ideas are the old-fashioned, aesthetic, secularist, equal-rights sort. She is a woman who carries rigid principles into the smallest concern of life. With Madonna-like features, good complexion and soft golden hair, she ought to be pleasant to look at: but as a matter of principle she dresses in yellow-green sloppy garments, large garden hat with bows of green silk—her hair is always coming down—and generally speaking she looks as if she had tumbled up out of an armchair in which she had slept the night, and her movements are aggressively ugly. But as Graham sees none of this what does it matter; they are devotedly attached: she has just enough money to make marriage —with no prospect of children—prudent, if not actually desirable for Graham. I doubt whether we shall be much of friends. We are both too set in our own mould, too completely filled up with work . . . to have time to discover the 'deeper affinities' which doubtless exist between two women who have both struggled with life and work."

[In fact, Mrs. Wallas had a daughter to whom she and her husband became devotedly attached. Beatrice Webb's ideas on the question of having children are revealing: it is apparent from Charlotte's later correspondence, especially with T. E. Lawrence, that Beatrice and possibly Sidney must have discussed these ideas with her on more than one occasion. Referring to a day spent with the Bertrand Russells and the Phillimores in the country, Beatrice wrote:

". . . So far as I can see there is only one serious criticism of the lives of the six persons gathered together in a Surrey cottage on this lovely June day—*no children*—all too intellectual or too strenuous to bear children! Whether the omission is 'intentional' or 'inevitable' does not matter much from the community's point of view. There is obviously some flaw in these marriages of pure companionship. Can we afford that these rather picked individuals shall remain childless? Is less highly-wrought material better to breed from? I, at least, can fall back with complacency on the 37 nephews and nieces who are carrying on the 'Potter' stock and so far unperturbed with ideas or enthusiasms."]

11

MARRIAGE

(1898–1902)

Charlotte had now got the double-decker flat in Adelphi Terrace conveniently arranged. The dining-room and large drawing-room were on the second floor, with the bedrooms, a study for G.B.S. and the kitchen on the third floor. There was no bathroom; the maids took cans of hot water into the bedrooms and filled a hip-bath. Charlotte had devoted servants, and treated them well, so domestic problems did not arise. It was a pleasant place to live in; the windows looked out over Adelphi Terrace to the river, and beyond the occasional hooting of passing craft, there was no noise.

They remained in Surrey, however. G.B.S. was getting no better, and Charlotte was becoming anxious. The house was proving too small, a source of irritation, as Charlotte liked plenty of space. She had intended taking G.B.S. abroad, to join up with the Webbs, who were on their way home from their trip, but G.B.S.'s condition made it impossible. She had written to Beatrice on November 6, 1898: "My dear Beatrice,

"Alas! to think that this letter only is going to meet you, instead of ourselves as I had hoped! I think you have our news up to a fortnight ago, and know . . . that we have taken another house, near here for the winter. It seemed the only thing to do, as another operation stares us in the face; and, of course, either London or travelling is impossible under the circumstances. The foot seems to have got decidedly worse in the last six weeks—but then G.B.S. has been most foolish, constantly walking on it in spite of all advice. We went up last Thursday to the specialist—Bowlby—who operated in the summer, and showed the foot to him. He said he was inclined to think that if it got fair play (that is, was kept *absolutely* quiet) it might heal still; but, if there was no change for the better, after trying this treatment for ten days, he would have to take out the whole bone, and, in consequence, take off the toe; that latter, apparently, being looked upon by the profession as a matter of no consequence.

"We move into our new house—Blen-Cathra, Hindhead, Haslemere—on Saturday next if all is well. I rather hope for good effects from the change, as this is a small, stuffy house and the other has lofty, airy rooms, besides being in a better situation.

"I shall be *very* glad to have you back for every reason; but, among others, for the selfish one that I long for a little advice and help from someone whose judgment and good sense I really feel that I can depend upon. I do feel rather isolated, for, though everyone makes all sorts of preposterous suggestions, no-one really gives me any feeling of confidence—the feeling I know I should have about you and Sidney if you were here. However, let's hope that long before you come the patient will be a sound man again, and there will be no need to help. Oh that ——— vegetarianism!

"I send you a few photographs which will amuse you. The Kodak has been a great joy to G.B.S. and nurse . . .

"The Wagner book is not out yet, but will be, I hope, in a week or so. Caesar and Cleopatra is at the 2nd. Act. I try to keep him from working as much as I can, but it is the only occupation he really cares for. Almost all books bore him, music is tiring, and seeing people more tiring still.

"Graham Wallas was down here yesterday. He is getting extremely fat and prosperous looking. He described Audrey, [his wife] with her large gold spectacles, kneeling in awe before the baby, hardly daring to touch it for fear of injuring it. I have not seen her as I hardly ever go up to Town.

"The Fabian Executive proposes that the new vol. of essays should come out in March, and hopes for one from Sidney embodying some of your experiences. I expect the Executive meetings are a funny contrast to what they used to be when G.B.S. and Sidney were there. I find them slow—*slow!* I am perfectly out of patience with the Fabians (*strictly* between ourselves): from my point of view it now consists of a parcel of boys and old women thinking they are making history, and really making themselves ridiculous. Possibly this may be an exaggeration.

"I will write to you at Port Said and hope there to be able to give you a more satisfactory account of our doings.

"Love to you both,
"Charlotte"

Before they moved to Blen-Cathra, Charlotte, on the doctor's suggestion, took G.B.S. down to Freshwater Bay in the Isle of Wight for a change of air. He improved rapidly, though he still had to use crutches, and spent most of his time working on *Caesar and Cleopatra* with his usual concentration. When they returned to Hindhead, G.B.S. at once tried riding his bicycle, to show Charlotte how well he now felt. He fell off and sprained the ankle of the bad foot. Mr. Bowlby was called down, and spoke severely, cautioning G.B.S. about possible permanent damage to the foot. G.B.S. agreed to exercise common sense, and let Charlotte settle him on a sofa where he could work, his foot properly supported and his crutches nearby.

Charlotte worked at her desk in the same room, taking dictation in longhand and writing letters for him to sign. She also drafted letters which he revised and wrote himself, handing them back to her again for copying, either in longhand or on the typewriter. Charlotte did not type his manuscripts, but she helped him to revise them, before they were sent to be typed professionally by a Miss Dickens.

The Webbs had returned from their tour and were back in London. Sidney Webb was trying to raise money in order to expand the School of Economics; he had already got promises and guarantees for a substantial amount, but he needed a great deal more. He wrote to Charlotte, asking if she would be willing again to help financially. Charlotte replied:

"28th. January, 1899   Blen-Cathra, Hindhead,
               Haslemere, Surrey.

"My dear Sidney,

 "If you want University Endowments from me you should not have married me to an anarchist. I have consulted G.B.S. as to whether I should send you a thousand pounds. He tells me that if I do so it will please you and Beatrice and probably secure Mr. H's[1] livelihood, besides providing outdoor relief for a certain number of stuttering nincompoops who are too feeble to earn their livings in the profession. On the other hand, he declares, it will extend the present social machinery for perverting and repressing research, for replacing Webbs by Marshalls and Shaws by Paters; and it will give us the trouble of preventing the creation of some more safe Tory seats. On the whole, he cannot conceive any method by which £1000 can be made to produce more widespread social mischief than the one you propose; but such is his affection for you that he urges me to enclose a cheque sooner than disappoint you. He is, however, very much concerned about you selling out on your own account to the extent of £1000. He suggests that if you were to produce Candida with that £1000, you would not only do some real good to Society but possibly get your money back with 100% to have over for the School.

 "I do not enclose a cheque because the £1000 is of course conditional as I presume yours is, on the £10,000 being raised. If you can tell me when it is likely to be absolutely wanted then I can see better whether I can help with current expenses—for instance, as to the printing of the reports. G.B.S. says 'Shelves be damned: the printing is the really important thing.'

 "You will understand that I am not so light hearted about giving money away as I was. I shall have to save for the purpose of putting my income out of danger . . . and we have now reached a time of life at which we realise what a very short time 20 years is. I regret to

[1] W. A. S. Hewins, first director of the London School of Economics and Political Science.

THIS IS A REPLACEMENT

find that G.B.S. maintains that the only guarantee one can have
for an investment being for the good of humanity is a dividend. I
quite realise now that it is you who are the sentimental idealist, and
he the shameless man of business.

                                    "Yours affectionately
                                              "C. F. Shaw
"P.P.S. You will perceive by the tone of this epistle that it is a joint
one, but your letter produced a great effect!"

G.B.S. was still working hard on *Caesar and Cleopatra,* and
Charlotte had her days well filled, helping with his correspondence,
seeing that the household ran smoothly so that he should not be disturbed, and keeping a watchful eye on G.B.S. himself. He was
absurdly casual about his foot, which had been fairly well for some
weeks, but had begun discharging again, and he said cheerfully
that he supposed another piece of bone would have to be removed.
In April, he tried to ride a bicycle in the road outside Blen-Cathra,
fell heavily, and sprained the same foot yet again. Charlotte lost
patience with him.

"This sprain is a great disappointment," she wrote to Beatrice
Webb. "He was getting on so well, and it makes me so angry to
think of the carelessness that caused it."

Charlotte intended to make a post-nuptial settlement, and had
asked Sidney Webb and Frederick Whelan[2] to be trustees. She also
decided to make a new will, and wanted the Webbs to be the
trustees of that. Then there was the question of moving again; she
favoured the sea:

"I am worried about the future. I hardly like to leave the house
for the night, and yet I must be away for 2 or 3 nights if I am to
look for another house. I am inclined to think it would be a good
thing if we went to a *hotel* at Margate for a few weeks in May—
just to see how the land lies."

G.B.S. had finished *Caesar and Cleopatra,* and was now working on a play which he intended for Ellen Terry, and which he was
calling *The Witch of Atlas.* He was always happy when he was
working at high pressure, and Charlotte found herself strangely
contented, knowing that she was being of great use to him, and

[2] Another Fabian.

that she therefore had a real, even if small, part in what she had come to realize was his essential existence. Because of her watchful care, too, his foot was mending. The wound had healed, and he could now hobble about without crutches. He was able to go to London occasionally, and when Charlotte did not accompany him, was punctilious about returning by an agreed train, so that she could meet him with a cab.

Charlotte had not gone to Margate, but had reserved rooms at a hotel in Ruan Minor, near Cadgwith in Cornwall, for a September holiday. After that she planned to take G.B.S. abroad. Meanwhile, there was the play for Ellen, and something new: a suggestion from Frederick Whelan that G.B.S. should stand for Parliament. The Fabians had already discussed the possibility of putting forward candidates, and now Whelan wrote proposing G.B.S. as one of them. Charlotte answered for her husband on July 12:

"Your letter came this morning, but, as G.B.S. started 5 minutes after reading it, to London, for the day, I have as yet had no opportunity of discussing it with him. I will not however lose a post in writing to tell you that G.B.S. is favourably disposed towards going into Parliament theoretically, and that he is in-clined to agree that a Fabian party in the House is highly desirable in the present state of affairs. I think a great deal hinges on the question *when* will N. Kensington be vacant, and *when* would the fight have to begin. G.B.S. has only been anything like well for a very few weeks and I am absolutely certain that if he had to go to Town and work hard *now*, he would break down again at once. Two or three months hence would be a different matter. Can you give us any information therefore as regards dates?

"Of course I understand the Liberal Party would not help much: we should have to work the thing for ourselves. I think that could be managed. I imagine it to be *a sine qua non that G.B.S. should stand as a Socialist.* I feel sure he would never condescend to slip in as an 'advanced Liberal' or 'Progressive Radical'! Anyway, *I* should absolutely object to that.

"If you will let me know about times and seasons, and if I see the smallest probability of anything coming of this, I will go up to Town and talk to you about it; unless you can manage to come down here . . ."

Nothing came of the idea, rather to Charlotte's relief. G.B.S. himself was too engrossed in the play he was just finishing to be able to think of anything else. He viewed the coming holiday in Cornwall, and the sea voyage to follow, with no great enthusiasm, writing to Ellen Terry in July, 1899:

". . . it is proposed to go to some hole in Cornwall named Cadgwith, to sea-bathe my weak ankle. Then round the Mediterranean in an Orient Steamer as far as Athens and back. I submit to this mainly because the steamer calls at Tangier. I want to see a Moorish town, as the Witch of Atlas scene is laid in Mogador, except the second act, which is in the mountains."

In August, Charlotte and G.B.S. left Ben-Cathra and went to Ruan Minor, where G.B.S. enjoyed swimming, and persuaded Charlotte to learn. He was writing regularly to Ellen about the play he had written for her—"Ellen's play"—which he had re-titled *Captain Brassbound's Conversion,* and he had got to the stage of discussing royalties and other business details for the production. It came as a considerable shock when Ellen Terry wrote to tell him that she did not think Lady Cecily Wayneflete, the principal character, would at all suit her, and suggested Mrs. Patrick Campbell for the part.

G.B.S. had trained himself to be philosophical about disappointments. He did not want Mrs. Patrick Campbell for Lady Cecily, he wanted Ellen. In any case, there would be many difficulties about getting Mrs. Pat, who was in great demand for leading parts. He argued good-naturedly with Ellen Terry in a series of letters, and finally told her that the play was now free to be offered in the open market, and she need not think of it any longer.

The Mediterranean voyage, on the S.S. *Lusitania,* was not a success. Charlotte, who loved being on the sea, found to her dismay that G.B.S. disliked being cooped up in a cabin, with nowhere to work but public rooms or on deck, where he was liable to constant interruptions. In any case, conditions were against an attempt at sustained work. The weather was unpleasantly humid, the pitching and rolling brought on Shaw's headaches, and he was not at all in the mood to look at "sights." He found the Sea of Marmara windy, he disliked Constantinople for its smells, and the Grecian Archipelago, which should have been a group of exquisite islands in a turquoise setting, was glimpsed through cold sleet. At Athens, he wrote to Ellen on October 12, 1899:

"Charlotte, who *will* cultivate French acting and thinks the Comédie Française the most perfect thing on earth, insisted on my going to hear that bellowing donkey, Mounet Sully, as Othello. Good Lord! The 4th. act ended at 12.30; the fifth began punctually at one. Poor Moony Silly grinned like a fairy queen in a fifth rate pantomime and howled like a newsboy. Shakespeare won the third act triumphantly; and Mooney got the credit of it. A horrible experience."

He was thankful to get back to England.

They settled down at Adelphi Terrace for the winter. G.B.S. took up his committee work with zest, attended meetings of the Fabian Society, and spent regular hours of each day writing. Charlotte, remembering the chaos of his business papers at Fitzroy Square, and the fact that he had sometimes found out-of-date cheques during his infrequent tidyings-up, now kept proper accounts for him. Each item was meticulously set down in a notebook:

"*1898*

Royalties on Devil's Disciple—first time on tour—

Brooklyn 20-25 Dec. 4 perf. Philadelphia, 29, etc.	£195—	2—9
Chicago	165—	3—6
Boston, Washington, Baltimore, Milwaukee, Sioux City	486—	5—8
Grant Richards, Plays Pleasant	56—	0—0
Daily Chronicle. Wagner and Morris reviews	18—18—0	
Morning Leader. Wagner Review	5—	0—0
Mrs. D. C. Barker, of Gaskyns, Rudgwick, 10% on receipts of amateur performances of 'Arms and the Man' at Rudgwick on the 8th. and 9th. June.	3—13—0"	

Charlotte was also doing a certain amount of social work. Mary Ward wrote to ask her to be "hostess" at one of the Evenings held at the Passmore Edwards Settlement during the ensuing session. "We hope that each friend will provide a little singing or reciting or violin playing, to help make the evenings more enjoyable . . ." One cannot see Charlotte entertaining the Settlement in this way, but she supported them with donations.

The first call on her time was her job as secretary to her husband. He was living the life of half a dozen men: writing plays, attending the St. Pancras Vestry, turning out numerous articles on all kinds of subjects from Free Trade to Ibsen, jotting down a fantastic number of ideas in words or phrases—his notebooks are full of them. He kept up a large correspondence with actors and theatre managers who were likely to do his plays, and wrote long letters, packed with argument, to Sidney Webb and others, about the policies of the Fabian Society.

Beatrice Webb wrote in her Diary on October 30, 1899: "The Shaws have taken up their residence in Charlotte's attractive flat over the School of Economics, and Sidney and I meet there on Thursdays to dine sumptuously between our respective lectures. Charlotte and Shaw have settled down into the most devoted married couple, she gentle and refined, with happiness added thereto, and he showing no sign of breaking loose from her dominion. What the intellectual product of the marriage will be I do not feel so sure; at any rate he will not become a dilettante, the habit of working is too deeply ingrained. It is interesting to watch his fitful struggles out of the social complaisancy natural to an environment of charm and plenty. How can atmosphere be resisted?"

It is equally interesting to speculate what these "fitful struggles" were. There never was a being less socially complaisant than Shaw; he felt passionately about his principles, and the fact that he was now living in comfortable and civilized surroundings made not the slightest difference to either his ideas or his work, in the sense that Beatrice Webb meant. On the contrary, the care which Charlotte took of him released energy which went into even more revolutionary articles, more talks at meetings of progressives, more plays. Mrs. Webb had not only got hold of the wrong end of the stick; she had got hold of the wrong stick.

Early in the spring of 1900, Charlotte took Blackdown Cottage, a house in the country, near Haslemere. The Webbs went down to stay with them in May to talk of Fabian affairs, and Beatrice, for some reason, found herself ill at ease. She wrote in her Diary:

". . . A minor element in my unhappiness was the discomfort that we had imposed ourselves on the Shaws, and that Charlotte Shaw did not want to have us. Perhaps this is a morbid impression. But it is clear that now that she is happily married we must not presume on her impulsive hospitality and kindly acquiescence in our proposals. All this made me glad to get to work again—to enjoy the mental peace of research, unhampered by human relationships, except the one ideal relationship of marriage."

Charlotte tired of Blackdown Cottage, and found one she liked better, Piccard's Cottage, near Guildford. G.B.S. did not much mind what house he was in so long as there was a room for him to work in. He was writing a preface for *Three Plays for Puritans,* and preparing it for publication. Charlotte tried to get him to work at a lower pressure, without success. His foot was quite better, he could walk and bicycle, he often went to London for the day—what was she worrying about?

The Boer War had broken out the previous year, and G.B.S. was writing a Fabian pamphlet and taking part in public discussions about it. Charlotte heard from Sissy that Hugh had gone out to South Africa with the City Imperial Volunteers, and asked her to come down to Surrey with Cicely for a holiday. But Sissy did not like George Bernard Shaw, and made excuses.

Charlotte had carried out her intention of making a will, which included an annuity of £600 to Shaw's mother, and the residue of her estate absolutely to G.B.S. if living. If not, £300 to his sister Lucy, after her mother's death, legacies to the London School of Economics for "economic teaching," to the Phonetics Institution National Gallery of Ireland or other gallery or museum in Ireland for a publicly owned orchestra in Ireland and an endowed theatre there, "to bring the masterpieces of Fine Art within the reach of the Irish people."[3]

G.B.S. did not influence her in the slightest over the personal bequests. They saw little of Lucinda Elizabeth and less of Lucy,

[3] See Appendix.

who disliked and was envious of Charlotte. Lucinda Elizabeth had no emotional feelings one way or the other regarding "Carlotta," though she was a little in awe of this reserved, well-bred woman whom her son had married. Charlotte managed to keep her own intense dislike of her mother-in-law within bounds, and was polite and outwardly friendly on the few occasions when they met each other; but G.B.S. was aware of her feeling, and took care not to press his relatives on her.

The provisions in her will for institutions were the result of consultation with G.B.S. She shared his ideas that to help individuals one must help "causes" first, if they were good ones. Her private account books at this period, and, indeed, until the end of her life, show the strength of her convictions on the point; she gave hundreds of pounds to all kinds of societies and groups which were, she felt, doing excellent work in a quiet way for the advancement of culture and the widening of education for "ordinary" people.

She rented Piccard's Cottage again in the spring, and Studland Rectory, near Corfe Castle, for their 1901 summer holiday. They liked being near the sea; Charlotte had become as keen a swimmer as G.B.S. He found Studland "a very enchanting place—to look at. It also has the curious effect of reviving every malady, every cramp, every pain, every bone fracture, even, from which one has ever suffered. And I have neatly slit my big toe into two symmetrical halves by stepping on a sharp flint whilst bathing."

Charlotte did her best to stop G.B.S. from working on "things dramatic" during summer holidays, but he had a large correspondence which he insisted must be answered. A letter from Sidney Webb about the political situation and the attitude of the Liberal leaders set G.B.S. gleefully dictating a twelve-page reply for Charlotte to send. Sidney had quoted Beatrice's opinions, and G.B.S. quoted Ibsen's *Pillars of Society*—Beatrice did not care for Ibsen:

". . . If B. had sat at Ibsen's play . . . she would have discovered that Ibsen had something to tell her of more importance to you at present than the old fashioned stuff about capital truth and capital freedom and capital emancipation of women. . . . That something was the exclamation of the cornered hero, 'We pillars of society are only the tools of society.' Now Rosebery, being a peer and a

political pillar, is necessarily a political tool. He is at present scream-
ing for somebody to come and handle him, exactly like the madman
in 'Peer Gynt' who thinks he is a pen and implores people to write
with him, finally cutting his throat by way of mending his nib.
There is really a lot to be learned from Ibsen if Beatrice would only
read him in the proper spirit. Your strength as always lies in your
willingness and your capacity to be the tool wielder just as the
official people's weakness has lain in their coveting the pomp and
glory of prominent tooldom. You are married to the only woman
in England who dare ask Rosebery to dinner and ask him whether
he will take beer or whisky. That is a tremendously strong position,
but only so long as your own sense and grip of it remain unclouded
and firm. If you once succumb to the fatal English weakness of wor-
shiping the idol you have yourself fashioned, with the marks of a
potter's thumb all over its still moist clay, you are lost. Handel did
not attain his summit as a musician by effacing himself in his
admiration of the majestic sounds produced by the bellow blower
who supplied his organ with wind. Rosebery is at present blowing
the bellows very hard. So is Asquith; so is Campbell-Bannerman;
so is Chamberlain; so are the whole boodle of them—all like so
many 'Pied Pipers of Hamelin'; but the children (meaning the
British Public) won't follow because there is no tune."

They liked Piccard's Cottage, keeping it until the following year,
and going up to London for periods at a time.

Early in 1902, the Secretary of the School of Economics asked
Charlotte to settle an account for some fixtures which had been in
the upper part of the Adelphi Terrace house when she had taken
over the rooms. The School, which had grown enormously, was
moving to its own building behind the Aldwych. Charlotte thought
the amount asked excessive, but felt that she was in an awkward
position and was not sure what to do about it. Shaw, irritated, dictated a reply to be sent to Sidney Webb:

"24th. March, 1902.   Piccard's Cottage,
                                                      Guildford.
"Dear Webb,
        "Those fixtures at Adelphi Terrace are destroying our do-
mestic life. Whenever I sit down to work at a play Charlotte cuts

in with them and wrecks my inspiration. So for Heaven's sake let's get them settled out of hand.

"On examining the list, I find that McKillop[4] has mistaken his profession. He should have been a house agent of the most unscrupulous type. Out of an unblushing total of £92. 9. 6, £24. 18 is for linoleum and oilcloth valued at 2/- a yard after six years' wear and after mutilation of the most horrible character to accommodate your bookcases. Naturally, I ask what you will pay me for not insisting on its instant and ignominious removal. Further, there is £10 for 30 lockers which nobody wants, but which we are prepared to leave unmolested; £14 for a W.C. which you stole from the first floor; and £3. 9 as the modest total for the acute disutility of gas brackets, mostly arrived at by charging 1/- for articles worth ½d. at the Marine Store. In short, if you knock £50 off, and take half the balance you will arrive at a figure of about £20.

"For the sake of the School and in consideration of my personal regard for the parties concerned, I am willing to offer £25. On a strict business footing I should offer 12, which is about what McKillop expects, if I may judge by the gleam in his eye when I mentioned that amount to him; but Charlotte's anomalous position as Governor and Trustee makes it advisable that the price should be clearly excessive. It is of course to be considered whether the things should not be removed and sold in the open market as a matter of principle; and if any of the Committee have the slightest doubt that the offer is a thoroughly sufficient one, and that the School would be out of pocket by not accepting it, such a sale ought to take place."

They returned to Adelphi Terrace in February, and the following month Shaw had a visitor whom he treated so oddly that if it had not been for Charlotte, he would not have spoken more than a few words to the caller—and would thereby have missed one of the most valuable contacts of his life.

Siegfried Trebitsch was a young Austrian dramatist, a friend of Schnitzler and von Hofmannsthal, who wrote theatre articles in the Viennese journals. On a visit to London in 1901, he brought a

[4] Secretary of the London School of Economics and Political Science.

letter of introduction to William Archer, whom he greatly admired as a translator of Ibsen. Archer found the Austrian intelligent and forward-looking.

"I write about the lions of the London stage—Pinero, Henry Arthur Jones, Sydney Grundy," Archer told him. "But there are unperformed plays which are worth a dozen of the others. Especially Shaw."

Trebitsch was interested, and asked whether he could obtain Shaw's plays. He returned home with *Plays, Pleasant and Unpleasant* and the recently published *Three Plays for Puritans.* The plays all made a considerable impression on him, especially *Candida,* which he found enchanting, a modern fairy tale. He read all ten plays straight off, and at once began to talk about them to theatre managers of his acquaintance. He did not at first think of translating them himself. He had published novels, short stories and plays, and was trying to make his own way as a creative writer. But he recognized originality, and he was determined to persuade a manager to put on at least one of Shaw's works. It would be a beginning.

Nobody was in the least interested. Trebitsch next tried Entsch, the head of a theatrical publishing firm, to see if he would publish translations of the plays, but Entsch said he would have nothing to do with this crazy Irishman, and advised Trebitsch to get on with his own work and not bother with foreign plays which could not possibly have a chance of success. Trebitsch was discouraged, but he did not give up. He had already translated some of *Candida,* and thought it intensely alive. He now decided that he must translate all the plays of George Bernard Shaw himself, and somehow get the German intelligentsia interested. Later in the year he went to London again, especially to see Archer, who gave him a warm letter of introduction to Shaw.

It was one thing to be ardently enthusiastic about the plays, another to approach Shaw in person. Trebitsch, for all his lively, extrovert nature, was a diffident man, and he spent some time in front of G.B.S.'s door in Adelphi Terrace, trying to summon up courage to knock. There was also a streak of caution in him which made him wonder if this was a wise step. He thought of his own work. If he turned into a translator, what would happen to the stories, the novels, the plays of his own that he intended to write? Then he remembered *Candida*, and he knocked at the door.

The maid took his letter of introduction, showed him into a sitting-room, and went upstairs. After a minute or two a middle-aged, well-dressed woman came in, shook hands, and said she was Mrs. Shaw. Trebitsch told her who he was and why he had come. She talked pleasantly for a few minutes, and Trebitsch was aware that she was quietly taking stock of him, either, he felt, to get rid of him or to allow him to see G.B.S. Then a tall man with bright, merry eyes and a reddish beard trimmed to a point, "an amiably mirthful giant," appeared in the doorway. Mrs. Shaw disappeared into the background, and presently went out.

Shaw told the visitor to sit down and asked him the object of his visit. When Trebitsch replied boldly that he was determined to translate Shaw's plays into German, and became enthusiastic, G.B.S. strode to the door, mounted the stairs outside and called out:

"Charlotte! Here's a young lunatic Archer's sent me who won't listen to reason. You come and calm him down."

Mrs. Shaw returned to the room, alone, apologized for Shaw's behaviour, spoke encouragingly to Trebitsch, and went to the door. Trebitsch heard her calling up the stairs, saying that the visitor appeared to be serious and sensible.

"Come down and listen to what he has to say," she ended.

G.B.S. appeared again and sat down opposite Trebitsch. Charlotte now took part in the conversation. Why, she demanded of her husband, should he not become known in Germany, since Shakespeare was accepted there as a national poet?

Now G.B.S. asked questions about Trebitsch's own work, and when the Viennese writer produced the galley proofs of the French translation of his first novel, together with a list of his published books in German, Shaw appeared to be satisfied. He began to talk about copyright, a subject of which Trebitsch knew little, but one which Shaw expounded with force.

Trebitsch left soon afterwards, not knowing what kind of impression he had made. A few days later he received a short letter:

"17th. March, 1902.   Adelphi Terrace,
                                                              W.C.
"Dear Sir,
        "My husband has been thinking over your proposition and
we shall be very glad if you will come to lunch here tomorrow
(Tuesday) at 1.30, and talk it over with him.
                                                "Yours sincerely,
                                                "C. F. Shaw"
    Trebitsch tried not to feel too elated, but he could hardly wait
until the morrow. At 1.25 he presented himself at Adelphi Terrace,
and luncheon was served punctually at the half hour. It was an excellent meal, but the young man noticed that though there was a
meat course for himself and his hostess, G.B.S. ate only vegetarian
dishes. Shaw brought up the subject of food, and urged his guest
to follow his example, adding:
    "That's the only way you'll be able to get a lot of work done.
Above all, give up those poisons, black coffee and wine."
    Charlotte unobtrusively looked after the needs of the two men,
but took no part in the conversation, nor did she remain when the
table had been cleared and they continued to talk. It was apparent
to Trebitsch that she approved of him, which was a relief. Shaw
talked mostly of the legal aspects of translation rights, and made
several suggestions. In the end, Trebitsch agreed to a proposition that he should have the rights for a year, during which he would
translate three of the plays. If he did not find a publisher or a
theatre manager for them within that time, he would give the
rights back to Shaw.
    Trebitsch returned to Vienna. He chose *The Devil's Disciple*,
Candida, and *Arms and the Man* for the three translations, and at
once began work on them.
    The young Austrian's visit brought great satisfaction to Char-
lotte. She had identified herself closely with her husband's work
during the past four years; she was sure he was a genius, and if
Trebitsch helped the world to appreciate him he had her approba-
tion. At forty-five, Charlotte was not very different in some ways
from the girl whose strongest characteristic had been an infinite
capacity for hero-worship.

12

HELPMEET

(1902–1905)

Within a year, by dint of unwearying labour and ceaseless importuning of publishers and managers, Siegfried Trebitsch had the satisfaction of seeing *The Devil's Disciple* put into production at the Raimundtheater in Vienna. At the same time he was able to persuade a noted German publisher, S. Fischer, to bring out the plays in volume form. Fischer actually founded a subsidiary company for the publishing of theatrical work in order to accomplish this in due form.

Charlotte was jubilant at the news. She wrote to Trebitsch in February, 1903:

"I should greatly like to subscribe to a Vienna press cutting agency, so that I may get any notices that appear in the papers about plays. Could you tell me the name and address of a good one.

"I regret so much that I am not going to Vienna for the great first night! It was impossible to manage it, but I look forward eagerly to hearing what happens. *Do* wire if it is really a success. Bad news will travel fast enough. . . . My kindest good wishes to you."

They went to Italy for Easter, Charlotte planning a route which took in Parma, Perugia, Assisi, Orvieto, Siena and Genoa, where she saw a very old friend, Dr. Breiting, who had attended her father when he had been taken ill in Genoa nearly twenty years before. G.B.S. was bored. He disliked the constant travelling, he was unable to work anywhere (which was what Charlote intended: she wanted him to have a rest), and he wished to get back to people he knew and could talk to. Perhaps it was this feeling which prompted the tenor of his reply to Janet Achurch, who wrote to him in May. The actress had played Candida for the Stage Society, and Lady Cecily for a single Stage Society production of *Captain Brassbound's Conversion,* a performance which had depressed G.B.S., who had thought her totally unsuited for the part. Janet Achurch had convinced herself that Charlotte Shaw did not like her and was influencing G.B.S. against her in consequence. Shaw replied:

"You do not understand the nature of Charlotte's objections to you. It is not a question of like and dislike in the ordinary sense: she has exactly the same objection to my mother, my sister and everybody who forms part of the past in which she has no part. The moment you walk into the room where I am you create a world in which you and I are at home and she is a stranger. That is the real difficulty of marrying at forty; and it must be faced until in the lapse of time the new world so grows up and supersedes the old that it need no longer be jealous of it. It is just the same with me: the moment her old friends call I become a mere chance acquaintance. I don't mind (indeed I generally plead business and bolt after coruscating enough to satisfy curiosity): but Charlotte *does* mind, and so would any woman. These situations require very considerate handling. If you were to divorce Charlie and marry a man whom you have never seen before, you would find for many years that almost any woman he was at all intimate with knew him better than you, and had a larger stock of common experiences with him."

Charlotte did, in fact, dislike Janet Achurch, because she distrusted her. She admired the actress and was wary of the woman; it seemed to her that the Charringtons were out for what they could get from G.B.S. It may have been instinctive antipathy on both sides—Charlotte's eyes could be very penetrating, and Miss Achurch had a cat-like feel for hidden hostility. It is true that Charlotte discouraged this particular friendship, though it is doubtful if Shaw's too-tidy analysis in his letter to Janet Achurch was accurate. The actress aroused antipathy in men as well as in women. Richard Mansfield, the American actor, writing to Shaw on April 14, 1895, had described her as a "massive, middle-aged woman" and had gone on to say, referring to Janet Achurch's performance in *Candida*:

"I couldn't have made love to your Candida if I had taken ether. I never fall in love with fuzzy-haired persons who purr and are business-like and take a drop when they feel disposed and have weak feminine voices. My ideal is something quite different. I detest an aroma of stale tobacco and gin. I detest intrigue and slyness and sham ambitions. I don't like women who sit on the floor or kneel by your side and have designs on your shirt bosom. I don't like women who comb their tawny locks with their fingers and claw their necks and scratch the air with their chins . . ."

*   *   *

Charlotte was happy. G.B.S. was well, and she had the satisfaction of knowing that it was because of her ceaseless care for his comfort that he was able to work steadily and without strain. She had brought order into his life, and she noticed that he reacted to the change in many little ways. In the Fitzroy Square days he had not appeared to mind the squalor which surrounded him. Now, an innate fastidiousness began to show itself. He appreciated her thoughtfulness in trying to vary his vegetarian diet as much as possible, and occasionally remarked on the excellent way the servants ran the ménage. Housekeeping, however, was not Charlotte's forte; she chose good servants, treated them well, and left them to do their work. Her own life was full of interest. She served on the committees of the London School of Economics and the School of Medicine for Women, and she was also on the play-reading committee of the Stage Society.

G.B.S. was finding a great deal of pleasure in being able to

entertain friends in a civilized home. Harley Granville-Barker
visited them and stayed for hours, talking with animation of his
repertory projects, and of other theatre matters. Members of the
Fabian Society Executive dropped in, or were formally invited to
dinner. There was always good talk. Charlotte's earlier habit of self-
questioning and doubting the use of her existence had disappeared;
she felt that all her former life had led up to this marriage. Her
destiny was to be the helpmeet of a great man. Of that she was
sure.

The country house she took for the summer of 1903 was Maybury
Knoll, near Woking, a favourite part of Surrey with them both.
They stayed there for most of the summer, returning to London at
week-ends. Charlotte was meeting many people connected with the
theatre, and though she usually kept in the background, Shaw's
friends were well aware that his wife possessed considerable intelligence and unbiased judgement. Alfred Sutro sent a play to G.B.S.
for his opinion; G.B.S. passed it on to Charlotte to read, and reported to Sutro that she was much affected.

"I shall read it this afternoon and fortify Charlotte with my
opinion for the S.S. [Stage Society] Committee on Wednesday. You
know the S.S.—the most stupendous Philistines in these isles; but
fortunately they will accept even works of genius to checkmate each
other; and this helps out the few good people who want good
work."

Shaw was extending his own activities. There were elections at
the London County Council, and the Webbs were anxious to have
as many progressives as possible on that body. G.B.S. stood with Sir
William Geary for St. Pancras, and threw himself into the campaign
with zest. Sidney Webb and Robert Phillimore had been returned
unopposed for Deptford, and Sidney and Beatrice now turned
their attention to getting G.B.S. in for St. Pancras. They had
mobilized the entire Fabian Society to work on his behalf; St. Pancras was not a Liberal borough.

Beatrice Webb wrote in her Diary on February 27, 1904:

"Whether this effort will win what would be a forlorn hope to
any other Progressive candidate, and will counteract the enemies
G.B.S. makes in our own ranks, we cannot tell. The Shaws have

been good friends to us, and we would not like them to have a humiliating defeat. What that erratic genius will do, if he gets on the L.C.C., heaven will know some day."

On March 7, she wrote:

"G.B.S. badly beaten; elsewhere the Progressives romping back with practically undiminished numbers. . . . G.B.S. showed himself hopelessly intractable during the election: refused to adopt any orthodox devices as to address and polling-card, inventing brilliant ones of his own; all quite unsuited to any constituency but Fabians and 'Souls.' Insisted that he was an atheist; that, though a teetotaller, he would force every citizen to imbibe a quartern of rum to cure any tendency to intoxication; laughed at the Nonconformist conscience; chaffed the Catholics about Transubstantiation; abused the Liberals, and contemptuously patronised the Conservatives—until nearly every section was equally disgruntled. His bad side is very prominent at an election—vanity and lack of reverence for knowledge or respect for other people's prejudices; even his good qualities—quixotic chivalry to his opponents and cold drawn truth, ruthlessly administered, to possible supporters, are magnificent but not war. Anyway, we did our best for him . . . and he and Charlotte are duly grateful. He will never be selected again by any constituency that any wire-puller thinks can be won."

G.B.S. took his defeat with a laugh—was it of relief? Charlotte did not know. He was working hard on a new play which he was writing at the request of W. B. Yeats for the Irish Literary Theatre, a group that put on plays at the Abbey Theatre in Dublin. It was to be called *John Bull's Other Island,* and when he discussed the characters with Charlotte, which he usually did, he found her surprisingly argumentative. They had had brushes on the subject of the Irish character on several occasions, and Charlotte, who knew the Irish far better than her husband, hoped that he would not exaggerate types too much. G.B.S. retorted that she had a romantic view of her fellow-countrymen which he did not share.

In the spring, Charlotte rented a house in Hertfordshire which she liked better than Maybury Knoll; this was the Old House at Harmer Green, a mile or two from Welwyn, a "16th. or 17th. century house—a gem," as G.B.S. described it to Ellen Terry. They stayed here for some weeks, then Charlotte was offered the loan of a friend's flat in Rome. G.B.S. refused to go. Not only had he to finish the play for Yeats, but Granville-Barker was putting on *Candida* for several performances at the Court Theatre, and there would be rehearsals to supervise. Charlotte went to Rome without him, and passed a restful month visiting old friends. She did not see Axel Munthe; he was rumoured to be in Capri. Charlotte received this item of news with bare interest: Munthe belonged to a different existence altogether. She did, however, seek out Sartorio, and was glad to find that the pastel he had made of her had survived and was in good condition. She arranged to have it sent home, and left Rome soon afterwards, arriving back in July.

G.B.S., as she suspected, had been overworking, and Charlotte took him to Harmer Green. Hardly had they settled there before she suggested a holiday in Scotland. G.B.S. was extremely irritated. No! A thousand times no! The Irish Literary Theatre had turned down *John Bull's Other Island,* much to his chagrin; it was to be produced instead by Granville-Barker at the Court Theatre in November, and there was still a considerable amount of work to be done on it.

[He later wrote in the preface to the play:

["Mr. Yeats got rather more than he bargained for. . . . It was uncongenial to the whole spirit of the neo-Gallic movement, which is bent on creating a new Ireland after its own ideal, whereas my play is a very uncompromising presentment of real old Ireland."

[G.B.S. could not understand why Irishmen should object to seeing their least attractive characteristics exposed on the stage.]

Charlotte let the firework display fizzle out, then quietly insisted that they should consider Scotland. If he was going to have the long strain of rehearsals for *John Bull* in the autumn, all the more reason why he should have a good holiday first. He had to give way, and they started for Scotland, G.B.S. taking a portmanteau filled with papers and notebooks.

It was not a restful holiday. They travelled to Alness, Rosemarkie in the Highlands, Edinburgh and North Berwick.

"Oh, these holidays, these accursed holidays!" G.B.S. wrote to Granville-Barker. He could find "no decent place" where he could either bathe or write. Nevertheless, he did manage to do quite a lot of writing, for besides finishing the revision of *John Bull's Other Island,* he worked on a one-act comedy, *How He Lied to Her Husband,* for Arnold Daly, the American actor who had played Marchbanks in the New York production of *Candida,* and who had asked him for a curtain-raiser.

John Bull's Other Island was produced at the Court Theatre in November, with Granville-Barker in the part of Father Keegan, and was a great success.

They spent Christmas, 1904, at Harmer Green. G.B.S. had always refused to keep the festive season and did not send Christmas cards to anybody; but they received so many that Charlotte was forced to send cards in return, inscribing greetings and including his name, in spite of his protests. At any rate, he declared, it was a relief to be in the country at this time, away from the vulgarities of the commercialized displays of tawdry tinsel in London.

Siegfried Trebitsch sent Charlotte a book for Christmas, and told her he was unwell and was wintering abroad. Charlotte replied:

"G.B.S. is not at all well. I wish I could persuade him to go with you to Egypt: I know that is what he wants—sun and rest! However, he will not move for anyone, and he works all day. . . . I am sorry your nerves are so bad. Did I ever send you a little book about vegetarian diet? I believe you would be quite well if you would give up meat, etc. and tea and coffee! I have done so with excellent results."

She had not, in fact, become a strict vegetarian by conviction. G.B.S. had long mocked at a carnivorous diet, though he had never seriously tried to persuade her to give it up entirely. She had phases of vegetarianism, especially when she was ill, but she could always return to her former diet without heart-searching.

Charlotte was literally right when she told Trebitsch that G.B.S. worked all day. He wrote relentlessly, beginning a new play almost as soon as he had finished the last one. He told Charlotte that all he needed was a theme—and there were enough themes and to spare in his amazing brain. Once started on page 1, the scenes grew. He revised and revised, but the foundation was established when he began, and the play was quickly built. Now forty-nine years old, he had written thirteen plays, including a masterpiece, *Man and Superman*. Charlotte was certain it was a masterpiece when he gave her the manuscript to read. She generally had definite opinions on her husband's work, and though G.B.S. did not always agree with her, he trusted her judgement. In this instance he agreed with her. It was, he said, one of the best things he had done, for it was packed full of his most firmly held beliefs.

In April, 1905, they went to stay with Beatrice and Sidney Webb, who had taken a house at Sandgate in Kent. H. G. Wells lived not far away, and Beatrice gave a dinner party for them. The guests—"carefully selected," according to Beatrice—were the Prime Minister [Mr. Balfour], the Bishop of Stepney, Mrs. Reeves, Mr. Thesiger, and "a new L.C.C. Moderate." Beatrice later wrote in her Diary that the P.M. thoroughly enjoyed the mixture of chaff and dialectic which flew from G.B.S. to Wells and round the table. Charlotte, beautifully dressed in a white gown, with her thick hair coiled round the back of her head, was content to listen to the brilliant conversation, and made friends with Mrs. Wells, who seemed to her to be a woman of charm and sense, mercifully unintellectual.

On their return to London there was a letter from Trebitsch to Shaw, and Charlotte replied for him:

"11th. April   10 Adelphi Terrace, W.C.

"Dear Mr. Trebitsch,

"I am to tell you that 1897 is the date of The Devil's Disciple. . . .

"G.B.S. wishes to know if the poetry of Dante Gabriel Rossetti and Swinburne is known in Germany, as Wilde's Salome should not appear extraordinary—quite the contrary—to anyone who was familiar with the poets of the Pre-Raphaelite Movement. This is probably why Salome is from the English point of view overrated in Germany. G.B.S. is being bombarded in all directions for contributions to the Schiller celebrations, but he says he has nothing to say. It is almost impossible always to get anything out of him unless he is really master of his subject, and he never journalizes in the sense of writing clever talk about things he doesn't understand.

"Yours very sincerely,
"C. F. Shaw"

Charlotte had taken over a good deal of G.B.S.'s correspondence, answering the dozens of letters which reached him daily from strangers and acquaintances, using her judgement as to which might be useful to him, politely but firmly fending the others off. Trebitsch sent frequent reports of the interest G.B.S. had at last aroused in Germany. Charlotte wrote to him in May, 1905:

"G.B.S. says you ought to try to see his plays done in English here. . . . You cannot see 'Man and Superman' until Sunday, May 21st., that is the day it will be produced, but both the other plays you could see before. 'You Never Can Tell' will have matinées on the 18th. and 19th., and 'John Bull' is being played every evening. So come about the 16th. or 17th. and stay over the 21st. and you can see them all."

Trebitsch accepted the invitation, and travelled to England to see the plays and stay with the Shaws at Adelphi Terrace. They liked him as much as ever, and the Austrian paid particular court to Charlotte, whom he considered to be his friendly angel; he did not forget that it was she who had been responsible in the first place for his good fortune in becoming Shaw's German translator. Trebitsch had had to make a difficult decision. The corpus of Shaw's work was growing. Was he, Trebitsch, to spend the rest of his life translating George Bernard Shaw? If so, it was no use having ambitions for a career of his own as a writer. One of his bitterest moments had been when a publisher in Vienna had offered to take his next book if he could assure to him the rights in forthcoming translations of Shaw, whose fame was becoming established throughout Europe and America. Trebitsch had refused to leave the faithful S. Fischer. The other publisher's blatantly cynical offer had shaken him into taking stock of his future. Was he to go down to posterity as the man who had given Shaw to the German-speaking world or as a novelist and dramatist in his own right?

He chose Shaw.

13

AYOT ST. LAWRENCE

(1905—1906)

Captain Brassbound's Conversion was on the stocks again. Ellen
Terry had at last agreed to do it, and arrangements were going ahead
for its production at the Court Theatre early in the following year.

Charlotte was particularly glad that the play was to be done;
she knew that G.B.S. had been irked by Ellen Terry's previous
decision, and he was looking forward to seeing her at last play the
part he had written especially for her. In July, Charlotte persuaded
him to accompany her to Ireland, to see her old home. Shaw had
not been back to his own country since he had left it as a young
man, and he did not particularly want to go now. But he was in
very good spirits, and as it might seem ungracious to refuse Charlotte's plea that he should visit Derry, he agreed to go.

It was with real excitement that Charlotte made the journey;
she had long wanted her husband to visit her childhood home.
If she had expected him to be equally excited, she was disappointed.
G.B.S. was hardly even interested. Derry was a house, like other
Big Houses in Ireland. Had it got a sitting-room well removed from
the drawing-room, where he could work in peace? He could think
of nothing but *Captain Brassbound's Conversion*, and he was also

working on a new play, which was to be about a girl who went into the Salvation Army.

Sissy had come to Derry for a holiday at the same time, and Charlotte hoped that her sister would be able to get to know G.B.S. and appreciate his unique character. Mrs. Cholmondeley was perfectly ready to be friends with her brother-in-law. She had read and heard so much about him during the last five years that her earlier suspicious distrust of him as an adventurer had changed to curiosity. She looked forward to becoming properly acquainted with him.

G.B.S. was not at first responsive. He felt that his sister-in-law still disapproved of him, and he remained in his sitting-room for most of the day, working on *Brassbound*, revising the scenes and making out cast-lists for Charlotte to copy and send to Granville-Barker. The new play was growing, too. Charlotte spent part of each morning with him, hard at her secretarial duties; the rest of the time she and Sissy visited friends in the neighbourhood and tenants on the estate. G.B.S. occasionally joined them for walks, and gradually the general atmosphere became easier. G.B.S. found that Sissy was not in the least formidable; she was, in fact, an agreeable and intelligent woman, who listened to his talk and smiled at his witticisms and generally proved to be very different from what he had always imagined her to be.

When the time came for them to leave, Sissy invited him to come and stay at Edstaston. Charlotte was to make a round of visits before returning home; G.B.S. was not going with her as he had to see Granville-Barker in London. He accepted Sissy's invitation, and two weeks later was writing to Beatrice Webb:

"5 October, 1905   Edstaston, Wem, Shropshire.
                     (Home of Charlotte's brother-in-law,
                                  Col. Cholmondeley.)

"I am here until Friday next week, when we shall come up for the Fabian, and make an end of our holiday.

"Charlotte and her sister enjoyed Derry so extraordinarily that I got a sort of secondhand enjoyment—largely mixed with resignation —out of it. . . .

"Mrs. C and I, in view of our previously rather distant relations, laid ourselves out to conciliate one another, and rather more than succeeded. I have the important advantage in such matters of not being nearly so disagreeable personally as one would suppose from my writings. I am now completely adopted on the usual lunatic privileged terms in the Cholmondeley household. I have taken several photographs of Mrs. C., and taught her to swim. The Colonel has presented me with a watch which tells the date and the phases of the moon. I play accompaniments to Mrs. C's singing, and the past is buried. . . .

"I send you an article on Education which I wrote for Great Thoughts. The editor asked me for a few lines & sent me five guineas. I was so touched by this departure from the usual yellow press practice of trying to get a column out of me for nothing that I wrote the article and returned the cheque.

"We have not yet got a country house. Charlotte is still in Ireland. This evening she crosses to Holyhead on her way hither from Mitchelstown Castle. She has been doing a round of Bandons and Castletowns & Kingstons & other Irish peers in their castles. They wanted me to come; but the worm turned at last. I fled to England and recovered my tone with such delirious joy that at the Salvation Army meeting at the Albert Hall on Monday, where they put me in the middle box on the grand tier, I sang magnificently, making everybody else in the box regard me as another Sankey or Alexander. It did me a lot of good.

> "When the roll (drum, drum) is called upyon—der
> When the roll (drum, drum) is called upyon—der
> When the roll (drum, drum) is called upyon—der
> When the roll is call dupyonder
>   I'LL BE THERE."

G.B.S. enjoyed himself at Edstaston. He made as favourable an impression on Hugh Cholmondeley as he had done on Sissy, and he enchanted their small daughter. Cecily was always to remember how this tall, laughing uncle treated her with the courtesy accorded to an adult, and the way he made everybody laugh. When G.B.S. left Edstaston, it was with a warm invitation to return.

Charlotte had always kept an Annuary, a kind of abbreviated diary, and was used to copying passages of prose and poetry which she liked into her commonplace books; she liked writing. During the winter of 1905–6, something new interested her: translating. Because of her good knowledge of the French language, she read a great many French books. There came into her hands a copy of *Maternité,* by Eugène Brieux. She later described, in her Foreword to *Damaged Goods,* the effect *Maternité* had on her:

"I read it from cover to cover without a pause, and when I laid it down I felt an event had occurred, and a new possession come into my life. I knew at once I must translate the play into English to make it accessible to those of my countrymen and women who could not read it in the original French. I spent many mornings of that chilly winter and spring trying to make the work as perfect as I could.

"I was at that time a member of the Executive Committee of the Stage Society, and my fellow-members, moved by my enthusiasm for the play, suggested that it should be performed by the Society. It was finally arranged that this should be done; and the MS was sent to the Censor to be licensed. A reply quickly came from that official to the effect that permission would not be granted, with a note saying, 'Inform whoever is responsible for this play that it will *never* be licensed in England.' Under these circumstances the play had to be given in the hole-and-corner way, and under the disadvantages and difficulties a banned play has to encounter. I shall not easily forget the zeal and devotion with which the artists worked; or the impression the play made upon many of them, even under the crushing circumstances of rehearsal morning after morning in an unwarmed and semi-lighted hall in a most depressing part of London. The performance was a dignified and competent one."

Charlotte had written to Brieux for permission to translate the play, and he had sent her a courteous reply, remarking that he was surprised as well as pleased that it should be done in English.

Maternité was produced by the Stage Society on April 8, 1906, and Charlotte determined to publish it, as a matter of social importance. Two of Brieux's other plays had been done into English: *The Three Daughters of M. Dupont,* translated by St. John Hankin, and *Les Avariés,* translated by John Pollock under the title

Damaged Goods. The Stage Society had already given a performance of *The Three Daughters of M. Dupont,* but had not had the
courage to produce *Damaged Goods,* which was even more outspoken on social evils usually ignored by polite society. Charlotte
suggested that all three plays should be published in one volume,
with a preface by her husband, and the other translators agreed.
Brieux readily gave permission, but explained that he had assigned
his literary rights in the plays to a P. V. Stock. Charlotte com-
municated with M. Stock and bought from him the rights to publish English translations.

Now came the task of finding a publisher. Charlotte sent the
plays to leading firms, but none of them would agree to publishing
Damaged Goods, explaining in their several ways that the prejudices
it aroused would be too strong. Charlotte was angry but not discouraged. She could wait. She was convinced the day would come
when a more realistic view would be taken of works of art which
dealt with serious subjects. Meanwhile she would go on translating
M. Brieux's plays, and soon began on *La Femme Seule.*

The work on the new translation could only be intermittent,
as she spent many hours a day writing and copying letters for
G.B.S. He no longer made jokes about having an unpaid secretary;
he now took Charlotte's assistance completely for granted, turning
to her when he was in any difficulty. He rarely discussed the
development of a play with her, but liked to tell her about the
characters. He was sometimes impatient of her comments, and
would argue and justify his points. Charlotte could not keep up
this kind of argument, but would quietly remind him that he had
asked for her opinion, and she had done no more than give it to
him.

She was able to save him a great deal of trouble by dealing with
his enormous correspondence, and simplifying the business side of
his work. He had long appreciated her down-to-earth attitude in
business affairs; she knew every detail of her own investments, and
could instruct her solicitors in the clearest terms. G.B.S. often left
her to reply to letters which angered him. In February, 1906, she
was writing to Trebitsch:

"G.B.S. tells me to let you know that he has nothing to do with this new version of Cashel Byron produced in New York. He did not authorize it: it is a piracy made without consulting him; so he is not able to do anything for you in the matter of the rights of translation. If you really want them it would be better for you to write direct to America about them."

G.B.S. was exceedingly annoyed by literary piracy, which was practised by some unscrupulous American publishers, but he could not do much about it. Charlotte, always indignant on his account, balanced the upsets in his life with positive pleasures. The one which he enjoyed greatly was being host at his own table. Famous people wished to meet him, and Charlotte took every opportunity of bringing this about. Her luncheon parties were already well known, and Charlotte made sure that interesting people were included. Shaw, in his own phrase, liked to "coruscate," and Charlotte was content to be a good hostess, and to allow him to indulge his natural vanity—for this was how she had come to regard his strong vein of exhibitionism. She recognized that it was part of the complex psychological make-up of an individual who was naturally shy, and though it irritated her—and was to do so very often—she had, after eight years of marriage, trained herself to accept it as part of her husband's genius.

August Rodin, the French sculptor, came to London, and when Charlotte heard that he wished to meet Mr. Bernard Shaw, she wrote asking him to lunch. Rodin was a man with a delightful personality, and Charlotte was pleased by a suggestion which came up at the table that he should make a bust of Shaw; she arranged to go with G.B.S. to Paris the following month. They could not go earlier, as *Captain Brassbound's Conversion* was opening on March 20, and *Maternité* was due to be produced early in April: engagements which demanded the presence of the Shaws.

Siegfried Trebitsch was also on a visit to Paris when Charlotte and G.B.S. arrived there in mid-April; he was having a short holiday with Rainer Maria Rilke, who was Rodin's secretary. The Shaws stayed at the Grand Hotel on the Quai D'Orsay, and Trebitsch at once called. He accompanied the Shaws the following day when they went to Rodin's studio.

It was an experience which always remained vivid for Trebitsch.

Rodin seemed to fill the entire studio with his tremendous energy, talking to himself as he worked. Charlotte was in high spirits. G.B.S. was being immortalized by a great artist-craftsman: this would be one of her husband's enduring memorials. Shaw was later to say that the Rodin bust was the only portrait which told the truth about him, and declared that Charlotte had complained to Rodin that all artists, caricaturists and photographers aimed at producing the sort of Mephistopheles they imagined Shaw to be, without ever taking the trouble to look at him. Rodin had replied: "Madame, what there is I will give you."

[Shaw gave his own account of the circumstances of the making of the Rodin bust in a letter to Jacob Epstein many years later. He wrote:

[". . . I have sat to so many well-known sculptors and painters that H. G. Wells complains that he cannot move about Europe without knocking against some image of me. That gives me an experience that you lack; so I will tell you all about it. I began with Rodin, who, never having heard of me, made every possible excuse to avoid a job that had no interest for him. But my wife would not be put off. She ascertained from the poet Rilke, then acting as Rodin's secretary, what his terms were. Rilke named £1000 for a marble, or £800 for a bronze. She then wrote to Rodin explaining that her husband was a famous writer with a great knowledge of art; that she wanted a memorial of him; and that he had refused to sit to anyone but Rodin, declaring that he would go down to posterity as a fool if, being within reach of Rodin, he selected any lesser genius. She also lodged £1000 in his bank on the understanding that it was a contribution to the general expenses of his activities, and that it placed him under no obligation to do a bust of me, or, if he began such a work, to continue it or finish it, or postpone any more important work for it.

["Rodin could not resist such treatment. He asked would it be possible for me to come to Paris and sit to him there in the studio provided by the French Government for the completion of his *Gate to Hell* (which he accordingly took care not to complete). We were there next morning. I suppose he rather liked us; for after a little talk he asked, with some hesitation and an evident fear that

he might be going too far, whether it would be at all possible for
me to make daily journeys to Meudon and sit to him in his home
studio . . . and for the next month I spent my days at Meudon and
became quite at home there. It was a curious experience, for the
bust, which began at the end of fifteen minutes work like a brilliant sketch by Sarah Bernhardt, went through the whole history of
sculpture since the Middle Ages. When it reached the twelfth century it was such a jewel that I begged him to let me take it away;
but he said he could 'carry it further'; and to my horror it became
successively a Bernini, a Canova or Thorwaldsen, a Gibson or
Foley, before it finally became a Rodin. . . .

["Now for the merits and failures of the bust. When my wife
said something to him about the way in which artists persisted
in drawing my reputation instead of drawing myself, he said, 'I
know nothing of Monsieur Shaw's reputation; but what is there I
will give you.' He should have said, 'What I can see in him I will
give you.' . . .

["As we talked and talked, in that lingua franca of philosophy
and art which is common to all languages, I made myself known
to Rodin as an intellectual and not as a savage, nor a pugilist, nor
a gladiator. He gave that in the bust unmistakably. But I am a
comedian as well as a philosopher: and Rodin had no sense of
humour. . . . Accordingly, the bust has no sense of humour; and
Shaw without a sense of humour is not quite Shaw, except perhaps
to himself."]

On May Day, Charlotte and G.B.S. went out to see the demon-
strations usual on that day, and found themselves in the Place de la
République, where a noisy crowd had gathered. Suddenly the police
began to charge with their batons, and Charlotte was pushed
roughly hither and thither. G.B.S. got her away, but she was so
indignant that she wanted to run back and throw stones at the
gendarmes. Shaw, amused, took her firmly by the arm and led her
to the hotel, Charlotte bursting into fresh spasms of rage all the
way.

They came back to Harmer Green, where Charlotte had again
rented the Old House, but they did not intend to stay beyond the
end of June, as she had taken a house at Mevagissey, in Cornwall,

for the summer. There was, as usual, a great deal of correspondence for her to answer, including several letters from Siegfried Trebitsch, who was worried about his business relations with G.B.S.

"I am very, *very* sorry you have been so bothered about this agreement, but, you know, my husband will never, under any possible circumstances, sign anything he has not read," Charlotte wrote to him. "Also he never parts with a copyright; either in five years or fifteen or fifty—it is all the same: he keeps the copyright until the Law takes it from him and gives it to the public. And I think he is quite right. You will have the script of Mrs. Warren and You Never Can Tell very soon now. . . . I suppose you have got the separate 'Stage Society' edition of Mrs. Warren, with the special preface? That is most important."

On July 7, she returned to him the first act of the German translation of *Man and Superman,* which Trebitsch had sent to Shaw some weeks before, for approval. Charlotte apologized for the long delay in replying.

"You know it is very slow, tedious work for him [G.B.S.] to go through these translations. He does not know German well, and he has to plod along with a dictionary—and it takes ages. He has been really dreadfully busy since we came from Paris, and it has been literally impossible for him to give much time to the books. . . .

"You will probably see in the newspapers today or tomorrow that the Court in New York has at last settled that Mrs. Warren's Profession is *not* indecent and is fit to be performed! This is very important, and I must say I am glad of it."

A week later they went to Mevagissey, where G.B.S. was soon enjoying himself in the sea. He and Charlotte went swimming every morning, and sometimes in the afternoons. For once, Shaw had no urgent work on hand; he could relax completely. Charlotte was accordingly contented. The house was comfortable, they had brought their servants—a married couple, Henry and Clara Higgs, who had been with them for five years—and there were guest rooms for friends. It was all exceedingly pleasant.

Robert Loraine came for a short stay; he had been John Tanner in the American production of *Man and Superman,* and the Shaws were fond of him. Granville-Barker was another visitor, but he came with a definite purpose. What play was Shaw going to let him have next? G.B.S. told him that he had no ideas ready for a play, and Granville-Barker was so obviously disappointed that Charlotte felt sorry for him. Something was working in her own mind. She and G.B.S. were friendly with the famous physician, Sir Almroth Wright, who was developing his new opsonic method for treating tuberculosis. On one occasion, when they had paid a call on Sir Almroth at St. Mary's Hospital, an assistant had interrupted their conversation with an apology and an urgent enquiry. Could Sir Almroth add another patient to the limited number he was treating by the new method? The physician had replied with another question. "Is he worth it?"

As they left the hospital, G.B.S. had said to Charlotte that there was a play in that situation, but had not mentioned it again. Now, watching Granville-Barker's disappointed face, she thought of it, and though she never interfered with G.B.S.'s work, she ventured a suggestion. Was there indeed a play in the situation they had found at the hospital? Perhaps—a dilemma?

Shaw made little comment, but she saw that he was listening. The next morning he went swimming, and in the afternoon he was writing in his notebook. True to his tenet that if he had a theme he also had a play, the first act was written at an astonishing pace; and, in fact, *The Doctor's Dilemma* was ready for production within three months. Granville-Barker produced it on November 20, 1906, with himself in the part of Dubedat.

*   *   *

Early in September, 1906, Charlotte was annoyed to find herself drawn into a quarrel which H. G. Wells was carrying on with the Fabian Society. Wells had joined the Fabians in 1903, being sponsored by G.B.S. and Graham Wallas; but he did not find a political home there, in spite of his advanced ideas. Sidney and Beatrice Webb, G.B.S., Graham Wallas, Sydney Olivier and the others were intellectuals, firmly convinced of the soundness of their principles and the importance of working steadily at problems until the best possible solutions could be found. They could also be depended upon to keep their heads in fierce controversy and argument.

Wells was an entirely different type of man—an individualist, quick-tempered and given to making wild assertions when he was angry. He was fundamentally in sympathy with the aims of the Fabians, and if he could have overcome his frequent irritation during the debates, and had learned the discipline of arguing rationally without losing his temper, he would have been of real use to the Society. At first, he got on very well with the Webbs, the Shaws, and others of the Old Gang, as he called them; G.B.S. liked him personally, and Charlotte, though she had reservations about H.G., especially when he exhibited ill-bred manners, was very much attached to his wife, Catherine. But their private meetings were few. In public debate at the Fabian Society, Wells antagonized people by his violently assertive manner. He disapproved of the Society's slow methods, and strongly criticized their set-up in general. Early in 1906, he wrote a paper which he called "Faults of the Fabian," and read it at one of the meetings. He accused them of many things, including smallness: small hall, small stall of "not very powerful tracts," a small outlook. He contrasted their ideas with the bigness of the world they were trying to change by their puny efforts: big business, big buildings, big newspapers which influenced multitudes of people. Wells insisted that the Fabian Society must move with the times and expand, must take larger premises, engage a larger staff, publish books, and generally acquire prestige by imposing themselves on the public mind as a force with which modern society had to reckon.

It was an ill-natured tirade, but it contained many shrewd points which appealed especially to the younger members. There was enough support for Wells to cause the Executive to agree to the formation of a special committee to go into the whole question of Fabian future policy. Charlotte and two members of the Executive, Headlam and Taylor, were put on this committee, and Catherine Wells acted as secretary. Wells drew up a report setting out his proposals, to be submitted to the Executive, and sent a copy to Charlotte to sign, though, he said, he would understand if she were not in perfect agreement with his ideas.

Charlotte drafted a reply which she showed to G.B.S., who revised it and added a paragraph at the end clearly designed to soften the impact of Charlotte's plain speaking, and to indicate that their personal relations with Wells were not affected.

"10, Adelphi Terrace, W.

4 September 1906

"If I am not 'in perfect agreement' my dear Mr. Wells! You must know quite well that I can't sign this report.

"You have let me in in the most abominable manner, you treacherous man, over this business. You must remember that before the Committee was formed you assured me over & over again that the past work of the Society formed no part of our business: that we were to devise forms of activity for the future & sketch out new work. I explained to you then that if your committee meant criticism & discussion of the past work & methods of the Executive I could not be on it, as I was part of the Executive & it reduced the matter to an absurdity that I should criticize myself. But in spite of this misunderstanding—as I conceived it—the committee has been nothing from its very first meeting but a Com^tee of Public Safety to try the Executive; with the foregone conclusion that it was to be condemned.

"Don't misunderstand me. I don't object to criticism of our methods & proceedings. We welcome it; & shall presently begin to enjoy it when the time comes to defend ourselves, but you cannot reasonably expect me to plead my own indictment. Try to realise that I am an accomplice of the Executive; that I am married to the Exec (just as poor Jane[1] is married to the committee); that I *am* the Executive; and that I really believe in the Exec and approve of it and am in a state of continual astonishment at all it has done with its means. If I had to choose between the Com^tee and the Exec to govern the Society in future, I shouldn't think twice about backing the Executive.

"I have been very anxious all through our sittings to keep friendly to your committee & I feel quite friendly still. But I don't agree with you, & I won't sign the report. I *know* what happens at & about the Executive and you don't; and what you have put in the

[1] Catherine Wells was called Jane by her friends.

report about it is not what I know but what you don't know. There
are certain things in the report I like and should have been so glad
to help to push. . . . But the impossible triumvirates, the magnificent publishing business, the grand suite of offices, the bringing
everything to the test of ordinary business success . . . all this you
would have had to cut out to get my signature; and then what
would be left?

"I don't know what the other members of the Executive will do;
I have not seen or heard from either of them for months. Mr. Headlam is always original, & may produce a minority report. Mr. Taylor
is so new a member that he is not yet really one of us. What I will
do I cannot say until the report has been discussed. What I *won't*
do is quite certain: I won't sign.

"G.B.S. has a scientific play nearly finished which he would like
to send to you. If only there were any chance of its being finished by
next Sunday I should propose a Folkestone week-end; but it has only
reached the end of the 3rd. act & there are to be five."

The result of the controversy is a matter of Fabian history; there
were noisy debates, with the Executive replying, point by point, to
Wells's proposals. Some of his suggestions were later adopted in a
modified form, but he made such outrageous personal attacks on
members of the Executive during the debates that he lost the sympathy of those who were at first inclined to support him, and the
Executive were the victors. G.B.S., with much tact and good nature, prevented Wells from resigning from the Society after such a
decided rebuff, and Wells continued to attend some of the meetings
for two years, after which he sent them a last indignant letter and
left.

The Shaws now looked for a permanent country home; they had
given up the Old House at Harmer Green. Both Charlotte and
G.B.S. liked Hertfordshire, with its unspoilt rural atmosphere, and
Charlotte obtained lists of houses in the vicinity of Welwyn. Among
those she went to see was the Rectory at Ayot St. Lawrence, a
pretty hamlet not far from Wheathampstead. The Rectory was a
late-Victorian villa, available because the Rector did not need such
a large house and could not afford to keep up the grounds. Char-

lotte did not care very much for the villa, but the gardens were attractive, and she rented the place for a limited period, to give her time to look for just the kind of house they wanted permanently; they hoped to find one with the beauty and character of the Old House at Harmer Green.

The Rectory had eight bedrooms, a dining-room, study, and a small drawing-room. They moved in at the beginning of November, 1906, and Charlotte engaged two maids to help Mrs. Higgs, while Higgs took over the large gardens, with an odd man to help him. Charlotte, used to efficient servants, treated them with the good manners and consideration natural to an Irish gentlewoman, though the wages she paid them were not overgenerous. Mr. and Mrs. Higgs received less than 30/- a week between them, but they had well-furnished quarters, and a liberal table. Charlotte kept strict accounts in her housekeeping books; every item, however small, had to be noted down by Mrs. Higgs:

"Parcel to post, 4d. Oranges and lemons, 1/. Beetroot, 3d."

The head of the household might be a vegetarian, but Charlotte provided plenty of meat for her staff, and for guests. There are daily entries in the butcher's books of steak, legs of mutton, filet veal, cutlets, rib beef, pork sausages and poultry.

No. 10, Adelphi Terrace was also well-staffed, and Charlotte had no housekeeping worries; they could go up to London at any time and find everything in order and ready for them. In January, Charlotte made her first appearance on the London stage, in what she was wont to describe as "the hole-and-corner" kind of performance. In order to establish copyright, a play had to be performed on a stage, a performance which was usually a read-through by friends of the playwright's. Harley Granville-Barker had written a play, *Waste,* and the copyright performance took place one morning at eleven o'clock, the "actors" being Charlotte, G.B.S., H.G. and Catherine Wells, John Galsworthy, William Archer, and other friends of Granville-Barker's.

The Shaws went to France in March, motoring in a hired car through Beauvais, Laon, Rheims, Crecy, Amiens and Rouen, the last of which they found highly interesting because of the Jeanne d'Arc associations. Soon after their return they were off again, this

time on a motor tour with Lion Phillimore to Woburn, Oxford
and Beaconsfield. G.B.S. was excited by motor-cars; he intended to
buy one and learn to drive it himself.

Their social circle was constantly widening. Charlotte met George
Meredith; Mark Twain lunched at Adelphi Terrace, as did Rodin
again, and Yvette Guilbert. The Fabian Society summer school that
year was being held at Llanbedr, in North Wales, and Charlotte
asked Sissy to join them there. She looked forward to some mountain air; she was feeling the strain of attending to her husband's
correspondence as well as dealing with increasing social duties.
Besides the minutely detailed household accounts, and her own
investments, she kept accounts of Shaw's professional earnings:

"J. Forbes Robertson, royalties on his first tour performances of the
Devil's Disciple at Leeds on the 3rd. 4th. 5th. & 6th.

£ 30—14—8

Ellen Terry performance of Captain Brassbound's
Conversion 14 Sept, at Grand Theatre, Fulham,
at Lyceum Theatre, Newport 26 Oct '07   39— 2—6
To Curtis Brown the literary agent, right to publish
in 'Collier's Weekly' article 'Aerial Football' Nov 3

185— 1—9"

It was time to engage a paid secretary, and G.B.S. offered the post
to his half-cousin, Georgina Gilmore, "Judy." In the 1907 account
books of G.B.S.'s earnings, Charlotte's handwriting changes to
that of Judy Gilmore, though Charlotte dealt with Income Tax
returns. She also kept in her own care personal correspondence
which affected G.B.S.

Charlotte was still working on the translation of *La Femme
Seule,* which she was determined to see produced. She had got to
know Lena Ashwell, a fine actress and an active supporter of the
women's movement, and hoped that Miss Ashwell would be available to take the chief character when the play attained a production.
Meanwhile, the secretarial work at Adelphi Terrace continued to
overflow onto her own desk. Siegfried Trebitsch usually wrote to
Charlotte; he was more certain of getting his questions answered
than if he approached G.B.S. direct. Charlotte corresponded with
him on her own account, too.

"I am going to ask you to do me a great favour if you will and can. Some weeks ago I read in a magazine that a German company has lately taken to extract from coffee all the harmful part. The part that affects one's nerves and gives one gout. I am aware that it is very widely known in Germany. But I can hear nothing of it. It has occurred to me that perhaps you can, if you would, find out something for me about this coffee and where I can get any. I shall be so very grateful to you if you can. I enclose, on a separate sheet, all the particulars I have heard of it."

Trebitsch sent two pounds of the coffee, and Charlotte, writing to thank him, said that both she and G.B.S. had been ill with influenza, and G.B.S. was beginning to rehearse his new play, *Getting Married.* Trebitsch had translated Shaw's book on Wagner, and said in his next letter that he had the chance of getting parts of it published in serial form. Charlotte wrote back at once.

"G.B.S. is most agitated about your publishing some of the most interesting chapters of the Wagner book by themselves. He says it is most dangerous and that the book should be read as a whole. . . . Will you please let me know exactly *what* portions you are publishing separately."

All through the early summer months Trebitsch pressed G.B.S., through Charlotte, to write articles for him to translate, or to send more plays. On July 7, 1907, Charlotte wrote to him:

"There is no chance that G.B.S. will write small or hurried articles about the recent plays of Ibsen, even if it was possible for him to find the time to do so just now. Surely it is better to make it clear that the Quintessence of Ibsenism is an *old* work that he has left behind long ago. It would be a fatal thing to make it appear 'up-to-date,' as there was so much of it that belongs to an early stage of G.B.S.: and it would only do him great harm if it was announced as being a quite recent and final view of Ibsen, or anything was done to encourage people to think that it is. I (personally) beg you to be very careful about this. . . ."

Three weeks later she was writing:

"The difficulty about the Devil's Disciple is this. G.B.S. does not wish you to have the typewritten copy because it is not correct and is not in a fit state to translate from. As soon as he can get the time he will correct the play and get it ready for the printer and then you will have it at once. He has various things to do, however, before he can attack this job. One is to do 'Brassbound' for you—Also Wagner!

" 'Socialism for Millionaires' will be sent to you at once."

Charlotte also helped her husband with a different type of correspondence: love-letters from women. A great many female adorers pestered G.B.S. He was impatient with them, but could not hurt their feelings, and he often answered their letters. Besides, he liked giving advice, and as these fervid correspondents usually asked for advice—on their love problems, their souls, their marital difficulties and frustrations of all kinds—G.B.S. could not resist the temptation to give them the benefit of his wisdom. The result was he often got so involved that he had to turn to Charlotte for help.

Erica Cotterill was one of the most extraordinary of these uninhibited correspondents. She was a young woman in her twenties when she first began to write to Shaw, in 1906. It is probable that she had seen his plays at the Court Theatre, and had convinced herself that the author was a kindred spirit. She possessed some literary talent, but was completely undisciplined. Shaw did not at first answer her long, chaotic letters, but Erica pursued him with such formidable persistence that he gave in, and occasionally sent a reply. She urged him to see her, and in the end he allowed her to come to Ayot. Erica brought with her a play she had written; she may have had some wild hope that Shaw would read it then and there. As he took no interest in it, Charlotte, with her usual kindness, told the girl to leave the play and she would read it herself. She kept her word, and wrote to Erica from Adelphi Terrace on July 1, 1907:

"Dear Miss Cotterill,

        "I am sorry I have not been able to answer your letter before, but I have read your play twice.

    "I think it is quite a remarkable play, for a first play. But you will not be surprised if I find fault with it, & you must not be vexed if I write only about its faults as that is what will help you most & I have so little time.

    "It wants cutting. As I read, bits of it interested me so much that

I read eagerly. Other bits bored me & I wanted to stop reading. . . .
You can indicate the character of Ivy & the men without all those
pages of dialogue. . . . Do not let a single sentence remain in the
play that is not absolutely *necessary* for the development of the
plot & the characters. . . . You must actually put yourself into the
skin of all your characters . . . you must see with their eyes, &
understand with their understanding, or else you will fail with
them. . . .

"Now shall I send the play back to you and will you cut it? And
then will you send it back to me & let me place it before the
Reading Committee of the Stage Society? Whether they accept it
or not it will be very interesting for you to hear what they say
about it."

No more was heard of the play. Erica continued to bombard Shaw
with letters, interspersing declarations of undying love for him with
requests for advice on literary matters. G.B.S. seemed unable to take
the obvious course of ignoring her letters; from time to time he
wrote her long replies. In April, 1908, after giving her a lesson
in getting a contract, he added:

"Now that I have taught you some respect for business and the
law, let me assure you that marriage is more sacred than either, and
that unless you are prepared to treat my wife with absolute loyalty,
you will be hurled into outer darkness for ever.

"The privilege of pawing me, such as it is, is hers exclusively.

"She has to tolerate worshipping females whose efforts to conceal
the fact that they take no interest in her are perfunctory, and who
bore her to distraction with their adoration of me; but it is my
business to see that her patience is not abused. . . . Whenever I get
anything in the nature of a love letter, I hand it straight to
Charlotte . . ."

The affair, if it can be called such, went on sporadically for two
more years. G.B.S. once talked to Hesketh Pearson about it:

"Erica opened fire with an impassioned plea that we should meet.
I warned her that nothing would come of it. But her correspondence
became longer and warmer; so I started giving her a little advice.
Instead of putting her off this incited her to more eloquent appeals,
and at length I met her, hoping that a rational interview would

abate her enthusiasm. It had precisely the opposite effect, and she did a monstrous thing: she took a cottage in this village in order to see me and be near me. I at once explained the whole position to my wife, so as to prepare her for possible incidents and intrusions. Though I had strongly advised Erica to remain invisible, she stupidly called at our house. Charlotte of course was furious and showed by her manner that the girl's behaviour was highly improper. Then, as you know, Charlotte wrote forbidding her to call again. This did not prevent Erica from maintaining a barrage of letters to me, several of which would have led an ignorant reader to believe that we had been sexually intimate . . . Erica lived in a fanciful world of her own. However, as the whole affair was extremely distasteful to Charlotte, who accused me of encouraging the girl, you must keep this to yourself until no one's feelings can be hurt by reference to it."

(Hesketh Pearson, in *Horizon*, November, 1958.)

The following is the letter he referred to:

"11 October 1910   10, Adelphi Terrace, W.C.

"Dear Miss Cotterill,

"I think I had better write to you to explain exactly why I intentionally shewed you that I strongly disapproved of your presence in my house, and that I did not—and do not—intend that your visit should be repeated. You might easily think that I was merely annoyed by your coming at an inconsiderate & unusual hour—as indeed I was—or that I disliked you. That was not it at all. I should object to your coming at tea time just as much as I do not particularly dislike you. On the contrary, it is because you are in some ways rather fine and sensitive, so that it is very difficult to be unkind to you, that I am determined to put a stop at once and for ever to any personal intimacy between us.

"The matter is a very simple one. You have made a declaration of your feelings to my husband; and you have followed that up by coming to live near us with the avowed object of gratifying those feelings by seeing as much as possible of him. If you were an older and more experienced woman I should characterize that in terms which would make any further acquaintance between us impossible. As you are young and entirely taken up with your own feelings, I can only tell you that when a woman makes such a declaration to a married man, or a man to a married woman, there is an end of all honourable question of their meeting one another again—intentionally at least. You do not understand this, perhaps; but you will later on, when you are married and know what loyalty men and women owe to one another in that very delicate and difficult relation. The present case is a specially difficult and dangerous one; for my husband is not a common man: if you become at all intimate with him he would become a necessity of life to you; and then the inevitable parting would cost you more suffering than it can now. I could not trust him to keep you at a distance: he is quite friendly and sympathetic with everybody, from dogs and cats to dukes and duchesses; and none of them can imagine that his universal friendliness is not a special regard for them. He has already allowed you to become far more attached to him than he should; and I do not intend to let you drift any further into an impossible position.

"If I must end by saying that this letter does not admit of any argument or reply, and that I do not mean it to lead to any correspondence between us, do not conclude that I am writing in an unfriendly spirit. It would be no use to discuss the matter now; and later on, when you are married and as old as I am, it will not be necessary. Meanwhile believe that my decision is quite inevitable and irrevocable.

"Yours sincerely,
"CHARLOTTE F. SHAW"

The handwriting is Charlotte's, but it is not her letter. G.B.S. dictated most of it.[2]

---

[2] Draft in Hanley Collection, University of Texas.

14

RIFTS

(1906 – 1912)

If, as seems possible, Charlotte Payne-Townshend had, in 1898, been unconsciously influenced by the Webb marriage into thinking that she and G.B.S. would achieve a similar partnership, by 1908 Charlotte Shaw must have known that this was an impossible hope. Her own marriage was totally different from that of the Webbs. Sidney and Beatrice were complementary to each other to an extent that was exceedingly rare. Beatrice's mind was of the same high quality as Sidney's—and they had the same objectives to work for. More important still, their emotional life was entirely satisfying, and likely to deepen with age.

There was no such harmony between Charlotte and G.B.S., either on the mental or the emotional level. Charlotte's intelligence matched that of her husband—she was, in fact, more intelligent than he was in many ways—but he possessed creative and intellectual powers far above the ordinary, and Charlotte was no intellectual. Her old dream, talked of so often with Louise Mock in the Roman days, the dream of walking by the side of a splendid man on terms of complete equality, had long since vanished. Charlotte still believed passionately in equality for women, and here was the splendid man, different from anyone else, and she had married him. But—walking by his side, sharing his thoughts and working with him? Charlotte found that G.B.S. was not a sharer in that sense. He was kind and generous with his time, his advice, and his money: qualities which Charlotte possessed, too. He was companionable enough when he was not writing, but as he had a tremendous timetable of lecturing, debating, attending committee meetings, producing articles and pamphlets when he wasn't at work on a play, they had actually very little time together, alone.

For mental stimulus, Charlotte instinctively turned to the spiritual life, which had so obsessed her in her earlier years. G.B.S. was never willing to discuss religion or philosophy with her. He was always ready to *talk* about his ideas: he was developing his theories of Creative Evolution, and Charlotte was an intent listener when he began on the subject. He did not, however, encourage her to put forward her own ideas. He thought them muddled—as, indeed, they were—and he had little sympathy with her efforts to formulate a creed by which she could live. His comments were so destructive, even when kindly said, that Charlotte stopped trying to talk to him about her inner life; but she did not cease her continual search for some form of religious belief which had a meaning for her. Charlotte's commonplace books for this period are filled with quotations, odd thoughts which came to her, phrases read or overheard, sometimes misquoted.

"Earth's packed with Heaven, and every common bush afire with God. But only those who see take off their shoes. The rest stand round and pick blackberries" [sic].

"Of all the unpractical dolts with whom we have to deal, the so-called 'practical man' is the worst. He is the Philistine of Philistines. His title is so conferred on him—most often by himself—because his vision is centred on the minor expendiencies to the exclusion of all that is capable of really ennobling life."

She wrote prayers:

"Infinite beauty of health within me, heal me of the blindness of heart which cannot see Thee: heal me of the hardness of heart which cannot feel Thee: heal me of the ignorance of attachment which makes me unfit to love. Grant to us such strength . . . as may support us in all dangers and carry us through all temptations."

The separate life she was making for herself did not conflict at all with her devotion to G.B.S., which was real and strong. She planned unceasingly for his comfort, easing away from him the small burdens of everyday existence, looking after his health, anticipating his needs. It was a devotion, however, which took no account of Shaw's own phobias. One of the things which he detested was travelling. Charlotte could never believe that he was serious about this. She herself loved travelling, and she was sure that it was the only way to stop G.B.S. from overworking. When he was in London, there were always demands on him: callers, Fabians and others wanting him to take the chair or to speak at meetings, actors and actresses begging for introductions, all kinds of people asking all sorts of favours.

It was a relief to get down to the peace of Ayot; they usually spent the middle of the week at Adelphi Terrace and went to their country home from Saturday to Tuesday or Wednesday. They still rented the Rectory, which they liked no better than they had done at first, but they had not been able to find the house they wanted, and at least it was comfortable. They might, they thought, even build a house if they could find a suitable piece of land. Meanwhile, Ayot was quiet; G.B.S. could work in the study he had fitted up for himself, and if he had been able to have his way he would not have left it except to come to London or to go to the Fabian summer schools.

Charlotte found Ayot dull. Used as she had always been to travelling from the time she was a girl, she could not endure the idea of staying at the Rectory for weeks together. She declared that G.B.S. needed more change than he was getting. Charlotte had convinced herself that the severe migraine headaches were due to his concentrated bouts of writing. Frequent trips abroad were essential for him, she said. G.B.S., as usual, protested vigorously. Charlotte listened—and went on with her arrangements for the next trip.

In July, 1908, they started on a long tour, beginning in Sweden. G.B.S. sent Granville-Barker a picture postcard of August Strindberg, the Swedish dramatist, and wrote on the back:

"Stockholm.

"This great man reached the summit of his career when he met the immortal G.B.S. at the Theatre Interne at Stockholm on the 16th. July 1908 at one o/clock in the afternoon. At 1.25, he said in German, 'At two o/clock I am going to be sick.' On this strong hint the party broke up."

The journey soon became intolerably tedious to G.B.S. They travelled to Lübeck and Munich, where they saw *Candida* and *How He Lied to Her Husband* at the Residenztheater. Shaw wrote to Granville-Barker:

"I shall never be the same man again. . . . The Eugene was a perfect H. G. Wells hero, only needing a terrier, a straw hat, a bicycle agency, a copy of the Sporting Times to make him complete."

Shaw's chief outlet was writing to Granville-Barker. Charlotte kept a watchful eye on her husband in case he should begin "something dramatic," and this annoyed him still more. He agreed with her that he needed a holiday, but he did not want always to be on the move. Charlotte replied that if he remained in one place he would inevitably begin to work, and that by travelling from place to place he would be drawing mental refreshment from fresh scenes. G.B.S. wrote to Granville-Barker on August 11 from "a delightful mediaeval walled town called Nordlingen," which he liked; but they had only stopped there on the way to Rothenburg:

"I used to want change: now I want rest, especially as the worries of travelling used to be a complete change from the high and strenuous activities of my prime, whereas now the vulgar worries of business are just like the travelling worries: and the only sign of improvement in my condition is that whereas I was crushed I am now exasperated. Another day in Munich would have driven me mad: the day after tomorrow I shall feel that another day's motoring will murder me."

On August 19, he was writing from Heidelberg:

"I am fed up with vagabondage, and with the cat and dog life I lead with poor Charlotte, who takes every unguarded expression of my loathing of travelling as a personal insult to herself. Another month of it would end in a divorce. I held out fairly well until Munich; but 3 weeks is my limit: since then I have been very bad company for myself and worse for her. Dont allude to this in correspondence: it is not safe until we are back again at our ain fireside."

* * *

G.B.S. usually hired a car when they were abroad, and now he decided to have one of his own. At the end of 1908 he bought a car and engaged a chauffeur. In March of the following year Charlotte suggested a tour of Algeria and Tunisia, and invited Sissy to accompany them. Both she and Shaw had been ill during the previous winter, and the idea of a trip into certain sunshine, leaving the cold and damp behind them, seemed a good idea, provided, G.B.S. stipulated, that they were not away too long. They took their car and the chauffeur, and sailed from Southampton. G.B.S. wrote to Hugh Cholmondeley from Algiers, reporting that Sissy was well, and added a postscript:

"Conversation just occurred as follows:

Sissy   Oh, I am *so* anxious for news of Hugh.

G.B.S.   (reassuringly) Depend on it, he's quite well. No news is good news, etc. etc. etc.

Sissy   Oh, it's not that. I want to hear how he got on in the point to point.

        (Curtain)"

Shaw, a good photographer, took many pictures, noting down the focus, condition of the light and other technical details in his small notebooks. But he quickly tired of the trip. The cities were interesting enough; not so the small towns. At one place the sanitary arrangements consisted mainly of the stairs—and Charlotte was calmly bent on continuing the journey! They had tyre bursts, and the dust and the heat were trying. G.B.S. marvelled that Charlotte and Sissy, usually so fastidious about their personal comfort, could put up with the conditions they met. As for himself, taking photographs now palled. He wanted to get back to England.

Sissy went with them again in the spring of 1910, this time to France for a tour of the Pyrenees. G.B.S. had tried to persuade them to take the car and chauffeur and go without him, but Charlotte, as usual, put forward unanswerable reasons why he should have a holiday. He was at odds with her, and in a state of suppressed fury for most of the journey; he took to darting in and out of churches at every stopping-place, sure that Charlotte must loathe him for his bad temper. He made comments on the hotels in one of the small notebooks which he always carried in his pockets. Of the Hôtel du Cerf at Alençon: "Very respectable—almost archdecorously." At Le Mans: "Le Dauphin good, but tried to put us into 'the annexe' —a penitentiary in the next street—2 or 3 minutes' walk to the hotel for meals—serious in wet or cold weather. Offer implied that rooms were better. They weren't. Hotel good. Electric light—radiators (too hot) everything good and clean."

At Tarbes, Charlotte fell ill, and G.B.S. wrote to Granville-Barker on April 10:

"On Friday Charlotte's temperature was so unyielding and her condition so moribund that I had to take serious measures, as Mrs. Chumley was anxious to call in a doctor. . . . So I fell on Charlotte with my fists in the most violent Swedish manner, and in spite of her protests that she could not bear to be touched, pummeled her and thumped her and banged her and kneaded her and wobbled her and rolled her about from head to foot with such miraculous effect that her temperature fell half a degree in ten minutes and Mrs. C came back to find her remonstrating in a voice of thunder though she had left her moaning and hopeless quarter of an hour before. Next morning she was normal; so I put her into the car and rattled her off to St. Jean de Luz & Biarritz to see how she could stand it."

Snow stopped them driving over the mountain passes. G.B.S. wrote again to Granville-Barker on April 15:

"Two more assaults on Ax have failed at the final passes. As my spirits rise at each rebuff, and the tempers of the ladies are affected in the same way, the situation becomes very strained at moments. There is a tendency to attribute to me the Acts of God—as if I made the snow expressly to baffle and annoy my fellow-travellers. Further excitement is provided by the institution of *vin compris* at meals. Kilsby [the chauffeur] partakes of the wine of the country at lunch; and when he starts immediately afterwards on mountain roads rushing corners on his wrong side & explaining cheerfully that he feels as if he could drive through anything, the effect is all that could be desired. For three days we have led the life of lost dogs, and our behaviour to one another shews it."

Later that year they went on a long tour of Ireland. Charlotte was always a champion of the Irish when she was in England, but she grew angry when she came up against the bigotry of the north, and the legends chalked up on the walls: "No surrender," "No popery." As they drove south, the dourness disappeared, and a lazy laisser-faire took its place. Many years in England, too, made her notice the slatternliness which she had once taken for granted. It was not an enjoyable tour; G.B.S. was very prickly all the time. He spent his fifty-fourth birthday in Ireland, but forbade any celebration; he disliked being reminded of his age.

Back in London, they gave luncheon parties, entertained Prince Eugen of Sweden to tea, went to the opening of *The Dark Lady of the Sonnets*. Shaw settled to an intensive stretch of work, and Charlotte herself had plenty with which to occupy herself. She had had the idea of making a selection of passages which she liked from her husband's works, and had arranged for Constable to publish it under the same kind of arrangement which Shaw had with them; Clark of Edinburgh was to print the book, and Constable to do the distribution. She was also preparing Brieux's three plays, *Maternité, The Three Daughters of M. Dupont* and *Damaged Goods,* for publication. She had never given up hope that they might be made available to the English public, and at last it was possible to bring out the book. Brieux had been elected a member of the French Academy, which now made him acceptable, for, as she wrote, "mud that may be thrown with impunity at a struggling social reformer and propagandist, must not smirch the robe of one of the Immortals."

The tours to the Continent continued. In the early summer of 1911, G.B.S. had an attack of neuritis, and as the doctor said he was to be "quiet for a bit," Charlotte took him for a tour which makes one dizzy even to read the bare details in her Annuary:

"Folkestone, Amiens, Rheims, Nancy, Gerardmer, Ballon

d'Alsace, Belfort, Pontarlier, Annecy: driving about Chambery country. Briançon, Gap, Grenoble—excursions to La Grande Chartreuse, Chamonix, Thonon les Bains, Diablerets, Thun, Oberarlberg, Oberammergau, Munich, Salzburg, Ischl, Innsbruck. Over to Brenner: bridge carried away. Put car on train. . . . Over pass to Trient, on to Bolzen up the Mendel. I walked to summit & saw sunset on the Dolomites . . . Tonale Pass . . . started for the Stelvio but were turned back by floods. Bergamo . . . Milan, Ivrea, Courmayeur, over Petit St. Bernard to Albertville: Bourg, Brou, Tours, Angers, Rennes . . ." and so back to London.

Shaw was thankful to be home again. He had been able to get some rest at Annecy, where they had stayed for a few days at the Beau Rivage Hotel, and he had put in solid hours of correspondence, writing mostly to Granville-Barker about a new play.

They spent Christmas in Shropshire with Sissy and Hugh. Cecily was married, and it was very quiet at Edstaston. It was also rather dull. G.B.S. got on well enough with the Cholmondeleys, but they had little in common. He was withdrawn and obviously very much preoccupied with his own thoughts. Sissy and Hugh put it down to the new play which he was writing, but Charlotte knew that his peculiar behaviour was due to another cause. They found it difficult to talk when they were alone together, they sparred over trifles. It was a relief to both of them when they left Edstaston and returned to Ayot and London.

G.B.S. had lectures to give in Coventry and Southampton; Charlotte immersed herself in the business connected with *Selected Passages*. She also worked on her translation of *La Femme Seule*, the Brieux play which she hoped the Actresses' Franchise League would put on.

At the end of March, 1912, Charlotte suggested to G.B.S. that they should go to Rome for a few weeks. He refused in uncompromising terms. Charlotte said that she did not feel well and needed a change; G.B.S. pointed out that there was nothing to prevent her from asking Sissy or a friend to go with her. There were scenes, and, in the end, Charlotte went alone, sailing on the *Orsova* for Naples on April 12. She became ill on the voyage, and did not fully recover during her stay in Rome. Louise Mock still lived there, and the two friends picked up the old threads; but

Charlotte felt unhappy and unsettled. Something was going wrong with her life.

A few weeks later G.B.S. was writing to Beatrice Webb (who wanted him to be a contributor to a journal which she and Sidney were starting) that he was too old [he was fifty-six] to undergo the strain of providing a regular feature in a periodical; and he warned her about the dangers of a husband and wife seeing too much of each other.

"I had to force Charlotte to take a holiday *from me*. Being very much in need of me, she quarrelled furiously with me the moment she suspected what I was at, until I wished her at the South Pole; and then she took leave of me (for a month after 14 years continuous adhesion) in a way that left Charles Ist. taking leave of his family simply nowhere. Of course it was an enormous relief to her, and quite a beneficial change for me. I had realized last year, when we took an inordinately long tour together, that it was a stupid thing for two people needing a change, to change everything—air, language, meals, habit, country—except the main condition of their lives, and to intensify that violently by isolating it in a foreign place where they knew nobody else. Now the moral of that for you is that though you may have come through a tour round the world without coming to a judicial separation, you should think twice before you complicate such dangerous experiments with a joint editorship. You will get on one another's nerves every week to such an extent that you have no idea of. . . .

"Just at present I have £6,000 to spend on a house for Charlotte; and she is as likely as not to insist on spending twelve. I should like, if it be legally possible, to get rid of that marriage settlement of mine for which Sidney and Whelan are trustees, and hand all the stock back to Charlotte, as I have stock enough of my own to secure my mother and sister against all contingencies, which was the sole object of the settlement."

The gratuitous innuendo in this letter would have hurt Charlotte sorely if she had read it. There had never been the slightest friction between them over money; each still paid a share of the joint expenditure of their two homes. If they had indeed bought or built a house, and it had cost more than the £6,000 which Shaw felt able to afford, Charlotte would have taken it entirely as a matter of course that she should pay the difference. Beatrice Webb had hoped that Shaw would put some money into the venture of starting the new journal. Shaw was genuinely opposed to the scheme, and as he had a habit of referring to his wife as "one of the firm" when he wished to avoid awkward financial entanglements, it is possible that he used her as an excuse for not supporting it.[1]

Judy Gilmore was now married and had been replaced by Ann Elder as Shaw's secretary, but Charlotte continued to deal with part of his correspondence, and some was sent on to her in Rome. One letter was from Trebitsch, who was being persistent about fresh plays for translation.

"Indeed G.B.S. is most tiresome, as you well know, about letters," Charlotte replied. "He writes to me—oh, yes!—but he *never* answers any of my questions, and it is quite hopeless to get him to reply about business."

She returned home at the end of May, G.B.S. meeting her with the car at Southampton. They spent a week-end with Granville-Barker and his wife, Lillah McCarthy, at their home at Stansted, in Kent; Charlotte was devoted to Granville-Barker, and got on well with Lillah. It was a pleasant, relaxed week-end, with much talk of the theatre, and their travels, and mutual friends. It would all have gone off very well if Charlotte had not happened to mention, during conversation, that she was planning to take G.B.S. on a summer tour of Germany for August and September.

*   *   *

It is extraordinary that Charlotte should have allowed this obsession with travel to take hold of her so completely, in spite of G.B.S.'s continual protests. She seems to have insisted, quite without rhyme or reason, that what he needed most was to go abroad. What was her real motive? Did she instinctively feel that other people absorbed him too much when he was in London or at Ayot, shutting her out? Was there another, unconscious, more complex reason?

In her Annuary for that year, 1912, there appears under the heading for June 26:

"G.B.S. read 'Pygmalion' to Mrs. Campbell."

[1] Shaw did, in fact, contribute £1,000 to the founding of the journal, *The New Statesman.*

15

MRS. PAT

(1 9 1 2 – 1 9 1 4)

The long affair between Bernard Shaw and Mrs. Patrick Campbell will hardly go down in history as one of the great love stories of all time; it is doubtful if real love ever entered into it on either side. It is still talked about, and has become part of the Shaw legend. While it was going on, many people regarded it as an extra-marital adventure on Shaw's part, though he was later to deny this very strenuously. The biographer's problem is to try to disentangle fact from fiction (and even a bare narration of fact can be misleading); above all, to attempt to find out how this friendship affected Charlotte and her relations with her husband.

Stella Patrick Campbell was one of the most talked-of actresses of the Edwardian era, and the personification of many of the disagreeable traits often attributed to star actresses: wilfulness, recklessness, arrogance, intense egoism. People who remember her have their favourite story of her rudeness to other players; Shaw himself wittily blackened her character when it suited him. She must have been a terror to act with, but there is another side of the picture. She was an exceedingly good actress—when she wished to be—and she happened to be born with a temperament which she could not control. The circumstances of her early life were such that it is surprising that she achieved the fame she did.

She was born Beatrice Stella Tanner in 1865, the daughter of an English mother and an Italian father. According to her own account, her grandfather was a wealthy Italian nobleman who fell into serious political trouble and was ruined. All her relations had a highly romantic aura: the Shah of Persia was godfather to a cousin, beautiful aunts married highly placed barons, consuls, famous artists. Beatrice, as she was called in the family, soon showed signs of being "different."

"I was neither a sweet, amiable nor amenable child. I was physically strong, very affectionate and imaginative, but temperamentally alien to those around me. I believe I was impatient with unintelligent people from the moment I was born: a tragedy—for I am three-parts a fool."

She had a scrappy education; her father had run through two fortunes and lost his money. Relatives came to their assistance, and an aunt paid for Beatrice to have a musical training. This did not last long, and at the age of seventeen Beatrice eloped with Patrick Campbell, a good-looking, feckless young man of twenty who earned less than £100 a year and turned out to have a delicate constitution. Within a very few years he had to go abroad for his health, and Beatrice was left with two children and no money; Patrick Campbell never earned enough to support them, moving from job to job in Australia and then in Africa, always optimistic, unable to keep a post for long.

Beatrice found herself the wage-earner. She had never been trained for a career, but she possessed striking good looks, a fine figure, and a good speaking voice. She had discovered, through playing parts for an amateur dramatic club, that she could act, and when she was offered a small part on the professional stage she accepted it thankfully, in spite of the fact that her aunts thought she was taking the first steps to perdition. She had made a beginning: she was earning money. The absolute necessity for making enough to bring up her children kept Beatrice Campbell on the long grind of the provinces—and it was a much longer and harder grind in those days than it is in these. For years she lived on a few shillings a week, sending most of her salary to her mother, who was looking after the children. Her splendid physique was a blessing now, but there were times when she was on the verge of a breakdown. The one stern discipline which emerges from a study of those early years is Beatrice Campbell's passionate determination to give her children a good education, and security. She had already accepted the fact that her husband would never earn a living.

Patrick Campbell joined the Army during the Boer War, and was killed in action. Mrs. Pat, as she was now familiarly known in the theatre, was well established on the London stage by this time, and much in demand by the leading managers and playwrights. She knew her assets and the strength of her popularity; she was well aware that the playgoing public came to see her, rather than the play, and that success was certain if a management was lucky enough to get her. She exploited her talent and her charm quite deliberately, coolly making bargains, using her caustic tongue uninhibitedly when the impulse seized her, or she felt she was being patronized. She was ambitious to be received in Society, and missed no opportunity to gain the friendship of prominent people. From the outside, she was a vain, spoilt, erratic charmer who delighted in making cutting remarks and who broke the nerve of the unfortunate actors compelled to play with her. In fact, she was an extremely lonely and frightened woman who found it impossible to handle her life with any degree of common sense. Her deepest emotions were tied up with her children; outside them she cared for hardly anyone. Though she spent the large sums of money she earned with reckless glee, she was always stricken with misery when she found that her son and daughter suffered as a result of her folly. All her life she lacked security of any kind. Her early unsatisfactory marriage had brought out what was ruthless and calculating in her nature, and she did not attempt to hide the unlikeable side. Her reputation for being tempestuous and difficult did not prevent managers from engaging her, nor playwrights from making every effort to secure her as the leading actress in their plays.

G.B.S. first wrote to Stella Patrick Campbell (she had dropped the Beatrice) in 1899, a year after his marriage, on some matter connected with the theatre. (He wrote *Caesar and Cleopatra* with her and Forbes Robertson in mind.) They exchanged several letters during the next ten years or so; then, in 1912, a regular correspondence developed. Shaw had begun to lace his letters with expressions of extravagant affection. He had written *Pygmalion,* and he knew that Mrs. Pat was interested—but on her own terms. She wanted to be the only star in that play. In July, 1922, G.B.S. sent her a long letter, full of the most exaggerated endearments, but mainly concerned to dissuade her from attempting management on the single-star system, which she was contemplating, having *Pygmalion* in mind. He ended:

"I must now go and read this to Charlotte. My love affairs are her unfailing amusement; all their tenderness recoils finally on herself. Besides, I love an audience."

He was sure that Ellen Terry, too, would be deeply interested in the state of his feelings, and sent her a letter on August 13, 1912, from Nancy, during the German tour which Charlotte had planned. He told her that he had written Eliza Doolittle for Mrs. Campbell, and had read the play to her. Then:

"I went calmly to her house to discuss business with her, as hard as nails, and, as I am a living man, fell head over ears in love with her in thirty seconds. And it lasted more than thirty hours . . . I am plying her with the most wonderful love letters."

Ellen Terry took this coolly and told him:

"*I'm* in love with Mrs. Campbell, too, or rather I'd like to be, but something tugs me back."

She knew quite well that Bernard Shaw found his brand of exuberant love-making useful when he wanted to persuade a particular actress to create an important part for him. In fact, Shaw actually wrote to Mrs. Pat on November, 1912:

"Stella, Stella

"Shut your ears tight against this blarneying Irish liar and actor. Read no more of his letters. He will fill his fountain pen with your heart's blood, and sell your most sacred emotions on the stage. He is a mass of imagination and no heart. . . .

"But don't cut him off utterly. He is really worth something,

even to *you*, if you harden your heart against him. He will tell you
that you are too great a woman to belong to any man, meaning, I
suppose that he is too great a man to belong to any woman. . . ."

Mrs. Pat carefully put this away with Shaw's other letters. Her
replies were more restrained. She would have liked Charlotte to
leave cards on her, but G.B.S. hedged. Charlotte, he said, was a
perfect dragon for cards, but she would take the view that Mrs.
Pat was only interested in her "celebrated man," not herself. In
any case, "she doesn't care much for women," and she had been
very ill lately. He ended the letter in a transport of romantic love-
passages—and did not read that letter, or any of those which followed, to his wife.

For the first time in their marriage, Bernard Shaw began to
keep something important from Charlotte. The extravagant attitudes, the epistolary posturings, the tempest of high-flown phrases
which poured from him so readily when he had a pen in his hand
had suddenly taken on meaning. He had became infatuated with
a woman who was an enchantress in the feminine sense, but whom
he half despised as a human being. She was, he knew, dishonest
and unscrupulous, using her powers of fascination with the most
ruthless precision, herself untouched. When, some years later, they
turned on each other and Shaw told her all this, his letters do not
sound heartbroken or disillusioned, but are more like exercises in
invective. He knew, right from the beginning, that this beautiful
actress with high talent but no heart was not worth the risk of
breaking up his home. Yet he did not stop the affair. The "great
enchantress" held him in thrall.

There were mischief-makers. One day, when the Shaws were
lunching out, "S.B." "very devilishly" asked G.B.S. point-blank
how Mrs. Pat was, and watched to see what damage that shell
would do when it exploded. It apparently did a great deal, for
G.B.S. told Mrs. Pat that he was extremely miserable for several
days. "When there are two people of whom one can stand almost
anything in the way of privation, and the other is so sensitive that
it is horrible cruelty to children to look coldly at that person (or
warmly at anyone else), why the hardy person must suffer and the
sensitive person be spared."

G.B.S. tried to spare the "sensitive person," but he was not very

successful. Everyone in the world of the theatre knew about the
affair, and though nobody would have dared to tell Mrs. G.B.S. of
the gossip, Charlotte was quite aware that her husband was constantly visiting Mrs. Pat at home, and was no longer pretending
that it was solely for the purpose of discussing the character of
Eliza Doolittle. He also met the actress at the house of his sister
Lucy, with whom she had become friendly. Although the brother
and sister had never got on, G.B.S. had for long contributed to
Lucy's as well as to his mother's maintenance, and a kind of pre-
carious acquaintanceship had succeeded the old hostility. Lucy
actively disliked Charlotte, and it is possible, as St. John Ervine
suggests, that the sister-in-law invited Mrs. Pat to her house when
G.B.S. was expected; Lucy was undergoing a bout of ill-health at
that period, and Charlotte must surely think it proper for a brother
to visit his ailing sister?

Whatever Charlotte thought on this point, she said nothing to
outsiders. People talked, but the Shaws' busy life went on, Charlotte composed and occupied. Her own health was in a poor state.
She had long had trouble with her chest, and now bronchitis and
asthma kept her in bed for days at a time. When she was well
again, Sir Horace Plunkett, an old friend, invited them to stay
with him at Kilteragh, his house in County Dublin, and Charlotte
was pleased when G.B.S. agreed to go.

They went off by car, G.B.S. at the wheel. He had learnt to
drive in 1908 on a Lorraine-Dietrich, which had its accelerator
pedal between the clutch and the brake. His reactions to that particular arrangement of pedals became automatic, and when he
changed to later cars with the accelerator to the right of the brake,
he could become dangerous. The chauffeurs he had, then and
later, had always to be ready to turn off the ignition when
G.B.S. mistook the pedals. Today, bound for Holyhead and Ireland,
they had scarcely been on the road an hour when G.B.S. suddenly
swerved into a clump of bushes at high speed, to avoid colliding
with another car, and stopped with a grinding jar against a tele-
graph pole. He was unhurt, but Charlotte was badly shaken, and
the car was put out of action; they had to hire another to take
them on.

There was a small house party at Kilteragh, and Charlotte, well looked after and among people she knew well, relaxed completely. The house was gloriously situated, the air was mild and fresh at the same time. She threw off her malaise and quickly became a centre of attention. G.B.S. wrote to Granville-Barker:

"Charlotte is in high spirits—almost in health. The domestic fiend of the last few months has become a green-eyed angel of the fireside."

To Mrs. Pat he wrote:

"Charlotte has suddenly got well, and changed from a fiend into a green-eyed mermaid, smiling and fascinating and dressing in diamonds and generally dispensing charm and childish happiness. What is more amazing, she actually refers to you without fury, even with raillery. 'Did you go to Brighton that day at Beachy Head?' Boundless contempt for both of us, but no more hatred."

As to that, it is unlikely that Charlotte even felt contempt, for something had come into her life which was aimed at neutralizing such a destructive emotion. It was, rather, a new aspect of an interest which she had never lost, and which was, from now onwards, to transform her entire outlook.

*   *   *

Charlotte had met James Porter Mills at Lena Ashwell's house, and had been so impressed by his ideas on philosophy and religion that she had gone to several of the lectures which he was giving in a small hall in Logan Place, near the Earl's Court Road. He was an American, odd, uncomfortable and, Charlotte found, rather unaccountable at times, but he was completely sincere. He was a doctor of medicine and had practised in Chicago for some years; his wife, who was even odder than himself, called herself a "Healer" and dabbled in Christian Science, giving lectures on the second floor of their Chicago house while he was seeing patients on the ground floor.

Presently Dr. Mills became worried; many of his patients grew worse instead of better, and some of them died when he felt they should have ultimately recovered. Why? He knew he was conscientious, and he could find no reasonable explanation. Then he fell ill himself—and his wife, the Healer, cured him. That made him

very angry, and he knew it was up to him to find out how it was
done.

"Being a husband he saw at once that his wife's way couldn't
be the right way; being a wife she quite agreed about that," Charlotte notes, in her account of the couple.

The Millses threw up their work and their prospects and their
home and their way of life, and as they had no children, they were
able to go out into the world together to "find out," armed only
with what money they had and a definite idea of *what* they sought:
a great power that could be used for good, and that would endure.
They journeyed all over Europe, went to Australia, travelled a
little in China and a great deal in India. They met many curious
people and found many strange, unexpected things. The result of
it all was the gradual shaping of a system of thinking and believing
on which to base a way of life. They called this system the "Teaching."

Dr. Mills was not at all brilliant, not even clever. At times Charlotte thought him a rather snuffy, bad-tempered old man; but he
had undeniable "power," and he was "different." He could not
write well, yet in the books which he published, lacking clarity
and without any vestige of style, he was able to convey something
that caught and held the attention. Charlotte felt quite certain
that she must study these ideas: it was almost a compulsion. For her
own instruction, and to get hold of the vital part, the root ideas, of
the Teaching, she took Dr. Mills's most ambitious book and resolved to pick it to pieces, to strip off the redundancies, and reduce
it to its elements. She was determined to understand as much of it
as possible, and to find out if there were any gaps or pitfalls. Charlotte had neither the courage nor the patience to put what survived
this treatment into her own words; she kept Mills's phraseology,
isolating the parts she thought important for understanding the
basic theory.

Her Annuary for 1913 and 1914 contains many references to
Dr. Mills's lectures. The long, difficult search for spiritual healing
which runs like a thread throughout her life, sometimes submerged,
at times of stress coming to the surface, is much in evidence at
this time. G.B.S. was at the climax of his affair with Mrs. Pat, and

was put to all shifts to avoid scenes with his wife. There was his end of a telephone conversation which Charlotte overheard, and lost her temper before she could control herself. G.B.S. wondered why one could not make one beloved woman happy without sacrificing another.

He and Charlotte went to the Continent, but she was ill for most of the time, and in a state of painful emotional upheaval, which she constantly tried to control. G.B.S. wrote to Mrs. Pat: "After two perfectly frightful scenes with me, in which she produced such a case against my career and character as made Bluebeard seem an angel in comparison, she quite suddenly and miraculously—at a moment when murder and suicide seemed the only thing left to her—recovered her intellectual balance, her sanity, and her amiability completely, and became once more (after about two years) the happy consort of an easy going man."

Home again, Charlotte resumed the lectures on the Teaching and tried to apply its lessons to her own existence. G.B.S. now treated her with especial courtesy and consideration. The Philanderer had discovered that he was exceedingly attached to his wife, and wanted to spare her feelings where Mrs. Pat was concerned; he took the greatest care that she should not know when he was with the actress. The fact that Charlotte guessed what he was up to most of the time, and that her feelings were lacerated as much by his evasions as by his actions, did not, apparently, occur to him.

In December, 1913, the Actresses' Franchise League produced Charlotte's translation of *La Femme Seule,* under the title *Woman on Her Own* at the Coronet Theatre, with Lena Ashwell and Nancy Price in the chief parts; and it got good notices. *Damaged Goods* was given a private production at the Little Theatre. G.B.S. was thick in rehearsals for *Pygmalion,* and was finding Mrs. Patrick Campbell, in the theatre, almost impossible to direct because of her egotism and venomous attitude to the other actors. But she was the Eliza he wanted, and G.B.S. had a great deal of patience. Their private association had no relation to the tempestuous scenes at rehearsals, a fact which Shaw found amusing and intriguing.

Early in 1914, Charlotte went to America with Lena Ashwell and Dr. and Mrs. Mills, hoping that the sea voyage would do her good. She stayed in New York and Boston, and returned after a fortnight, feeling refreshed by the change. She had missed the first night of *Pygmalion*, but went to see it soon after her return, and heard that Mrs. Pat had married George Cornwallis West. G.B.S. referred to it as an item of news, and went on to tell her of the troubles and tribulations of the rehearsals. Charlotte had always been a ready listener when he talked about his plays, and it was no different now. They found themselves on terms of the old friendship, when they had worked so much together. It was pleasant.

Their life resumed the familiar social pattern. Mrs. Annie Besant came to lunch, they visited the Webbs and the Granville-Barkers; met the philosopher Henri Bergson at one luncheon party and the composer Richard Strauss at another. Writers, musicians, politicians, visiting diplomats, notabilities of all kinds came to Adelphi Terrace. G.B.S. and Charlotte were asked out everywhere. Charlotte was always very well dressed, in the best of taste: she looked just what she was, a cultivated gentlewoman. They made a striking couple when they went out together.

Charlotte never attempted to step into G.B.S.'s limelight. If she had not been so reserved, she could have had some limelight of her own. A. C. Fifield, a publisher in a small way whom she wanted to help, had taken over *Selected Passages* from Constable's, and had also brought out a popular edition of *Damaged Goods*, for which Charlotte wrote a preface. In America, the Connecticut Society of Social Hygiene sold 10,000 copies of the translated play in pamphlet form.

It was, however, her study of Dr. Mills's book on the Teaching which mattered most to Charlotte. She was still working on it, and in the end she found what she was looking for: a clear knowledge and understanding of Mills's ideas, so far as they went. The old man, back in England, heard what she had been doing, and was pleased. He said it would be a valuable textbook, just what he wanted for his students, and he commanded that it should be published as a pamphlet. Charlotte was appalled, for she considered the style poor and the whole thing needed rethinking, but Mills was insistent. Fifield printed an edition, to which Charlotte gave the title *Knowledge Is the Door*, and a thousand copies were sold.

Then war broke out, and the classes stopped. Dr. Mills went

back to America. All the students of the Teaching whom Charlotte had thought the best became rabid militarists—she remained the only pacifist. She went for the last time to Logan Place and returned home feeling very depressed and unhappy. There was Lena, who cared about these things, but few other people to whom she could talk—*really* talk. Charlotte knew what it was to feel alone, in the deepest, most terrifying sense of the word.

16

WAR AND AFTER

(1914–1922)

The war naturally put an end to the Shaws' journeys on the Continent, but they continued to travel about in England, and they paid several visits to Ireland to stay with Sir Horace Plunkett, Lady Gregory, and other friends. Sissy sometimes joined them, especially if they were going to Parknasilla, a beautiful little resort in the south of Ireland which the sisters had known since their childhood.

In May, 1915, Charlotte and G.B.S. crossed back to Holyhead with a number of survivors from the *Lusitania*, and got into conversation with a woman who had lost both husband and father. The woman said that after the first explosion the passengers were got into the boats, ready to lower, when the captain sent an order that they were to get out again, as the ship was not going to sink. "The people cheered, and we all got out," said the woman. "Then came the second explosion, and everything went to pieces."

The flat, quiet recital brought a touch of horror into the sunny day, and Charlotte had her first realization of what the war could mean to civilians. She was still thinking of the woman when she arrived home and found that Harley Granville-Barker and Lillah, who had been in America, were now back and "in a very unsettled state." Granville-Barker had met a rich woman, Helen Huntington, in New York, and had been fascinated by her, though she was married and a great deal older than himself. Charlotte found this piece of news tiresome, and hoped he would not make a fool of himself: what a time to start that sort of thing! But the affair was serious, and by 1916 "Harley was up and down at Ayot," trying to get G.B.S. to help persuade Lillah to consent to a divorce. Charlotte could hardly contain her impatience with him.

Early in 1917, G.B.S. was invited by the War Office to visit the Front. Charlotte later wrote a full account of his adventures to Sissy.

> "Ayot St. Lawrence,
>
> 16 Feb. 1917
>
> "Dearest Sister,
>
> "You told me to tell you all about G.B.S.'s visit to the front.
>
> "It was the greatest possible success. Everyone was more than good to him & they extended his permit so that he was away nearly ten days instead of 3!
>
> He went off in a bitter N. easterly gale & I thought he would have a fearful crossing. But they had a private cabin for him on the steamer & he slept, warm & comfortable, all the way over. When he got to Boulogne he was met by a Captain Roberts with a car & driven straight off to the place where he was to stay. There are 3 chateaux 'Somewhere in France' (you must forgive me if I tell you things you know all about, as of course I must assume it is all news & go straight on). In one of these is housed the C. in C. & his staff. In another are the correspondents of the different newspapers— men more or less permanently out there. In the third are the 'distinguished visitors'; and there was G.B.S. I have photographs of the house, it is one of those typical 17th. or 18th. Cent. big French country houses in a kind of park with a great avenue of splendid trees in front leading up to it. It appears to have been very comfortable, fairly warm & G.B.S. was quite well fed on eggs, cheese, bread & butter & lots of dried dates & figs.
>
> "He was asked the first morning what he most wanted to see, & he said Ypres. They said it was a very 'unhealthy place' but if he

really must go they would see what could be done. So he was motored to Ypres. There he found the 'Town Major' who was a gigantic Irishman, who took them in charge & said 'If you want to see it all, I'll shew you, though I expect I'll be stopped by my own police—but we'll get round.' So they drove off to the principal square where the Cloth Hall is—or was. G.B.S. was very much struck by the fact that though all the houses are gutted the walls are nearly all standing—because the shells explode vertically & do almost no execution laterally. These skeletons of houses make splendid cover: the soldiers put bars of metal across & pile on top of them lots of bags of sand. This they call making an 'elephant dug-out.' Ypres is full of English soldiers living in these things, but this you are supposed *not to tell*. Why, I cannot imagine, as everyone knows the English have Ypres. Another thing G.B.S. noticed was that you go straight from the streets into the trenches. At the end of the road you will see a hole, or a door, & by that you go into the lines.

"Well: when they were getting near the big square—bang! a shell exploded in front of the car! I have never been able to ascertain exactly how far in front! But anyway it frightened the chauffeur & he stopped. The Town Major yelled 'Go on, man, go right on. A shell never comes in the same place twice.' So they went on. Then they saw what had been the Cloth Hall.

"Then he was taken to see the Tanks, & had a ride in one! He says they go about 3 miles an hour, but when you are inside you fancy you are tearing over the ground, the engines are so powerful & make such a commotion. The great creatures will subside gracefully down the side of an immense crater, lie wallowing at the bottom, & then the most absurd thing is to see them struggling & panting up the other side. Sometimes they slide back again.

"One very interesting day they took him to a place called by the Tommies Eatapples! Here there is a great camp for training the fresh men when they come out. It appears they would be quite useless if they were sent straight up to the front; they must be put into gas helmets & taught to go through gas: through the lacrimatory shell effects, smoke shells, &c. &c. Then they must be taught to go

through miles of dark galleries. This seems to upset them more than
anything. I think it would me!

"Then there came an invitation for G.B.S. to lunch with the C.
in C. & all the arrangements made for that day had to be counter-
manded. They had a very cheery lunch, I gather, & after lunch Sir
Douglas, to the great disgust of his people, who had made other
arrangements for him, said he should take G.B.S. off with him in
his car to see some experiments that were being made of the new
inventions. So they had a long drive alone together in an immense
Rolls Royce *closed* car, & G.B.S. says it was the only time in all those
bitter drives in that Arctic weather that he had a rug over his knees!
They appear to have had quite a heart-to-heart talk, & to have discussed everything!

"The experiments were of such things as heat shells—which are
supposed to set everything on fire—& don't: & of flamme werfe
(flame throwers) which are supposed to breathe out destruction—&
don't. The man who was responsible for one of them said 'How
amazing [annoying?], it's worked every time I've tried it until now.'
And an old general called out 'It's done exactly that every time *I've*
seen it.' G.B.S. said 'But it's all snow & ice & yet that shall set the
furze on fire?' 'Oh' said the general, 'they soaked it in parrafin!!!' [*sic*]

"He slept that night at Amiens because it was too far to get back
to his château & because the C. in C. said he wished him to make
the acquaintance of General Rawlinson who (I understand) commands at the Somme front. G.B.S. says the old hotel at Amiens is
just as it used to be, hardly any change (isn't it funny to think of:
do you remember the seagulls in the garden?) In the morning he
was taken round the Somme front & saw a lot of things & was under
fire to the extent that one shell was sent at his party—upon which
they quickly took cover. One very interesting thing he says is that
the Germans are practically not firing at all at present. The English
guns are going all the time—intermittently—but the enemy does
not reply except just now & then. He is reserving all his muni-
tions. . . .

"That night he slept again at Amiens & in the morning drove
back to his chateau, &, in the afternoon, said goodbye to his hosts
there & went off to spend a night with Robert Loraine—Major

Loraine—who is commanding an aeroplane squadron—(I understand, & I daresay you know, that the grades are wing, squadron, flight, in the air service, & that when Loraine becomes a flight commander he will be called Colonel). They live in huts, & when he got there G.B.S. really knew what cold meant. When he was dressing in the morning in his hut his money froze to his fingers! & he could not button any button without holding his fingers in a jug of hot water they brought him. The men's clothes freeze to the ground. He says Loraine is completely taken up with office work & organization, that he never flies now. His particular men do no observation or photographing, & they go up only one man in a machine. They are duellists! Their business is simply to fight. Loraine has a great, loud, braying horn, & when an enemy is reported in the air, he touches an electric button which makes this sound, & off go the men. He was shewing the horn to G.B.S. & he sounded it by accident, & in a moment, before he could say it was a false alarm, a machine was in the air. The others were not so quick, & were stopped, but this unhappy hero was in the air more than an hour looking for imaginary Huns. When he came down his only satisfaction was that Loraine told him he was much pleased at his getting off so promptly.

"The next day G.B.S. drove to Boulogne in Loraine's car—about an hour and a half—& there was the guest of a great friend of ours (Sir Almroth Wright—the original of Ri[d]geon in The Doctor's Dilemma) who is superintending a big Hospital there; &, incidentally, making many discoveries. The men in the hospital were practically the only wounded G.B.S. saw. He seems to have escaped horrors, & only saw one dead man the whole time. But he saw a regiment of men coming back from the trenches—they had been there for 16 days & were coming back for a rest—& he was greatly struck by their exhaustion. He said practically every one of them had their mouths wide open & gave the impression they were too exhausted to keep them closed. . . .

"Now I want very much to hear how your wrist is. I am practically well & can walk 2 or 3 miles then my knee gets a little stiff after that.

"Let me hear if you get this letter. It would be annoying if it was lost.

"The best of love to you both

"Your

"Sister."

* * *

Adelphi Terrace was damaged in an air raid, and soldiers' sheds and searchlights were put up at Ayot. Charlotte went to Ireland a good deal during the next few years, and G.B.S. sometimes accompanied her; at other times Sissy was her companion. The two sisters, though never intimate, had drawn together more than before; Sissy had two granddaughters, and Charlotte liked seeing them. They were later to remember her as being reserved and slightly aloof with them; but in her undemonstrative way she had a strong affection for her niece, Cecily, and was interested in Cecily's children, though she did not often see them.

During these years, Charlotte suffered much from ill-health, especially from a pain in her back. It was diagnosed as lumbago, and it caused her much misery, as no doctor seemed able to cure it, and it became chronic after a time. It was fortunate that she had such good servants; Higgs and his wife looked after her well when she was at Ayot. Their wages had gone up, and the staff increased by an undergardener. Kilsby had been succeeded by Fred Day, who had first been "vetted" by Charlotte—her instinct for the best type of employé rarely failed.

Charlotte had not lost her love of travel, and weakness and recurring illness did not prevent her from setting out for tours. When the war was over, and they were able to go abroad again, they sailed to Madeira, and enjoyed the voyage. G.B.S. was more resigned to Charlotte's peregrinations than he had formerly been, but he was testy if he could not find the conditions he liked. In 1922, he and Charlotte combined a stay at a summer school near Scarborough with what was to be a short holiday on their way to Ireland, but at Clevedon G.B.S. found "only the mud of the Bristol Channel," Tenby was full, Fishguard offered only harbour bilge to bathe in. He also found the Shavian cult at the summer school a nuisance, especially among the female members, remarking in a letter to Beatrice Webb on September 6, 1922:

"I grow old apace . . . I have lost all differentiated interest in women, and am bored by their redoubled interest in me."

There was another matter which was more than an irritation. Stella Patrick Campbell had written her life and had been trying for the past year to get him to agree to her putting in the letters he had sent her seven or eight years before. G.B.S. had refused, and when she wrote him wheedling appeals, refused again with brutal directness:

". . . you start from the position that the publication of intimate letters that were never intended for publication is not permissible among persons of honour. . . . If they are love letters from a married man to a woman who is not his wife, and who is engaged at the same time to another man whom she has subsequently married, the difficulty becomes a wild impossibility."

He insisted on revising the proofs:

"I have spent two days on the job, and have very carefully considered every point. Nobody can reproach you for publishing it as I have left it; and there is the requisite touch to set Charlotte right without which I would have seen the whole universe damned before consenting to the publication of a line. It will be hard enough on her as it is to see her husband as the supreme ass of a drama of which you are the heroine."

When the book appeared, Mrs. Pat was extremely angry because, as she said, the publisher had advertised it largely on Bernard Shaw's love-letters. She had tried to persuade G.B.S. to allow her to publish a particularly intimate letter dating from 1912, which he had forbidden her to use in any circumstances. He sent her a note with press cuttings, saying that even the sub-edited letters had upset his wife. Mrs. Pat replied:

"I am truly sorry if Charlotte is distressed, if only she had been kind to me we could have selected the letters together—If only she would pity—instead of despising actresses for not being as well educated and as well behaved as herself—"

What Charlotte said to G.B.S. about the publication of this book has not been recorded. Characteristically, she neither discussed it

with anyone nor allowed it to interfere with their social life. They
went out: they entertained at home: they visited friends in the
country. All London might be talking about Mrs. Pat's revelations,
but not in the hearing of Mrs. Bernard Shaw. Charlotte had her
own full, exceedingly busy life to lead, and she went serenely ahead,
leading it. G.B.S. had come to depend upon her in a way that
probably neither of them had thought possible in the early days of
their marriage. He had an efficient secretary in Miss Patch, who had
come after Ann Elder; she dealt with all the business side of his
work, the many strangers who would have encroached upon his
time, and the multiplicity of enquiries and requests for favours
which descend on men in the public eye. Charlotte continued, as of
old, to write to their long-established connections, like Trebitsch,
and to their mutual friends. She also acted as a sounding board for
G.B.S.'s ideas. He now relied a great deal on her judgment.
She knew every scene in his plays, and had once said that every
minor character in a Shaw play had the makings of a major character—a perceptive remark which G.B.S. valued.

Charlotte had also learnt where to put in a word which might
take root. G.B.S. had for long been interested in Jeanne d'Arc; they
had often passed through Orléans and Domremy on their travels,
and G.B.S. had talked of the Maid from time to time. Sydney
Cockerell, the Curator of the Fitzwilliam Museum at Cambridge,
one of G.B.S.'s oldest friends, knew of this interest, and early in
1923 sent him a copy of T. Douglas Murray's *Jeanne d'Arc,* because of the picture it gave of the Maid's personality, and the records
of her trial. G.B.S. was occupied with other things, and did not then
open the book; but Charlotte read it, and began to leave it casually
in her husband's way. He picked it up from time to time, and
dipped into it. Then, one day, he settled down to read it seriously.

Meanwhile, Sydney Cockerell brought someone into Charlotte's
life who was to transform it, to make her aware anew that she had
a mind and a soul of her own, apart from George Bernard Shaw.

17

T. E. LAWRENCE

(1922–1935)

Charlotte's long friendship with T. E. Lawrence, "Lawrence of Arabia," was, as she later wrote to Dorothy Walker, one of the strangest episodes in her life. It lasted from 1922 until Lawrence's death in 1935, and though there were times when Charlotte grew angry with this extraordinary man, she never lost her affection for him. It was a feeling which has been variously interpreted, and some of Charlotte's letters suggest that a thread of intense emotion became entangled in it during the later years—not surprising, perhaps, in an elderly, childless woman who had been starved of affection for most of her early life. The correspondence on the whole, however, suggests one of those rare friendships where two questing minds find stimulus and help in sparking off against each other. Charlotte was over sixty and Lawrence under forty when they first became friends, but the difference in age seemed not to matter.

Two more dissimilar characters could not be imagined: Charlotte, straightforward, intelligent, detesting personal publicity, and Lawrence, highly gifted, devious, intellectual—sometimes arrogantly so —a man of great complexity. Much has been written about Lawrence since his death, and distortions have inevitably led to legend; he was an individual who attracted enmity as well as loyalty. He was many-sided to a greater extent than most people, and the less pleasant aspects of his personality have often been presented as the whole man. An assessment of the real Lawrence has yet to be written. When it is, his long correspondence with Charlotte Shaw (only a fraction of which can be given here) should prove of great value, for it brings out the conflicts which were probably responsible for his continual restlessness and obliqueness.

Lawrence revealed himself to Charlotte as he did to few other people. He was able to talk to her of the dichotomy in his nature, of which he was well aware; and Charlotte was able to tell him of the things that mattered most to her in life. Both of them read a great deal, and liked discussing books. When Lawrence began to go to Ayot, it was G.B.S. who inevitably took the floor, and Lawrence felt overshadowed. G.B.S. was courteous enough, but he never took the trouble to understand Lawrence: this comes out unmistakably in a judgement of T.E.L. which Shaw made some years later. It was Charlotte to whom Lawrence could write with complete freedom; he was able to set down his thoughts and opinions, however prejudiced, knowing that though she might disagree with them she would take them seriously enough to argue. Lawrence greatly admired Shaw, but it was Charlotte who became his friend.

Thomas Edward Lawrence was born in 1888, of Anglo-Irish parentage, and educated at Oxford. He took a first-class degree in modern history, and was very much interested in archaeology, working on sites in the Middle East. This led to a knowledge of, and liking for, the Arabs, which gained him first prominence, then fame. He brought most of the Hejaz under Arab-British control, and in the 1914–18 war raised Arab levies which broke up the Turkish Fourth Army, and contributed substantially to the Turkish collapse.

After the war, unable to settle down to civilian life, Lawrence joined the R.A.F., serving in the ranks, but "Lawrence of Arabia" was a marked man, and he changed his name twice, first to Ross and then to Shaw. The disguise was thin, as he had many friends and acquaintances among prominent people; it helped, however, to sink his identity which, he declared, was what he wanted. His main pre-occupation, at the period when he first got in touch with Bernard Shaw, was the account he had written of his exploits in the Arab campaign, which was to be published under the title *The Seven Pillars of Wisdom*.

The Shaws met T. E. Lawrence through Sydney Cockerell, who wanted a portrait of G.B.S. for the Fitzwilliam Museum. Charlotte knew of this, and on March 13, 1922, she wrote to Cockerell:

"Do you remember G.B.S. saying he would give one of the three [Augustus] John portraits of himself to the Fitzwilliam. Again last week he spoke of it and said he had quite decided to do so. It is the one in the drawing-room—the larger one. Now we are going to have the house 'done up' next month, and the place will be full of workmen, and these valuable things rather get on my mind. Will you write a line to G.B.S. and tell him what I say, and suggest that you should have the picture *now*, that is, if you want it?"

Decidedly Sydney Cockerell wanted it, and he wrote at once to Shaw, who replied saying he could collect the portrait when he liked. Shortly afterwards, Sydney Cockerell was lunching in London with T. E. Lawrence, to discuss how they could help their mutual friend, Charles Doughty, author of *Arabia Deserta*, who was in financial difficulties. Cockerell mentioned that after lunch he was going round to Adelphi Terrace to collect Shaw's portrait, and asked Lawrence if he would like to accompany him. Lawrence hesitated. He preferred, he said, to admire great men from afar; he was not sure if it was wise to meet them in the flesh. Sydney Cockerell assured him that as it was a Saturday they would be unlikely to see G.B.S., because the Shaws usually went down to Ayot every week-end, and they would be gone by the early afternoon.

When the two men reached Adelphi Terrace, however, they found the Shaws still there. Introductions and polite conversation followed; G.B.S. realized that this was "Lurens Pasha" but did not refer to the fact. Cockerell and Lawrence left with the portrait.

About the middle of August that year, G.B.S. received a letter from Lawrence.

"You will be puzzled at my writing to you, but Cockerell some months ago took me round to you and introduced me, and you did not talk too formidably.

"I want to ask you two questions: the first one 'Do you still read books?' doesn't require an answer. If you still go on reading I'm going to put the second question: if you don't, then please skip the two inside pages of this note and carry over to my signature at the end, and burn it all without replying. I hate letter-writing—as much as I can—and so, probably, do you.

"My real wish is to ask you if you will read, or try to read, a book which I have written. It's about the war, which will put you off, to start with, and there are technical unpleasantnesses about it. For instance it is very long; about 300,000 words I suspect, though I have not counted them. I have very little money and do not wish to publish it: however, it had to be printed, so I got it done on a lino. press in a newspaper office. That means it's beastly to look at, two columns on a quarto page, small newspaper type which hurts your eyes, and dozens of misprints, corrected roughly in ink: for only five copies exist, and I could not afford a proof. The punctuation is entirely the compositor's fancy: and he had an odd fancy, especially on Mondays.

"That's the worst to be said on the material side. So far as concerns myself you must be told, before you commit yourself to saying 'yes,' that I'm not a writer, and successfully passed the age of 30 without having wanted to write anything. I was brought up as a professional historian, which means the worship of original documents. To my astonishment, after peace came I found I was myself the sole person who knew what had happened in Arabia during the war; and the only literate person in the Arab Army. So it became a professional duty to record what happened. I started out to do it plainly and simply, much as a baby thinks it's easy to talk: and then I found myself bogged in a confusion of ways of saying the easiest things, and unable to describe the plainest places: and then problems of conduct came along, and the people with me had to be characterised:—in fact I got fairly into it, and the job became too much for me. *Your* first book was not perfect, though it was a subject you had chosen for yourself, and you had an itch to write!

"In my case, I have, I believe, taken refuge in second-hand words: I mean, I think I've borrowed expressions and adjectives and ideas from everybody I've ever read, and cut them down to my own size, and stitched them together again. My tastes are daily mailish, so there's enough piffle and romance and wooliness to make a realist sick. There's a lot of half-baked thinking, some cheap disgust and complaint (the fighting fronts were mainly hysterical, you know, where they weren't professional, and I'm not the least a proper soldier): in fact all the sham stuff you have spent your life trying to prick. If you read my thing, it will show you that your prefaces have been written in vain, if I'm a fair sample of my generation. This might make you laugh, if the thing was amusingly written: but it's long-winded, and pretentious, and dull to the point where I can no longer bear to look at it myself. I chose that moment to have it printed!

"You'll wonder why, if all this is true (and I think it is) I want any decent person still more a person like yourself [here there is an asterisk with the footnote: 'ambiguous: but I wanted to avoid expressing my liking for your work'] to read it. Well, it's because it is history, and I'm shamed for ever if I'm the sole chronicler of an event, and fail to chronicle it: and yet unless what I've written can be made better I'll burn it. My own disgust with it is so great that I no longer believe it worth trying to improve (or possible to improve). If you read it or part of it and came to the same conclusion, you would give me courage to strike the match: whereas now I distrust my own judgement, and it seems cruel to destroy a thing on which I have worked my hardest for three years. While if you said that parts were rubbish, and other parts not so bad, and parts of it possible, (and distinguished those parts variously) then your standards might enable me to clear up mine, and give me energy enough to tackle the job again. (If you say it is all possible I will reluctantly get rid of your own books from my shelves.)

"All this is very unfair—or would be, if you knew me: but deleting that twenty minutes with Cockerell we are utter strangers, and likely to remain so, and therefore there is no pressure on you to answer this letter at all. I won't be in the least astonished (indeed I'll write another of the same sort to a man called Orage [editor of The New Age] whom I have never met, but whose criticism I enjoy: and my opinion of you will go up. Yours with many apologies
                                                "T. E. LAWRENCE

"Incidentally: I don't want people to know that the book exists. So whether you reply or not, I hope you will not talk of it."

Clearly this was not something to hand over to Miss Patch to answer. G.B.S. wrote to Lawrence, agreeing to look at the manuscript when he had time, but making no promise as to a date. The manuscript arrived at Ayot in the middle of September. G.B.S. glanced through it, and gave it to Charlotte to read, saying that it was obviously a very unusual work. Charlotte began to read the script with her accustomed thoroughness. The young man who had called with Sydney Cockerell had made little impression on her, though she remembered that he was slightly built and had very blue eyes. Now, reading his pages, something quite extraordinary happened. It seemed to her that she had gone back forty years, when she had read so many books about Eastern religions, and was reaching out for something that was beyond her understanding. Here was a kindred mind. She sensed undertones in the historical survey of the Arab world with which the manuscript opened, and was aware of a curious excitement. She was sure that this was a man far above the usual, and as she read on she knew that he had written a remarkable book. She said so to G.B.S., and he looked at it again, though he found it impossible to spare the time to read it properly, as he was going to a summer school in Yorkshire and had lecture notes to prepare. He wrote to Lawrence and suggested that Constable's might be interested in publishing it, and offered to put in a word there. Lawrence replied thanking him, and stated that he did not wish to have it published; he had felt bound to write it, and was very anxious to have Shaw's opinion, but he meant to show it to only six people.

On November 24, Charlotte wrote to Sydney Cockerell:

"I want to talk to you about a wonderful Ms. that has been given us to read by someone you brought to see us *if you know about it.* Do you? If you don't, I can't talk of it as we have it under the seal of secrecy. But I am carried off my feet by it!"

G.B.S. had not read the manuscript by December, and Lawrence grew impatient. He wrote to Charlotte, whose *Selected Passages* he had read. Charlotte replied:

"10, Adelphi Terrace, W.C.
31st. December, 1922

"Dear Mr. Lawrence,

"If you've been 'mad keen' to hear about your book I've been mad keen to write to you about it ever since I read it, or rather ever since I began to read it, and I simply haven't dared. I got from it an impression of you as an Immense Personality soaring in the blue (of the Arabian skies) far above my lowly sphere, and that everything I could say in the way of admiration, or comment, or question, could only be an impertinence. But the latest developments of your career have been so startlingly unexpected, and your later letters so human, that I take my courage in both hands and send you a word.

"Now is it *conceivable, imaginable,* that a man who could write the Seven Pillars can have any doubts about it? If you don't know it is a 'great book' what is the use of telling you so. I believe (though he had never said anything of the sort) that G.B.S. thinks you are 'pulling his leg' when you ask him. I devoured the book from cover to cover as soon as I got hold of it. I could not stop. I drove G.B.S. almost mad by insisting on reading him special bits when he was deep in something else. I am an old woman, old enough at any rate to be your mother; I have met all sorts of men and women of the kind that are called distinguished; I have read their books and discussed them with them; but I have never read anything like this: I don't believe anything really like it has been written before. When I find in your letter such suggestions as 'Should it be without the first person singular?' 'Is there any style in my writing?' I think— are you laughing at us! Why, foolish man, it *could* only have been written in the first person singular: it is one of the most amazingly individual documents that has ever been written: there is no 'style' because it is above and beyond anything so silly.

"You have been the means of bringing into the world a poignant human document, and now—have faith in the Power that worked in you. . . .

"I am greatly honoured by your phrase 'divine book of' selections please, not 'extracts,' since it was I who selected them. . . .

"Your book must be published as a whole. Don't you see that?

Perhaps little bits about the French . . . might be toned down . . . *but don't leave out the things an ordinary man would leave out*: the things people will tell you are too shocking. Publish the book practically as it is, in good print, in a lot of volumes. . . .

"Both G.B.S. and I have lots of experience about books & we would both *like* to put it at your service. By the way, don't call him 'Mr.' Shaw!

"Yours sincerely,
"C.F.S.
(Mrs. G.B.S.!)"

Lawrence was pleased at Mrs. Shaw's enthusiasm. He wrote to her from the R.A.F. early in January, 1923.

"Dear Mrs. 'G.B.S.'

"It's a wonderful letter, that of yours, and I've liked it beyond measure: though my doubts as to the virtues of the Seven Pillars remain: indeed, I'd be an insufferable creature if I was sure of it, for to me a good book is the best thing that can be done. However I'd been thinking it possibly a bad book, & your praise of it makes me more hopeful. At the same time, you know, it's more a store-house than a book—has no unity, is too discursive, dispersed, heterogeneous. I've shot into it, as a builder into his yard all the odds and ends of ideas which came to me during those years: indeed I suspect that it's a summary of myself to February 1920, and the people who read it will know me better than I know myself.

"Since 1920 I've had no experiences, & it's partly that newness today which makes the Seven Pillars seem to me so inadequate to their theme. This last adventure in the R.A.F. is a chapter in itself. It would be hard to remain inhuman while jostling all days and nights in a crowd of clean and simple men. There is something here which in my life before I'd never met—had hardly dreamed of . . .

"I've refused to sign any contract for any part of the Seven Pillars. . . . I'd like to publish the whole, but that's as improbable as that I'd walk naked down Piccadilly: not that I'd like that either, but the whole is the only honest thing.

"I showed my mother your letter. She likes you . . . because you praised my work, and mothers have (privately) an inordinate pride in sons. The horrors of the book strike her painfully, and she hates my having noted, or seen, such things. . . .

"It's very good of you and G.B.S. to offer me your help. It would be invaluable if I was publishing: but today I feel that I won't. It was only lack of food which frightened me into consenting: and in the R.A.F. they give us quantities of food.

"Yours sincerely,
"T. E. LAWRENCE"

By the beginning of 1924, a regular correspondence had been established and they were writing frequently to each other. Lawrence had taken a small cottage, Clouds Hill, not far from Bovington Camp, where he was stationed, and he spent as much time as he could there, reading books and listening to gramophone records; he was passionately fond of music. Charlotte sent books, including the Brieux translations, and records, for which he was very grateful, writing to tell her that R.A.F. friends who came to the cottage enjoyed these gifts along with him. He was still bent on denigrating his own book, writing on January 13:

"I heartily despise the Seven Pillars. I admire heartily G.B.S. . . . yet I would not like G.B.S. to do for my book what I (a worm) did for Doughty, a great writer. [Lawrence had written a preface for an edition of Doughty's book.] I'd like G.B.S. to review my book (if it were published normally): I'd be proud of his review, even if it were venomous: but I'd not prefix it to the volume itself, were it great slabs, casks, of buttery praise. Introductions are not honourable things, either for the introducer or the introduced . . . and when a pitiable flea presumes (on his technical knowledge) to play salesman to a book which is a wonderful book of art (the flea being presumed a Philistine flea) then the spectacle is a wholly horrid one. Haven't you sometimes felt oiked to find the names of holidaymakers cut with knives into the smooth walls of mediaeval ruins? Is there a difference between the cads and me?

"For the humour of the situation lies in my having consented to write an introduction to Richard Garnett's book 'The Twilight of the Gods': to be done soon, & (unlike the Doughty) to be paid for. . . . Oh, the sweet pill!

"More thanks,
"T.E.S."[1]

[1] Lawrence had changed his name to Shaw, and now signed his letters T.E.S.

G.B.S. had completed *St. Joan,* which had been produced in New York at the beginning of the year. He sent Lawrence a proof copy of the play. *Back to Methuselah* was on in London, and Lawrence, who had bought a motor-bicycle, managed to get up to London to see at least part of it. He wrote to Charlotte on March 3, 1924:

"Joan shall be read with extreme care—and delight. It's magnificent to be trusted with such a treasure.

"My Methuselah performance was fairish. The bike was raw & new, a man-killer. I'm afraid to death of it. However it enabled me to hear Part IV. Part V was something unearthly. It wasn't a play but a declaration of faith. Lilith's speech reads itself more beautifully within my brain than off the stage. The Second Part (least exciting in the book) gained most from the play acted.

"I'd go mad if I'd been able to hold a crowd like that: did you feel (with your fingers almost) the tightness of the crowd's attention? There, I've spluttered clean out of any ruins of a prose style I ever had: but these last six days have been marvellous: and Pte. Shaw isn't able to endure like the late Colonel Lawrence.

"The others are continuing to borrow all your books—except the Brieux."

A fortnight later he wrote again:

"I've read Joan, St. Joan—and want to say straight out that it is one of his best writings. Don't take me as a play-judge: I know nothing of the stage, & don't care very much for it: a play to me is only a particular art-form like a sonnet: but as writing Joan is magnificent.

"Some sea-change has come over G.B.S. in the last ten years. Perhaps it isn't new that he should be on the side of the angels— even when they are undisguised angels—but surely it's new that every one of his characters should be honest and kindly and even-minded? I like it, & find it essentially true, the more I see of men (almost I'm able to think gently of some sergeants—they mean less than appears—their official style has to be subtracted before you measure the manner & matter of their delivery): but people don't usually feel fair towards humanity till they are old & successful & ready to retire—and G.B.S. isn't the third, & probably will never be the first—just as I'll never be second.

"Seriously, it's done his art & heart good to get the doctrine of Methuselah off his breathing-works: and the poet in him is now going to have a little dance. Did you notice the balance in the prose of the fighting part of Joan? Take care: he may yet write an epic of blood-lust. All things are possible with a delivered evangelical. Wonderful lines in Joan were on p. 26, where the Archb. rebukes the lapdogs. Oh, I'd like to hear de Rais stammer out his desperate save-face from that!

"I shrink from Joan's very little dialect. It seems to me a literary manner, like italics; unworthy of an artist of Mr. Shaw's cut and sweep of spoken word. He gives Joan a loud simplicity without it— and I'm a detester & despiser of bumpkins. The best men in the ranks are not the bumpkin-spoken. A fellow worth listening to isn't the tyro, but the man who is trying once more, on top of ten thousand failures, to phrase precisely what his mind feels.

"Page 31 where the Dauphin snaps his fingers in La Tremouille's face. Excellent.

"Page 35 Who was Dunois' second wife? The jape about 'Staff Officers' lower down is a real deep thrust. It lightens up this scene, which to my mind doesn't hold quite as much metal as the preceding one.

"The next pages, where Warwick and Cauchon & the ancestor of the die-hard play together is a delight in its sheer skill of character-work. The three men stand out & live solidly & separately.

"Pp. 53-65: they are adequate: but Mr. Shaw doesn't know how men who have fought together stand in relation to one another (when there has been recognisable personal relations in the fighting line) afterwards. They understand so deeply that they never hesitate to differ fundamentally. The word 'pet' should come out of the last line of p. 53. They have a half section, a pal, a chum: not more than one, either comrade, or no comrade: there aren't degrees in fellowship. The development of the tragedy grows fast through this scene.

"I found pp. 66–95 intolerable. The shadow of the tragedy at the end lay over the first pages, & made the so-accurate historical 'placing' of the men a horror. Over their pages I galloped, to reach the crisis. Joan came in, & held her own, indeed increased her nobility. It was good to make her sign that confession—and then she died, 'off.'

"I have a prejudice against the writer who leaves the reader to make his top-scene for him. I funked it, in the death of Farraj, my man: faced it, in the plain narrative of my mishaps in Deraa the night I was captured. Here in St. Joan the climax will be a red light shining from the fire into the courtyard. Authors feel they aren't up to writing so tremendous a thing, & so they put a row of dots . . . . or swallow silently & leave the poor reader to stuff up their gap with his cherished & grudged emotion. It's indirect art & direct shirking. Of course if he'd dipped his pen in all his strength & written straight forward the play could never have been presented: but the more honour so. It would have cleaned us all to have *seen* Joan die.

"The fifth act is pure genius. I wouldn't have a thought of it otherwise than written: I'm most thankful to you for letting me read it.

"This is a rotten letter written straight out of a mazed head this Sunday afternoon in the cottage. Russell & Palmer (did you meet Palmer, a shy little doormouse of mine?) are playing jinks & Mozart on a gramophone behind me: & the birds are all shouting aloud in the soft sunshine outside. The day has been slightly overcast, and there is a taste of spring rain in it. I've only just finished Joan, after five days spent in reading her twice.

"It was my fault that I didn't see you during Methuselah, but I was innocent of the ringing up. The grime & oiliness of those dark 150-mile dashes sandwiched in between laborious days were thick on me when I twice called: & the guardians of your entanglement . . . were firm that neither you nor he ever saw anyone without appointment. When G.B.S. scoffs at my fear of publicity he should go down the first half-flight of stairs & look at that gate & imagine himself without it—imagine himself day-tenant of one-twentieth of a barrack floor, & owner of the handkerchief & money in the pocket of his government suit!"

In a letter later that month, Lawrence criticized Barrie, Belloc and Lowell Thomas, the American who had "made my vulgar reputation." He told Charlotte that *The Seven Pillars* was to be pub-

lished, 100 copies or so, at 30 guineas each, and "Your copy will be
made special somehow." Charlotte replied to this letter indignantly
defending Barrie and Belloc, and repudiating his criticisms of *St.
Joan,* which she considered a masterpiece without any fault. It was
clear that she felt at ease with him, setting her thoughts down at
odd moments in a way she had never been able to do with G.B.S.
She wrote:

"You have written to me about writing several times almost as if
you thought we differed about that: but I agree with you pro-
foundly—more deeply than you will understand—I think."

They discussed places they both knew. Lawrence wrote from
Clouds Hill in November, 1924:

"Ely: yes, a most glorious place, & to look away across England
from the Cathedral is marvellous. Something in the Norman style
strikes me as so logical & unanswerable . . . it's not argument, a
proposition, like the pointed work, which stands only by stress &
balance. Norman, Romanesque, rather, is a plain statement." And
again:

"My reading lately? Only the Swallow Book of Ernst Toller's. It
is most moving & excellent. I've been through it about six times,
gladly. . . ."

". . . In the cottage, with a huge fire." The New World Sym-
phony was being played on his gramophone. "The slow movement
is full of folk rhythms, & beautifully reproduced."

He often returned to the subject of G.B.S.'s writing:

"The Elizabethan age was Shakespeare & his fellows: & I feel that
this age will be Shaw & his fellows, when the detractions of the
next 150 years are past. It's stuff which has to be taken without
question, like air or light. How they will hate it, in thirty years!"

Charlotte had offered to read the proofs of the *Seven Pillars,* an
offer which Lawrence gratefully accepted. Pike, the printer, was
"an artist of great severity and carefulness . . . his pages are made as
beautifully as he can compass them"; but neither Lawrence nor
Pike was a good proof-reader: they tried to grasp paragraphs entire
and the misspelt word escaped them. Charlotte asked what form
her corrections should take.

"Any you please. My pleasure is only bounded by your pain. Do as much, in each batch, as come easy to you. . . . Read the thing as long as you can do so without boredom. . . . As the hesitant nervous author I'll value most such corrections as affect the manner & matter of the expression of ideas: because they will tend to make the book better, & I dread strangers seeing the thing in its existing unworthy clumsy form. . . .

"What a pother about a trifle! G.B.S. has brought forth twenty books; and I'm in a mess over one. The first no doubt is hardest, but the difference must lie between us. Of course his genius makes him feel sure what is important, & what isn't, & my blundering imitation confounds essentials & inessentials. Also, you know, it's the only book I'll write, & it's an apology for my first thirty years, & the explanation of the renunciation which followed them. . . ."

Lawrence went to his cottage as often as he could, with the R.A.F. companions who liked to listen to his records. He gave Charlotte descriptions of these visits, and the men:

"The Air Force fellows are like Oxford undergraduates in their second term . . . their first questioning, their first doubt of an established convention of law or practice, opens a flood-gate in their minds: for if one thing is doubtful all things are doubtful: the world to them has been a concrete, founded, polished thing: & the first crack is portentous. . . . They ask questions about every rule of conduct & experience, & about mind & soul & body: and I . . . answer succinctly & with illumination . . . Methuselah is a prime card to play . . . it puts one side quite quintessentially. G.B.S. would laugh to see himself the prime reaction against the carnality of barrack-life, but that's the way it goes. You get a reinforced masculinity by herding men together & segregating them for 20 hours of the 24 . . . and reinforced masculinity is a way of describing an animalism which is not the less bestial for being happy and deliberate."

Of G.B.S.'s Prefaces he wrote:

"The plays are creations: flames. The prefaces are sober plaited arguments, addressed to our lower intellects. If you 'feel' the play you are only annoyed at the repeat in a lower key. If you don't feel the play you're a low fellow, not worth arguing with. It's the yoking together of quick & dead which distresses me: though I'm silly to resent it, for probably it's G.B.S.'s sense of probity & humane responsibility which forces him to show us that his instincts are based on reason & common sense & human nature & decency. . . . I do like the prefaces, too, in certain moods: in other moods they are like the 2/3 (admission & entertainment tax) which you have to pay at Queen's Hall before you can hear Scriabin."

On June 23, 1924, he wrote from the Camp:

". . . Our selves are like matter (*are* matter?) subdivisible into atoms & thence eternally subdivisible according to the fineness of our investigating apparatus: and they presumably (logically & inevitably) build up conversely into aggregations cosmic & universal so far as our imaginations can reach—and infinitely beyond them into dimensions which we can't even imagine—but may doubtfully feel. . . .

"Oxford . . . am I Oxford? That subfusc place would deny it. Bradley sits on his sofa there, puffing a briar, & proves that he & it & we have no existence. I've a bad habit, if I feel a thing, of acting it straightway. Very unacademic, I assure you. . . .

"The book. THE BOOK, as you put it. No. of subscribers to date 34. Progress very slow: but not so slow as the printer. . . . More subscribers badly wanted . . . but patience. If I wait long enough they will come.

"Why do wet days usually provoke my writing to you? Is there something in the dash of rain against the glass which makes me willing to talk confidences? They usually are confidences, you know. I suspect that the rain & the wind give me a shut-away, secret, safe feeling."

He asked Charlotte to find an "unofficial" doctor for a sergeant who had been hurt in a road accident and faced the prospect of life with a permanently stiff ankle. Charlotte, who believed in osteopaths, at once sent him an address, and Lawrence replied:

"You are really extraordinarily good, to put yourself out for us. When I wrote to you I felt like a surgeon, exploring with his scalpel to find out the limit of his patient's appendix of good nature. You, being understanding, will feel how much easier it is to be kind than to ask another to be kind."

On August 17 he wrote from Clouds Hill:

"Yesterday was an occasion . . . I celebrated a birthday. By my pay-book (full of queer statements about me) it was my twentieth.

By my attestation form it was my thirtieth. By truth it must have
been my thirty-sixth. The day justified itself splendidly. . . .
Salmond, an Air Marshal . . . took me off to dinner with his wife
& brother . . . it's rich to eat at a table whose top does not physically
remind you of its past meals. . . ."

In September he sent her forty pages of proof, asking her to
"alter, mark, erase, add, abuse anything which hits you: either
technical or literary, or moral, or intellectual." Charlotte made
many suggestions in the margins of the proof-sheets, and sent them
back. Lawrence wrote:

"It will take me some time to work them into a fair copy (of
course I'm accepting all the changes, as made) since they affect
the spirit as well as the letter of the book. . . .

"I'm sorry to lose the list of names on page the second. It was my
only homage to the fellows who helped the show. Perhaps it can
be stuck in somewhere, someday. . . . The book really begins in
Chapter 10, which has not yet been sent to you, as it isn't ready.
May I go on sending the proofs? . . .

"G.B.S.'s punctuations strike me as literary, not conversational.
Stops aren't necessary, really, at all. . . . Please give G.B.S. my
most astonished thanks; and accept the same directly for yourself."

On November 29, Lawrence sent Charlotte a long description
of *Tess of the d'Urbervilles* which he attended, as a guest of
Thomas Hardy:

". . . and when it was over—at midnight on a stormy night I rode
to Southampton, back round the forest till dawn, because bed
wasn't any good after an experience like that.

"I was rumoured to be Mr. Hardy's son by his first wife. So that
doubles & quits the Rector who thought I was yours! Did you hear
that the poor man asked some of the Tank Corps in jail—next day
—about me: and came to the Hardys on the third day to see who
I really was. . . ."

*   *   *

Charlotte continued to send him regular parcels of books, sometimes at intervals of only a few days. She kept records; in 1925, the
books and papers she posted to him included:

9 Feb.	Lady Gregory's Plays.
	Charwoman's Daughter, Stephens.
	Blake by Chesterton.
15 Feb.	1st vol Antichrist Merezhkowsky.
	Mrs. Warren's Profession
	(Mercury, Observer, 2 Times Lt. Sup)
18 Feb.	Pierre le Grand 2 vol.
23	The Hour Glass
	Yeats and La Naissance des Dieux
2 March	Papers and Algernon Blackwood
	First 30 Years
9 March	Battle of the Books
19	Mr. Britling
20	Times Lit. Sup and Job, preface G.K.C.
30	Papers and Darrel Figgis "Children of Earth"
13 April	Three Kingdoms Storm Jameson
20 April	Oddta XIX Cent.
	The Plough and the Stars, O'Casey
25 April	Bruce Rogers
	Elgar's Music

Lawrence had become a welcome visitor to Ayot. He would turn up unexpectedly, stay for an hour or two, then hurtle away again in order to get back to camp. Charlotte wrote to him from Ayot on October 9, 1926:

"Back in the shelter [in the garden] A brilliant summer day. A crystalline dew left by the morning fog shining in the grass: gossamer twinkling from shrub to shrub: a red leaf here & there—no, many red leaves, & yellow ones. Did I say I hated Ayot? Of course I *do*—really. But today—I have visited the whole place round. A gateway: a corner round which a bicycle has often disappeared—& sometimes appeared. An armchair (which was painted red!) A porch, in which G.B.S. now sits. Ayot is justified—it lifts its head. Poor Ayot!"

When *The Seven Pillars* was published, Lawrence had a copy especially bound for Charlotte by a superb craftsman, McClelland, the only rival to Douglas Cockerell, who was then the leading bookbinder in the country. Lawrence was in an almost continuous state of depression, and Charlotte did something very unusual for her:

she sent him one of the notebooks in which she had made long analyses of Dr. Mills's Teaching. He wrote again, asking about Mills, and Charlotte now sent him a copy of *Knowledge Is the Door,* which she had found on the top shelf of a cupboard. She enclosed a letter:

"When I gave you the little notebook, & afterwards, I wanted to write to you some explanations of what was meant by 2 things, Principle & Meditation. Somehow I couldn't. I sat down again and again to do it, but, though it should have been quite easy, nothing came. So I left it. But . . . you said 'Sitting still is not the summum bonum. More bees and bats nest in you then, than thoughts. Perceive herein the influence of your notebook.' Then I felt how guilty I was, or that is the exact contrary of the influence the little book should have had."

She went on to tell him about Dr. Mills and the Teaching.

"Here are some specimens of our 'meditations.' The S & P stand for Primary and Secondary & if you care to know the meaning of that you will find it in the book.

S. 1. I will have freedom in desire, emotion, thought, sensation.
2. Infinite spirit, thou art thyself the substance of all my desire.
3. Infinite Faith & Life within me, thou art my freedom from fear.
4. I will be faithful to my truth: I renounce the old, animal states of darkness & inertia: I will serve the light of the world.

P. 1. My will in thee is joy not sorrow.
2. I am divine Intelligence thy Principle: have faith in me.
3. Be still, & know that I am the substance of all thy desire. Have faith in me.
4. Be still & know that I am power within thee. There is no power in conditions, there is no power in personality; there is only power in me, thy Principle.
5. My grace is sufficient for thee; *there is no condemnation.*
6. I am original Health, thy principle.
   I heal thy soul of ignorant desire;
   I heal thy heart of ignorant emotion;
   I heal thy mind of ignorant thought;
   I heal thy body of ignorant sensation."

There is no record of how Lawrence took these rather difficult, esoteric ideas, but he evidently treated them with respect, other-

wise Charlotte would have withdrawn herself: she was exceedingly
sensitive in anything which affected her spiritual life. He sent her
some poems which he had written, and Charlotte replied with a
letter which brought out a poetic strain usually buried beneath the
practical forthrightness of the personality she showed to the world.
She was in bed with one of her occasional attacks of "seediness,"
and immersed herself at once in Lawrence's verses, and her reply:

"Ayot,

14 March, 1927

"How about this:—

"The years like great big oxen tread the world

"And God the herdsman goads them on behind. (I blush to say
this line makes me giggle.)

"The nearest I can get to your splendid line. It is Yeats. I do not
yet know which of his poems it comes from, but shall presently
find it. I think it must have been this, lingering in your mind,
caused you to compose 'My thoughts like slow black oxen crowd
the plain,' which is incomparably better than Yeats; my only criticism of it being that I never saw *oxen* crowd a plain. They always
seem to come single spies (or dual) not in battalions. Buffalos, now,
little black ones, I have. I was at Paestum, so long ago that the
country there was all infested by brigands and it took an order
from a High Official (!) provided by an English Ambassador of
that day to enable us to go there. And we went in an extraordinarily
large and extraordinarily ramshackle carriage; my father, my
mother, my sister and myself; with 4 funny little wiry horses and
a coachman who threw his arms about and shouted all the time—
whether to attract the brigands or to repel them I never found out.
We had an escort, wild men, also with quaint, hairy, wise little
horses. The plain was—

Marshy, wild and bare

Wide, wild and open to the air—

brushwood and swamp—marecage—sunshine—yellow flowers—
beautiful indescribably. I can see it now. And everywhere, in the
ditches and waterholes and bogs and low woodland—buffalos—
crowds and crowds, wallowing, fighting, being happy—and dis-
liking *us* very much. We ate a lunch we had brought with us on

the steps of the greatest Temple—honey and figs and raisins—I
don't remember anything else. A long, lovely day!"

She wrote to him again the following day:

"Alas! Alas! I am still in bed. Quite a fierce little fever flamed up.
Now it has gone down again & I am normal and got up for a little
this afternoon. I am always ashamed of being ill: see the little
book. And now I know you have the little book because a most
wonderful letter has come to tell me so. G.B.S. sat by my bed and
read every word of it (But I had read it first!) He was quite beautifully stroked the right way; he likes the things you say about him
quite very much. You will find his Spectator review among the
ones in this letter.

"I am hoping, so very much, I shall get G.B.S. to ask our Eric[2]
to do a frontispiece for his socialism book. He is playing with the
idea now. He says he wants one like Dürer's Melancholia! Too
amusing—Eric confronted with that—how he would laugh . . .

"I send a vol. of Winston. For the first time my cherished privilege of making up your parcels has been ceded to another. I hate
her. But these are the penalties when one is so wicked as to be ill.

"From this deplorable chamber, on this deplorable day of east
wind & haze.

"Ti voglio bene,
"C.F.S."

There came a day when Charlotte found she could tell him
about something she rarely mentioned to anybody: her early life.
G.B.S., of course, knew the main outlines, but he had never been
really interested; when she had tried to talk to him of her early
years at Derry he had listened politely but had made bantering,
paradoxical remarks which dried up any more words.

It seemed natural to tell Lawrence. The *leit-motiv* of many of his
letters had been the necessity of being cleansed in one's mind and
soul. Charlotte had secreted an awful bitterness throughout her
life, and now she felt impelled to allow it to well up and flow over.
She wrote to Lawrence on May 17, 1927:

"I'd like to make this a real letter, if I can. I want to tell you
about myself.

[2] Eric Kennington.

"I had a perfectly hellish childhood & youth, after I got old enough to take things in at all. My father was Irish, in the sense that your father was: his family had lived in Ireland for generations and had married into families of which the same was true. . . . My mother was a terribly strong character—managing and domineering. She could not bear opposition: if it was offered she either became violent, or she cried. She felt (genuinely felt) she had sacrificed her life for us & my father . . . & she never ceased telling us so. She felt (quite genuinely) that we none of us loved her enough or considered her enough, or helped her enough (she would never be helped—ever) or respected her wishes sufficiently, or cared to spend our time with her.

"My father was gentle & affectionate, well-educated & well-read very, *very* good, honourable & straight. He was a marvel of patience with my mother, which was terribly bad for her. I think, now, she ought to have been *beaten*: it would have been better for us all, especially for herself. As it was my father led a most unhappy life, & died comparatively young of sheer tiredness. It was a terrible home. My sister . . . takes after another branch of the family & got through it best. I am, in some ways, like my father, but I have a lot of my mother's managing, domineering strain in me. I used to stand between my father & her, & stand up against her on my own account. But I have in me (what you have so much more strongly) a fearful streak of conscience, & sense of duty, complicated by a sensitiveness that is nothing less than a disease. The conscience has been my undoing. At that time I thought She is my mother: I owe her respect & devotion. I must bow to properly constituted authority (fearful little prig that I was, I used to go about mouthing that phrase to myself—I got it from some accursed book—& crushing down all that was best in me with it. 'Properly—constituted—authority' Lord!) & so I was a kind of buffer she hurled herself against. . . .

"Well, I needn't go on. . . . It warped my character & spoiled my life & my health & my mind. The older I got the more I felt it & the more I longed for freedom. . . . It is my belief that she first killed my father & then killed herself. Oh! Not murder in any legal sense—though it ought to be. But separated (mostly) from his home & his interests, & constantly snubbed & corrected he began to be often ill, & then he got internal trouble & died, I think of pure unhappiness. Afterwards she died: of brooding, & self-pity, &—well—and selfishness. It is really awful to think how glad I was. I sometimes still wonder whether my constant longing for her death had anything to do with killing her.

"Well. That's that.

"Now what about it all.

"It couldn't really happen now . . . girls have emancipated themselves & expect to go out into the world & live their lives as boys do. And yet, how burning a question, this of the exaction of parents, remains. . . . I am sure her little illnesses and 'nervous depression' & final collapse were self-induced. If she had had the teaching of the little book & *lived* it—the constant turning from the negative suggestion, the sinking of 'personality' in 'principle,' the keeping the high thought always on top, she would have saved herself alive, & done much more than that in her reactions on us.

"Another thought . . . the conflicts of temperaments is nature's way of averaging the race. Nature thrusts men & women into the arms of their opposites . . . ordinary, commonplace people are attracted by unlikeness: the strong by the weak, the passionate by the calm, the dark by the fair. In marriage this causes untold unhappiness . . . brought about by the clash of temperaments. We constantly blame only one, & probably the wrong one. For the troubles of my youth my mother seemed entirely to blame, but on mature reflection I see that is a wrong view. We were to blame as much as she was. We humoured her, we gave way, we were 'unselfish,' we effaced ourselves: in short, to look it squarely in the face—we were weak and gave way to FEAR. I believe that fear, concealed in a thousand disguises, is the worst enemy of the race, the most crippling disability we have brought down from our primitive ancestors, who, probably, lived always in fear (please consider this carefully—it applies to many things besides mothers). I was afraid of her. Afraid of the pain she could cause me, afraid of failing in my duty (that bugbear!) towards her. If I had had the pluck, the courage, the determination, the decent straightness to say 'Damn duty: I will take my life into my own hands & develop as

I know I can develop & let other people face their own problems, no matter how "wicked" it is according to my governors, teachers & spiritual pastors & masters'—I now believe that would have pulled her together, made her control herself, respect me & be a better & wiser woman.

"Then another thing.

"I don't believe, as far as I can remember, that I was born with a dislike of children—perhaps I was. But, anyway, my own home life made me firmly resolve never to be the mother of a child who might suffer as I had suffered. . . . As I grew older I saw many, & better, reasons for sticking to my resolution . . . I was told it was my duty to contribute my share to the maintenance of the race. I said I was living in what I considered to be an over-populated country, & I saw no immediate prospect of the disappearance of the race: also I did not desire to produce cannon-fodder. But they said I was a remarkable person & I should hand on my qualities. I said it did not appear that distinguished people had distinguished descendants: great men & women are 'sports' usually. And so on.

"But there is another side to this question. No one must say 'Because of my heredity, I will not have children.' The finest people come from the most unexpected &, apparently, the most unlikely & unfortunate combinations. You & I & G.B.S. are all instances of this. There is no way, so far, devised of finding out from what forebears the most useful & the finest specimens will come—even physically—not to speak of mentally. Besides we do not know what sort of men and women we want. We have no standard. Julius Caesar was an epileptic.

"There! I feel so much better for saying all that. I've never put any of it down in black & white before, & looked at it. The fatal mistake, I find, is to keep these things locked up like guilty secrets & brood upon them. Bring them out to the surface: let the daylight shine on them & the Sun of Righteousness will shrivel up the pettiness, & meanness, & make Wisdom & Beauty.

"Ever,

"C.F.S."

Lawrence was posted to Karachi in 1927, and they corresponded regularly. In one of Lawrence's letters he showed great interest in the trial of Roger Casement.[3] Charlotte wrote to him from Stresa, on September 15, 1927:

"You tell me you have my first letter from here. I distrust the ways of this careless country—but such a dear country!—How terribly hateful England appears to me now! You say 'This is to be the only letter to you this week.' But I have had two! two!! two!!! You spoil me.

"About Casement. You say 'This letter will not please you.' WHY? Your opinion of Casement is deeply interesting to me. I do so wish you had gone on to say how much you know about him because that might have saved me a lot of writing; &, perhaps, telling you things you know already. For I must inform you now of all I know of Casement in case any of it is new to you.

"When Casement was arrested & brought to England we were, of course, much moved, but really did not pay exceptional attention to the matter, as we only knew him in a general way, our paths never having lain together. But very shortly there appeared at Adelphi Terrace a Miss Gertrude Bannister & asked for an interview. We saw her. She was an Irishwoman of a fine type: sensible, shrewd, capable, responsible; at that moment teacher in a girls' school near London. She told us she was Roger Casement's cousin: that their two families had been brought up together as children and were like brothers & sisters, but that she and Roger had been special friends. It was evident that she was deeply attached to him. She said she had just come from the prison where she had taken him a change of clothes & some little comforts. Roger was soaked to the skin, you know, when arrested as the collapsible boat collapsed too soon & he & the other man had some difficulty in getting ashore. The people who took him would do nothing for him. She came to us in the first place for some money help, &, in the second, to ask if we would work with her to get together a little group of people to attempt to work up some real defence for him.

"Well, I liked her—and it was not difficult to persuade G.B.S. to

[3] Irish nationalist who, after a career in the British consular service which earned him a knighthood, turned rebel and visited Germany in 1914, as anti-British propagandist. Arrested in 1916, when he landed from a German submarine on the Irish coast, near Tralee.

do everything in his power. We got a little knot of people together —Casement's solicitor, Gavin Duffy, and others. So few! alas! (wartime, it was!) We had many meetings. G.B.S. wrote out what he thought Casement ought to do. That was, not to employ counsel; to *defend himself* (he was a fine speaker): not to deny anything, to acknowledge facts and to say they did not make him guilty: that his country had declared herself free and that he had a right to work for his country's freedom and be treated as, what he was, a prisoner of war.

"Casement wouldn't take his advice: he was just not big enough.

"He sent most grateful messages but said he was in the hands of his legal advisers and that they said they must conduct the case, but that he, Casement, should make a statement afterwards from the dock.

"They did for him. When the trial came of course precisely what we feared happened. F.E.[4] was damnable: treated the whole with consummate insolence, *de haut en bas*. Casement's counsel, Sullivan (a man I knew, to my sorrow, over other things), made an excited speech for hours and hours and hours—bored everyone to tears—and then broke down and fainted. They passed sentence, and then— Casement got up and made the speech G.B.S. had sketched for him. He made a profound sensation with it, and several of the jury said afterwards that if they had heard all that before retiring the verdict would have been different. Of course it was too late and could do nothing to change the result.

"It will always be one of my deep personal regrets that I did not go to the trial. I felt at the time it was like running after a sensation —thinking of myself, you see, & not of Casement. Gertrude told me afterwards he had said he hoped his friends would go, as it would help him to know that there was sympathy near him. But she did not tell me till afterwards. Also she, & a few other Irishwomen, went & knelt outside the prison at the time he was hanged. But they did not tell me. She said they thought I 'might not like it!'

"Well, now, there is this dreadful thing to tell you.

"Sept. 16

"During the meetings at Adelphi Terrace of our little gang,

4 F. E. Smith, a brilliant counsel, afterwards Lord Birkenhead.

after it had been going on for some time, suddenly a shattering piece of 'information' was flung into the middle of us. There were diaries. Casement's diaries had been seized: found in some trunks he had left in some lodgings—somewhere. And these diaries—! Then there were dark hints. The diaries had been written in Putumayo, I think it was—'notes—observations—impossible to describe —could not be mentioned before a lady—most unfortunate—!' Of course we got angry & said: 'Suggestions: hints to injure him.' Then Mr. Massingham (of whom you may have heard: an intimate friend of ours: Editor for years of The Nation, a paper he made famous for a sort of knight errantry, taking up the case of every under-dog and going for every highly-placed littleness & meanness & inefficiency) one of our little party, doing all in his power to help, went to Scotland Yard & demanded, as a prominent journalist, to be told the truth of this matter. And he came back and said they had *shown him the diaries.* Massingham was, of all the people I have met, one of the least squeamish; one of the least likely to be surprised by any ordinary or extraordinary moral obliquities, or impressed by any kind of human frailty; but he said he had never seen or imagined such things. He said he could not give time to read all through, but he sampled the writings very thoroughly; & he told us they were as bad as it was possible to conceive, & they undoubtedly appeared to be in Casement's handwriting.

"It was a crushing blow. We were (or rather our little committee was) rather knocked to pieces. Gertrude Bannister, who of course declared that her knowledge of Roger made much a thing appear to be impossible, could only say at last that his health had been knocked to bits in the tropics; that he had had a long nervous illness and, at times, had been practically 'off his head.' She could only imagine that *if* he had written such things (unless for scientific or medical purposes) he must have been mad at the time.

"To this day I have not solved this mystery. These diaries were never mentioned at the trial. Some of his enemies took great credit to themselves for this & made it out to be very generous—no doubt the diaries would have appeared quick enough (if genuine) had there been any chance of an acquittal, but you could go nowhere in London at the time without hearing this scandal whispered. It was put about in influential peoples' houses: discussed in low tones in drawing-rooms: shouted in Clubs: there were tiny, obscure little paragraphs in society papers—I don't know—I wish I did. The thing entirely killed any English sympathy there might have been for Casement; & I myself think, had it not been for this, even in war-time, they wouldn't have dared to hang him.

"I possess a copy of a diary of Casement's I prize very much. His diary from before he left America the last time to go to Germany. It covers the voyage, & some time he spent in Norway, secretly, with interesting sidelights upon the character of the then British Minister in Norway. Also the subsequent time in Germany & his start for Ireland in the submarine. It is this Figgis quotes. It has never been published, I think, but privately printed. Gertrude Bannister gave me the copy I have. I also have some writings of Casement's about world politics which show what a clear, logical thinker he was—I got these from America & some little poems. I wonder—will I ever have the chance of showing you these—& the copy of the speech G.B.S. sketched for him!

"I am so glad you are a friend of Casement. Perhaps some day you will find out about those diaries for me.

"Blessings always,
"C.F.S."

[In 1935, John Buchan had apparently suggested to Lawrence that he should do some more writing, for in a letter to Buchan from Clouds Hill, dated 1-4-35, Lawrence said:

". . . A novel—no, I think not: my writing practice has all been to put down more and more exactly what I have seen or felt: invention would come very hard. A biography—yes, I had wanted to write Casement, Sir Roger; but the obstacle is that the Government refuse all access to those confiscated diaries from which purported extracts were circulated to influential people when he was condemned; and without them there cannot be a life of him written."]

Charlotte and Lawrence had many mutual friends, and she would often write and tell him about her visits to country houses, to dinner parties where she had met interesting people, and the luncheons which had become an established part of her own pattern of hospitality. There were sad occasions, too. On October 10, 1927, she sent him a description of the cremation of H. G. Wells's wife:

"Now I've just come back from the cremation of Jane Wells at Golders Green. It was dreadful—dreadful—*dreadful!* I haven't been so upset . . . for a long time. G.B.S.'s sister was cremated there some years ago. Then he himself arranged a sort of service which consisted of his reciting some poems—I remember one was 'Fear no more the heat of the sun'—I was so fearfully afraid he'd 'dry up' (that is what actors call it when your forget your 'lines') and, in between, he gave us an address which was exactly right. He just dared any of Lucy's friends to sigh and lament and pull long faces about her—and he sent us away bright and cheery and hopeful, and full of 'go.'

"(But today! My stars!)

"The little chapel (you were there for Doughty, weren't you?) was full of people when we arrived: but Gyp, the elder son, took us up to an empty pew at the very front. He and his brother Frank and their wives were sitting in a corresponding pew on the other side. A moment after, H.G. came up the aisle with a tall old man— I thought—Balfour?—but he wasn't—a sort of stage Balfour—Dr. T. E. Page, who took his seat at a reading desk on the platform. H.G. (who had meant to sit with his boys) hesitated a moment and then came and sat with us. Then the organ began a terrible dirge. We all stood up—and stood for what seemed hours and hours and hours, while that organ played on our nerves and senses and knocked them to pieces. H.G. began to cry like a child—tried to hide it at first and then let go. After centuries of torment the organist stopped (if he hadn't I'm sure in two more minutes G.B.S. would have gone up to the organ loft and killed him) and we all sat down, and pseudo-Balfour began to read a paper, written, as he told us, by Wells. It was terrible beyond anything words can describe: a soul in torment—self torture. He drowned us in a sea of misery and as we were gasping began a panegyric of Jane which made her appear as a delicate, flowerlike, gentle being, surrounding itself with beauty and philanthropy and love. Now Jane was one of the strongest characters I ever met. She managed H.G. and her good curious sons and her circle generally according to her own very definite and very original theories—with almost unbroken success—*from the point of view of her theories*. Then there came a place where the address said 'she never resented a slight; she never gave voice to a harsh judgment.' At that point the audience, all more or less acquainted with many details of H.G.'s private life, thrilled, like corn under a wet north wind—and H.G.—H.G. positively howled. You are no doubt aware that he was not a conventionally perfect husband—and the slights Jane did not resent . . .

"O it was hideous—terrible and frightful. I am an old woman and there is one thing I seem, at least, to have learned. The way of transgressors is hard . . .

"But that is enough. To write like this will seem to you exaggerated—and in 'shocking bad taste!'

"The moment the coffin was shoved through the door into the furnace, and H.G. and the boys went round, G.B.S. and I trotted through another door into the garden and I took quite a little time to get quiet. Then we went into the yard to look for the car and found the rest of the congregation—mostly in tears (it was as bad as that). First thing I knew Lopokova flung herself into my arms sobbing and shaking. A tiny thing she is: she felt like a bit of thistledown that had been out in a rainstorm. Then Sydney Olivier, with red eyes, held out a shaking hand: and Virginia[5] herself, looking very stately and calm, and remote, relieved me of Lopokova. . . .

"G.B.S., of course, began to 'behave badly' at once, making jokes to everyone, and finally—putting H.G. into his car—he actually got a sort of grin out of *him*.

"Then we came back here. But I am ten years older!"

The Adelphi had been scheduled for demolition, and Charlotte had to look for another flat in London, because the Georgian terrace where they lived would disappear. She found a flat in Whitehall Court which had previously been occupied by Countess Russell, of *Elizabeth and Her German Garden* fame. G.B.S. had got used to Adelphi Terrace and disliked the upheaval, but they had to move, and the Whitehall Court flat had the advantage of being in a service block, with a restaurant. It was a good deal more convenient than

[5] Virginia Woolf.

10, Adelphi Terrace, and as they were on the fourth floor, they had a pleasant view of the river from the balcony.

Charlotte disliked the idea of the move as much as did her husband, and she wrote about it to Lawrence. A letter which she sent him on October 13, 1927, apparently refers to some observations he had made on the move.

"Our journey was as comfortable and successful as a journey could possibly be, and did not tire us. The arrival at Whitehall Court was as crushing as you predicted. It was exactly as you said: but it was not all the poor secretaries [sic] fault. The terrible truth is that the Adelphi Terrace furniture does not suit Whitehall Court and does not look right there. Partly inherent incompatibility, partly that our eyes, accustomed to it as it was could not bear it as it is. The rooms are much lighter at Whitehall Court, and the things look shabby and second-hand! The first view was awful, but already this week, after some repose at Ayot, it is better. I had a lot of things changed.

"How I would like a little time really *to myself!* But I know that cannot be until I follow Jane into that furnace, and I don't want to do that—yet. There is no address for letters there—

"C.F.S."

Charlotte's strong feelings on behalf of Ireland had not abated with the passage of years. On December 19, 1927, she sent Lawrence a long description of a luncheon at Trent Park, Sir Philip Sassoon's country house, when she suddenly and unexpectedly "let herself go," as she afterwards remembered:

"On Sunday a day at Trent (please, the cold is so intense my hands are paralysed—and if the writing is wobbly that is why—*not* old age!) Winston and Mrs. Churchill and Lord Hugh Cecil and other members of the peerage (a fresh pen & better?) and various fragile exotic-looking American women (really made of steel) with inconspicuous husbands. At luncheon I found myself between Sir Philip and an empty place. I thought 'Now *who*? I won't be able to bear one of those American men today, nor Lord D'Abernon!' About four minutes later there sailed into the empty place— Lord Hugh. I mentally thanked God, and turned to cope with Sir Philip who was chaffing me. Now I am no good at chaffing or back chat, I am slow and stupid and have no repartee. It didn't matter then in the least, for he waltzed on, not stopping for reply. If he was not entirely above suspicion I should have said 'too many cocktails.' But he is safe about that. Presently he began to scold the servants; and to do that in public always appears to me a deep offence. So I turned a shoulder, almost imperceptibly, but so that it made a barrier, and listened with my other ear. The Prayer Book. I thought so. Splendid! this will do. I had to wait a long time, for he was well started, and his other neighbour quite intelligent. After a while, at a suitable moment, I whispered 'Disestablishment?'

"You know Lord Hugh, of course: his little crumpled up, clever face, and his long, lean, ascetic-looking body, which doesn't prevent him from eating a hearty luncheon and doing full justice to excellent drinks (no doubt he fasts Fridays). He swung round as if a pin had been driven into him.

Lord Hugh. Disestablishment! Of course! *That* is the question—you may well ask.

Myself. Do you dread it, or do you want it?

Lord Hugh. (Emphatically: pulling himself together) I neither dread it nor want it. If it is to come, I am ready for it.

Myself. In Ireland the Disestablishment of the Church of the Protestant ascendancy proved to be a practically unqualified benefit—especially to the Church itself which, from a scandal, becomes a reputable and well-managed institution. Not too poor, either.

Lord Hugh. Ah, poor. The money, of course, must remain with the Church, under any circumstances.

Myself. The money! Would you keep the tithes, and the other worldly possessions?

Lord Hugh. Most assuredly. I could not for a moment consent that they should be alienated from religion, or devoted to secular uses. But I should be content to share them with other religious bodies. I would not consent to their being used for purposes of mere benevolence—hospitals, and such things.

Myself.   I see your idea. But—one has heard of the disciples of Our Lady Poverty! the incentive of Necessity: the disembarrassing oneself of the thick clay—?

Lord Hugh.   But—yes—of course—but—do you know how poor they are already?

Myself.   (Frankly laughing) Well, certainly. I have heard of poor curates. Perhaps the other view is out of date. (changing the subject) A very difficult and critical position, for a member of the House with a conscience, that division on Thursday. And the result— a simple No Popery vote—leaves a still more ticklish problem.

Lord Hugh.   Yes: indeed. A problem only to be solved by Divine Guidance.

Myself.   (Very deferentially) Lord Hugh—I speak most sincerely—I am really asking for information—Conscience I know. If we speak of conscience I think you and I will understand each other. But will you tell me—what is Divine Guidance?

Lord Hugh.   (Very kindly and earnestly: but hortatory-pedagogic) Divine Guidance is knowledge of the will of God coming to us through the direction of His vice-regents here: the government and authorities He has set over us, and His ministers and representatives. Do you know the Articles of the Church?

Myself.   Yes: fairly well.

Lord Hugh.   Perhaps you remember that one says (quoting) 'that prerogative which we see to have been given always to all godly Princes in Holy Scriptures by God Himself: that is, that they should rule all estates and decrees committed to their charge by God, whether they be Ecclesiastical or Temporal'—it is in obedience to such authority that Divine Guidance becomes manifest.

Myself.   You don't find it a disturbing thought that the power of such authorities almost always originated through violence and destruction?

Lord Hugh. (Very earnestly) No—not in the least. They could
            not be there but by the grace of God, sustaining them,
            and we must submit ourselves to His will. That is
            how we come to find Divine Guidance.
Myself.   I think I understand. You would say we must submit
            ourselves to properly constituted authority.
Lord Hugh. Yes: that is what I mean.
Myself.   (Reflectively) You don't know how it interests me to
            hear you say that. (A pause.) But how about rebel-
            lions? There have been rebellions history has more
            than justified.
Lord Hugh. Ah: rebellions. The justification of rebellions depends
            upon the amount of wrong rebelled against.
Myself.   My own country has rebelled continuously for some-
            where about seven centuries, and we think she has
            come out justified at the latter end. I'm Irish.
Lord Hugh. (Sharply: his face tying itself into ugly knots, and
            taking on for a moment an expression really cruel and
            fanatical) In my opinion nothing justifies murder.
Myself.   (Lightly and confidentially) Now will you, please,
            explain to me something I want to know *so much*.
            What is the difference between killing and murder?
            English and French killed Germans in the war. Was
            that murder?
Lord Hugh. Certainly not. Obviously not. It was done in obedi-
            ence to the authorities in defence of the realm. (Quot-
            ing another Article) 'It is lawful for Christian men,
            at the commandment of the magistrate to wear
            weapons and serve in the wars.'
Myself.   Yes: I remember. But will you remember that my
            country—the only Christian country who has kept her
            Church unchanged down through the ages, in the
            face of bitter persecution, and of temptation—my
            country proclaimed itself a Republic, and the author-
            ities and ministers of that Republic declared war
            against England. You can't have it both ways. Were
            the killings done by order of these ministers any more

murders than the killing of the English by Germans?

Lord Hugh. Obviously there is no similarity between the cases. The French, the English and Germans had the status of belligerents conferred by established authority. The Irish set-up has authority for their own convenience. You cannot give yourself the status of belligerent. You must receive it from—from—

Myself. (Interrupting) —a very properly constituted authority—

"I must really drop this silly nonsense, which seems to me now as if it only was written to make myself look clever & poor Lord Hugh a fool. *Which he is not.* I do not say all this conversation actually took place—what I am prepared to swear is that I have not misrepresented Lord Hugh's views, as they were unfolded to me, in any essential. What comes out of it for you & me should be a feeling of chastened satisfaction & relief—a dutiful thankfulness—that the Arabs were given (though late) the Status of Belligerents; and some gratification in having at last found out what that means; even though Michael Collins & his fellows remain written down as murderers.

"And that brings me to something I want to say.

"After a little hesitation I am sending you a book called Jane Carroll. The hero is, of course, Michael Collins. Her name I somehow don't feel inclined to write: but the veil is very thin: I don't think you can help knowing who she is. I have talked to her a lot about the book. She is what one calls a 'friend' of mine. I am fond of her personally & admire her in some ways, though she often makes me squirm! About this book, for instance. I think she is proud of it, & glad it has been written. That shocks me to the depths of my soul. I have never asked her if any of the incidents ever took place, but she told me once, 'I *was* in an ambush with him'— which makes me think none of the other things happened as they are described. Michael, of course, was not killed the way the book says: he was killed in an ambush by the republicans—given away, almost certainly, by the driver of his car. I told you I was in Ireland then: so was this friend: we were both in Dublin. Michael was

killed in Co. Cork. That time brought us together in a way nothing else could have done . . . Michael and a number of others had
made a vow to keep chaste & sober for 3 years at the time they had
declared the Republic, & (one can never *know*) I am almost ·
certain in my own mind Michael did not break that vow. If he had
I think it not improbable one of the others would have killed him,
as it describes in this book. The author of J C is not an Irishman,
but has lived 12 years in, or near, Cork. He has caught my friend's
little clever way of talking—her wit & readiness, & her—diplomatic
ability, remarkably well. She *is* beautiful, even still, & has a charm
far more rare than her beauty."

On January 16, 1928, Charlotte wrote Lawrence an account of
Thomas Hardy's funeral in Westminster Abbey. She had secured
a seat in the middle of the south transept:

"And now I have come from the burial of Thomas Hardy's ashes
in the Abbey. . . . G.B.S. was a pall-bearer. He walked to pair with
Mr. Galsworthy, but as the catafalque was high and great they
were completely separated from one another. It seemed absurd to
have an immense bier and a great and splendid pall, white, em-
broidered with royal crowns and many other emblems enclose one
small casket, but it made its effect. The service was very beautifully
sung and I have never heard anything better read than the lesson
'Let us now praise famous men.' The clergy came first and shocked
me. All except one looked full of worldly pomp & disdain; self-
conscious jacks-in-office—but that one, young, appeared wrapped
from the world. Then came the catafalque, & after some men
friends: finally Mrs. Hardy with Mr. Cockerell. The first time they
passed she looked erect & calm, but was so completely swathed in
crape that her face was invisible; as she passed back she was hang-
ing on to Mr. Cockerell's arm, & seemed completely broken. The
service at the grave (I did not see it) must have been terribly trying
for her. . . . Mr. Cockerell was splendid. He gives the impression
(sometimes) of restraining emotion, but I don't think he feels anything very deeply.

"Before me was Jack Squire and his pretty young wife. He
looked old and battered—getting grey on the top of his head—&
rather—well—Behind me was Mr. Tomlinson. I am very fond of

Mr. Tomlinson. I felt him there all the time, &, at a very moving moment, I just turned slightly to catch his eye & I saw him transfixed,[6] with tears rolling slowly down his face. When it was all over I managed to get close to him for a moment in the crowd, & told him (with difficulty, he is so deaf!) about Gallion's Reach. His poor, sad, tired little face lighted up—and he *laughed!*

"Then a wonderful thing happened. On that glorious organ an almost divine organist played the Dead March from *Saul.* I say advisedly that was among the most splendid things of my life. He began very low and soft and gradually opened out, making one's whole being thrill to each great phrase, up to a most marvellous burst of great chords—confident, assertive, triumphant. Ah, it takes Handel to say the last word. He never fails me. If anyone talks to me now of doubts and fears & minor keys, &—sad stories of the deaths of kings—I shall say—But I *know.*"

At the end of March, 1928, Lawrence sent Charlotte a manuscript copy of *The Mint,* his outspoken account of barrack-room life in the R.A.F. He had begun the draft of the book at Clouds Hill, and took the notes with him to Karachi, writing out the manuscript in pencil and then in ink. He had already told Charlotte about his intention of doing this book, and she had twice asked him to send her his draft. He appears to have sent her both versions, for she wrote telling him that the first reading, in "those large, corrected scraps of paper, was too difficult and too slow to give the book fair play. One was so checked by illegible passages, by references impossible to follow, by erasures, that one halts through it, often losing the thread, and with the rhythm gone, and it got no honest chance. But *now*—reading it straight on, easily without checks, it makes its full impression, and one can know all it really is, and estimate its worth to the extent of one's ability. *It is a splendid thing.* Heart searching in its depth and force . . ."

Lawrence's reply indicates how surely he felt he could count on her for sympathy and understanding.

[6] At the foot of this page in the original, G.B.S. has written in red ink: "Sic. but she means transfigured." This letter is part of Charlotte's correspondence with T. E. Lawrence which Bernard Shaw did not read until after her death.

"Karachi
8. 5. 28

". . . I have got your letter of April 15 before me . . . I've had an
Ayot feeling over me lately. . . . It would be good to see you again,
& talk to you, and see G.B.S. again, and talk to him. . . .

"Your liking it [*The Mint*] pleases me very much. I had not
expected that. It is so raw: deliberately so raw. Everything in it
designed to emphasise the flesh of man, leading a life which is only
of the body, & therefore growing, as I see it, very natural souls. . . .

"My mother is at a little London boarding-house. I wonder how
you will like her. She is monumental, really: and so unlike you.
Probably she is exactly like me; otherwise we wouldn't so hanker
after one another, whenever we are wise enough to keep apart.
Her letters are things I dread, and she always asks for more of
mine (I try to write monthly: but we haven't a subject we dare
be intimate upon: so they are spavined things) and hates them
when they come, as they do, ever so rarely. I think I'm afraid of
letting her get, ever so little, inside the circle of my integrity: and
she is always hammering and sapping to come in. A very dominant
person: only old now, and, so my brother says, very much less than
she had been.

"She has so lived in her children, & in my father, that she cannot relieve herself, upon herself, and from herself, at all. And it
isn't right to cry out to your children for love. They are prevented,
by the walls of time and function, from loving their parents. . . ."

In a letter written about the same time:

"Still at Karachi . . . I shall be glad when I know the best or
worst of my change and have got bedded down in the new camp.
Uprooting and re-potting are two discomforts for the plant.

"I'd like to howl and beat my head against the ground outside
the house of that unknown man in the R.T.C. who stole my St.
Joan proof from me. It is a wrong instinct, this cherishing of relics:
but it's wronger still of him to be cherishing my relic. . . . If you
see an unknown copy in the sale-room lists will you ask whose it
was? I'd like to bear the fellow a named grudge. He knew it was a
rarity, for I kept it always in my box, with my two or three treasures,
and not on my bookshelf . . . down with all relics, though . . . we

shouldn't have any relics. Yet I collect them . . . the flesh is un-
commonly contradictory, as material, isn't it?"

Lawrence had found his friendship with Charlotte a valuable
safety valve; he felt natural with her, able to say anything he
liked. He had also grown attached to her, and worried when she
occasionally mentioned that she had been laid up.

"Your illness grows worse in character," he said in a letter,
"every light you throw on it. You must have been dangerously ill.
Nothing of that sort was to be divined from your letters at the
time. I've looked back: they are tired, but quite calm. Do you
know, I think I treat you more confidently than you do me? At
least I seem to tell you everything that happens to me every week."

Lawrence continued to write very long letters; detailed analyses
of books which Charlotte had sent him, and his opinions on contemporary writers and public figures.

"17. 5. 28

"On the 23rd. my move is: to Peshawar . . . I will write to you
from there . . . and tell you what my new address will be, and how
the new conditions strike me. . . . I clutch my place in the R.A.F.
like a lifebuoy, because if it went from me I would sink, straight
away. I hope the Mint will not make Trenchard hate me. He is so
very kind and large: but it offends against his tradition of loyalty, &
perhaps he will think me a scab for betraying my service. . . .

"Last week I read Ethel Smythe's latest. I confess she slightly
jars me. Perhaps, in the days she remembers, women were oppressed: but I see little traces of it today. If many of them feel like
her, the boot will soon be on the other foot. . . . The other book
was Rose Macaulay's. I wonder how autobiographical it was? A
queer queer book . . . you say G.B.S. reads her particularly. That is
extraordinary. What do I read, particularly? D.H.L., Forster, Tomlinson, Theodore Powys, H.G.W., G.B.S., James Stephens, Yeats; I
suppose there are many others. But then I'm not 70 but 40. G.B.S.
has read everything, probably, in his time."

He had made a translation of the *Odyssey* while he was in
Karachi, and sent batches to Charlotte for comment. She was at
that time very much occupied with the Standard Edition of Shaw's
works, which she was helping G.B.S. and his secretary to get

ready; but she made time to go through Lawrence's script, and pencilled many comments in the margins before sending it back to India.

After his return to England, Lawrence kept in touch with the Shaws; there are not many letters relating to this period. G.B.S. and Charlotte gave T.E.L. a new motor-bicycle, and when they were at home he sometimes paid them flying visits, as he had done in earlier years. There were months, however, when they did not see him, and for Charlotte, at least, the bonds of friendship were loosening a little. It was inevitable that sooner or later she should become impatient with Lawrence's devious ways, though she still kept her admiration and affection for him. One of the last letters she wrote to him was on the voyage to South Africa which she and G.B.S. took in 1935:

> "In the Red Sea,
> 7 April, 1935

"The glow of the Suez Canal as came through this time will be unforgettable—the colouring beat everything I have seen in this region before, and that is saying much. Of course we thought and spoke of you. Here, too—

"We are well—frozen for the first 10 days, and now grilling, we survive.

"Port Sudan—yes—I wonder what its future will be. It has a noble range of mountains.

> "C.F.S."

T. E. Lawrence met his death soon afterwards: he was killed in a crash on the motor-bicycle which had been the Shaws' gift to him. Charlotte received a letter from Dorothy Walker, the daughter of Emery Walker, a friend of Shaw's in his younger days. Dolly Walker knew of Charlotte's friendship with T.E.L. and had written at once. Charlotte replied on June 24, 1935, after her return home to Ayot:

"Thank you dear Dolly for your letter. You understand! I was so thankful to be away when it happened. The South African papers made a giant deal of it but there was not the vulgar excitement there has been here. How he suffered from that all his life! I am not sure this is not better for *him*. He always dreaded pain &

the idea of death (as a sort of sign of defeat!) and now, you see, he has got off without knowing anything about it. I somehow cannot feel he is really gone—he seems to be here in this little house he came to so often."

Four years later, on March 6, 1939, she said in another letter to Dorothy Walker, after the publication of a collection of his letters:

"I think T.E. meant his letters to be published. He was an inexpressibly complicated person. In a sense he was tragically sincere. But, also, he always had one eye on the limelight. You say you are thankful I do not allow any of my letters to be published. Now I feel this book shows they ought to be published just to show how much better he could be than anything that's in that [word crossed out] I think he would always have grinned at the idea of any one 'mothering' him. But, in the end, he was very dreadfully lonely. The strangest contact of my life."

18

WIFE TO A FAMOUS MAN

(1922–1943)

Long ago, the Parisian palmist, M. Desbarrolles, whom Charlotte had consulted at the gay command of Edith Somerville, had foretold:

"Marriage of love with a distinguished person, long life. Loves distinguished persons, and wide search for distinction in herself or husband."

Many people still living remember Charlotte as always being in the background, standing apart from the distinguished person whose wife she was; the limelight which isolated G.B.S. from others wherever he went make this impression inevitable. So far as Charlotte was concerned, she preferred to remain in the background on public and social occasions. She detested publicity as much as G.B.S. enjoyed it, but she understood her famous man very well, and was quite fiercely insistent that he should be appreciated for his genius, and should always get his due. There were times, nevertheless, when she suddenly became impatient of his incorrigible acting instinct. Leonora Ervine remembers an occasion when guests arriving for a luncheon party were received

by Charlotte alone. Turning to Mrs. Ervine, Charlotte whispered:
"I do wish G.B.S. wouldn't wait to make an entrance, but would
receive with me!"

Sure enough, when all the guests were assembled in the drawing-
room, G.B.S. made his entrance, and was soon "coruscating."

They were settled at Ayot St. Lawrence and now had no
thought of moving; G.B.S. had bought the Rectory after renting it
for twenty years, and kept bees and pigeons as a hobby, the
gardener adding the care of these to his other duties. G.B.S. and
Charlotte both suffered much from minor illnesses as they grew
older, Shaw easily catching cold and influenza, and Charlotte
having a great deal of trouble with pains in her back. They still
went abroad as much as they could, and now it was G.B.S. who
was quite glad to go travelling. He found that when he was away
he could write without interruptions; at Ayot and in London there
were visitors, telephone calls which he could not avoid answering,
decisions to make. More than ever did he dislike being distracted
from the one thing that mattered to him: his work.

In January, 1925, they went to Madeira, staying at Reid's Hotel
in Funchal. Charlotte wrote to Sydney Cockerell:

"We are well, among flowers & sunshine & lizards. Bathing every
day & staying in a most exceedingly comfortable hotel. G.B.S. looks
about 20 years younger than when he left London! Our grumble
is the climate: it is very relaxing & in spite of all our mercies, we
feel suicidal most of the time. G.B.S. is doing a lot of work. He
writes from breakfast to 12 o'clock: then we go & swim. He is busy
with a little book on Socialism; it began as a sort of text-book, but
is developing into bold generalisations qualified to startle be-
ginners."

The "little book on Socialism" was to be his reply to a request
made to him by Sissy, who had written asking him for a leaflet on
socialism, as she wanted to explain it in simple terms to her
Women's Institute in Shropshire. [The leaflet grew into *The
Intelligent Woman's Guide to Socialism and Capitalism*, and took
G.B.S. three years to write.]

He was ill again after his return from Madeira, and on June 1,
1925, Charlotte wrote to Sydney Cockerell:

"I am glad to say G.B.S. continues to improve, & now only needs
to get his strength back. We are going to stay with the Sidney
Webbs on Saturday next for some days—that will be his 'change
of air'—you know they have a little house in Hampshire now.
G.B.S. is engaged to debate with H. Belloc on the 9th. & we are
rather dreading that, but he wants to do it, if possible: he would
go up to London for the day for it. He will stay quietly here at
Ayot till Saturday. . . . He is *not* writing a play on St. Teresa!"

They motored to Scotland in August, "leaving nothing to be
explored but Faroe, Iceland and the North Pole," as Shaw remarked in a letter to the Webbs. Beatrice was writing her auto-
biography, and she sent them a draft of the first four chapters, for
their comments. G.B.S. replied from Malvern, where they were
staying for a few days:

"The book is certainly unique: I cannot recall anything like it
before." After a long critique of several of the sections, he added:

"The Victorian reserve about your love affairs is funny in these
shameless psycho analytical days. It even suggests that they were
affairs instead of states of mind. . . . To what extent was your
sociological work relieved and saved from staleness by interests and
trains of imagination that were more or less sexual—say romantic?
. . . had you ever an intellectual hero, and a lump of a fleshly hero
simultaneously? Did you ever tell your love . . . how far did you
find yourself a critically judging self-controlling agent and how far
the helpless instrument of a force that landed you in interests that
appalled you by the incongruity of their objects?

"That is the sort of thing that might quite safely and decently
be put in without mentioning a single name or a single specific
incident. It would be, and indeed should be done lightly and un-
affectedly; but a complete finger-on-lip attitude produced the Victorian effect of at one stroke omitting a side of life without which
any picture of it must be scientifically incomplete . . ."

Charlotte enclosed a letter, saying that she was flattered at
Beatrice's request that she should also criticize the manuscript.
She agreed with G.B.S. about the personal romances:

"These necessarily modify a young woman's life to such an
enormous extent that to leave them out makes the subject a sort of

Frankenstein monster—outside human categories." She then went
on to attack a part of the manuscript which had not particularly
interested G.B.S., but about which she felt strongly herself.

"About Uncle Brian.[1] I was deeply disappointed that you leave
your association with him so slightly sketched . . . you say nothing
of what he taught you, what you gained from him, & what effect
it had upon you. I was eagerly looking forward to hearing about
this. Indian religions are a very profound subject. I have often
wondered, in later years, what Uncle Brian knew about them, &
what his attitude towards them was. I was too undeveloped at the
time I knew him to find out anything about his mind. . . . The
Christian part of the diary seems to contain nothing markedly different from the experiences of many thoughtful, impressionable
English girls of that date. The girls who later on in the century
turned to rationalism. I find a slight reminder all through of your
attitude of 25 years ago, which gave me such a shock when I
met you then. 'One metaphysic is as good as another,' you used to
say. There is a new spirit in the world now; &, if you retain the
passage in which you say something like: 'If I had my time over
again I think I would remain in the English church' . . . you will
find, I think, that that declaration, & the somewhat patronising
attitude of a good deal of that particular bit of your chapter, will
strike a number of people as far more cynical than you recognise it
to be."

Beatrice Webb wrote in her Diary, May 1, 1925:

"G.B.S.'s letter is encouraging. Though he is evidently puzzled
as to what will be its effect—whether it will be a success or a
failure on publication. Charlotte does not like it (I gather from
her letter) in the main because her uncle, Brian Hodgson, is not
sufficiently appreciated! . . . And then Charlotte does not really
like me any more than I really like her: our continued friendly and
mutually respectful relations, and quite genuine loyalty and friendliness towards each other are a testimony to good manners in the
widest sense—to tolerance and kindliness on both sides."

There was a curious ambivalence in Beatrice's attitude towards

[1] Brian Hodgson, a distinguished Orientalist. The family connection with
Charlotte is not clear.

Charlotte, for, in spite of this entry in her private Diary, she liked receiving letters from Charlotte and wrote to her in affectionate terms.

The Shaws went to Stresa in the summer of 1926, as they both needed warmth and sunshine. Charlotte wrote to Beatrice Webb from the Regina Palace Hotel, where they were staying:

"Well, my news is good. G.B.S. really does seem brighter and better & stronger. I don't mean that he is anything like he was before his illness, but he is so very much better than he was when he left London, that it seems to be like a cure. We have been most fortunate in finding kind people here who have adored him, & spoiled him & taken every care of him. First, just across the water 3 miles or so from here Albert Coates has a villa. He is a very celebrated conductor—as you of course know—but what we did not know is that he is a magnetically charming person. He was brought up in Russia, where his father had a business, & has all the Russian spirituality with the English firmness & character. His wife we like too, & they have had a succession of interesting friends staying with them, among them a Prima Donna from Moscow who has never sung (in public) out of Russia, & who, G.B.S. thinks the best singer he ever heard. She used to sing to us for hours when she was here. It is at the Coates' villa we bathe—he has a large grassy garden, sloping down to the Lake, quite in the country. Here it is all roads & big hotels; but we prefer to live here & go over there, for the sake of comfortable rooms & good food. The Lake & its surroundings are lovely beyond description, & change so beautifully from day to day that it is impossible to get tired of them.

"Just at this moment G.B.S. is off at another corner of the Lake having his portrait done. You may possibly remember that some time ago (1912 we *think*) a bust was done of him by Prince Paul Troubetzkoi. We did not like it & had nearly forgotten it when suddenly Troubetzkoi turned up here. He has a villa on the Lake, a big studio & an astonishing wife. We lunched with them & he immediately entreated & insisted that he should do a figurine—a little statuette. He has done it & is now at work on a bust. It has been splendid as it has kept G.B.S. employed & amused going over day after day & sitting. You see, my great struggle has been to keep G.B.S. from working, & the luck has been in getting the Coates with their bathing & their music & Troubetzkoi with his artistic talk & his sittings to second me. I think both the figurine & the bust will be good in a way—but, to me, that is a secondary consideration!

"We have not yet settled the day we return, but I suppose it will be in the early part of October. G.B.S. seems very reluctant to go, & I dread the change of climate for him more than I can say. You see, for the last six months in England he really *never was warm* (to speak generally). Here he has got over that shiveriness and has been comfortable—but then it is really *hot* here—it has never been below 70 since we came, night or day, & sometimes over 80. . . ."

G.B.S. had his seventieth birthday while he was away, but, as usual, he would allow no celebration. Charlotte had tried to stop mention of it in the Continental press. Some months before, Siegfried Trebitsch had written to tell her that the anniversary was to be suitably celebrated in Austria and Germany, and she had re-plied by return post:

"You appal and horrify me! *Don't*, we pray you, have anything to do with such a thing. Stop it: smother it in every way you can. The Germans are sentimental, there is no doubt: and sentimental people are always unkind. They think of their own sentiments and not of the feelings of the other person. Can anything be more unkind than to call the attention of all Europe to the fact that a man is 70? If he was 17 or 170—not 70! . . . G.B.S. is really *very vexed about this.* I have seldom seen him more so. . . ."

*   *   *

In 1928, the Shaws began a friendship which was to bring them both a great deal of happiness. They became close friends with a boxer.

Gene Tunney's first contact with G.B.S. was a correspondence about doing a film of *Cashel Byron's Profession,* Shaw's novel with a pugilist hero. Tunney, an Irish-American, was the undefeated heavy-weight world champion, having defeated Jack Dempsey in 1926 and again in 1927; he retired from professional boxing in 1928.

The idea of the film was neither his nor Shaw's, and Gene Tunney refused the part because he was not an actor and was out of sympathy with the kind of man Cashel Byron was. In the summer of 1928, Tunney and his wife came to England, and the good-looking ex-boxer was fêted and asked everywhere. A dinner, to which the Shaws were invited, was given for him in London, but the Shaws were in the South of France. G.B.S. wrote to Tunney direct, regretting that they could not come to the dinner, and suggested meeting at some other time, away from cameras and journalists.

On December 14 of that year, Gene Tunney and Polly, his wife, went to lunch with the Shaws; the other guests included the Max Beerbohms and Maurice Baring. The attraction between the Shaws and the Tunneys was instantaneous. Before the end of the lunch, Charlotte and G.B.S. had decided to change plans they had made for going abroad the following spring, and to join the Tunneys for a holiday on the Adriatic island of Brioni, about which the young American couple were enthusiastic.

The linking between them, so quickly formed, was probably founded on the power some people have in bringing out the best qualities in others. Gene Tunney possessed the essential simplicities, complete sincerity, and the kind of uncomplicated goodness which sometimes goes with great physical strength. He and Shaw found that they had a lot in common, mainly about diet and not smoking or drinking. Tunney thought Charlotte one of the most charming and gracious women he had ever met, possessed of great kindness, and with beautiful manners: an opinion he was never to modify in any way. After more than thirty years he remembers her benign personality.

"It was wonderful to be with G.B.S., but Charlotte was a good half of it."

They all spent a month on Brioni in 1929, as they had planned. Polly Tunney was as delightful as her husband, and Charlotte felt at ease and happy with them both. The Tunneys had a boat, and there were water excursions; or they would go by horse-carriage to local beauty spots. On one of these trips they went to a lakeside restaurant for a meal. Gene Tunney praised the local wine and ordered a bottle, pouring out glasses for Charlotte, Polly and himself. Then the teetotal G.B.S. held out his glass, saying that he would like to taste a little of this highly recommended wine. Later in the holiday, on an occasion when G.B.S. was making remarks about drink, Gene Tunney laughingly teased him about the wine he had had on the day by the lake, saying:

"How can you pronounce a wine good or bad when you don't drink?"

Shaw replied:

"For thirty years Charlotte and I have entertained people, and we have always served wine with the meals, but Charlotte knew nothing of wines and left the selection to me. I always tasted them, and with no tobacco or meat to mar my palate I had the most excellent taste in wines—to such an extent that Charlotte used to complain of the size of our wine bills, because I only ordered the very best!"

Mr. Tunney does not give Charlotte's comment on this typically Shavian statement. What he remembers clearly is the fun they had together, and Charlotte laughing a lot. He says:

"After their arrival in Brioni, Mrs. Shaw heard me addressing G.B.S. as 'Mr. Shaw.' This went on for several days, after which, on one of our numerous long walks together . . . upon my addressing him as 'Mr. Shaw' . . . he stopped and said: 'Charlotte has heard you call me Mr. Shaw and she has pointed out to me that all my friends call me G.B.S. so, if it is only to please Charlotte, do call me G.B.S.' "

*   *   *

Charlotte had a bad year in 1930, beginning in May, when she became ill during a stay at Buxton in Derbyshire. G.B.S. wrote to Lady Astor:

"I should have liked to talk to you on the telephone; but it is so situated that I cannot be sure that Charlotte will not hear what I say; and I am deceiving her (as we all are here) about her illness: she thinks she has tonsillitis, which is not alarming, whereas she really has scarlatina.

"One of the tricks of scarlatina is to start on your glands when it has finished with your throat, in which event your restored normal temperature suddenly shoots up again. That is what happened to Charlotte yesterday . . . her temperature had risen to 102 and she was in despair. She said to me very earnestly 'Have I got mumps?' 'No,' I replied with conviction: 'you havent got mumps.' This morning I did what I wanted to do on Thursday when I returned to London. I engaged a nurse. When I first suggested it Charlotte wouldnt hear of it. 'I couldnt bear it,' she said. 'She would be trained to be cheerful and to keep up my spirits. She would WARBLE at me all the time.' And so she was left to me and to the unskilled and overdriven chambermaids. But after six days without washing she welcomed the nurse, who is an excellent young woman. She does not warble; but when I took the doctor for a drive and the patient became anxious for my safe return, she cheered her up with a faithful account of all the most frightful recent motor smashes in Buxton.

"So Charlotte is still in bed in a fairly high fever; and the doctor says she will have two days of it, or rather the remainder of two days, one and a half having already elapsed. She is improving visibly; and the mump is yielding instead of gaining."

To Beatrice Webb he wrote on May 6 that Charlotte was mending satisfactorily, her temperature normal and her temper reassuringly fractious. She had developed conjunctivitis, too, which was not only painful but prevented her from reading. A few days later he wrote again to Lady Astor, saying that Charlotte was peeling, and eating voraciously, and was at last out of pain.

In October, 1930, G.B.S. was writing to Sydney Cockerell: "Charlotte bruised her ribs over the arms of her chair, and yells when embraced, but is otherwise well."

A few days later she had a fall in Hanover Square, coming down heavily on her shoulder and hip and cracking a bone in both places. The hip joint was not injured, and the bones remained in position, but she had to lie still in bed to give the cracked bones a chance to knit together.

At the end of 1931, the Shaws sailed to South Africa, which Charlotte enjoyed until the serious accident which might have ended in tragedy. She was sitting in the back of a car which G.B.S.

was driving to Port Elizabeth, with a friend, Captain Newton, beside him. At one point G.B.S. stepped on the accelerator instead of the brake, with immediate consequences. He wrote various accounts of the mishap to different friends; the card which he sent to T. E. Lawrence, in February, 1932, from Knysna, Cape Province, runs:

"I have surpassed all my previous exploits as a motorist by driving our hired car at full throttle over a ditch and hedge surmounted by 5 lines of barbed wire, through a bunker three feet deep (a sunken path), and to a standstill in rough country with one strand of barbed wire still holding. Neither the car nor its driver was disabled; but you must make Lady Astor shew you the letter I am sending by this mail detailing the consequences to poor Charlotte. She is lying up here quietly for repairs . . ."

Charlotte had been badly hurt by heavy luggage falling on her, and she had multiple injuries, as well as deep bruising on her back and one leg. They remained at a place called the Wilderness until she recovered, and G.B.S., never able to stop himself writing, was soon at work on a book which was to become *The Adventures of the Black Girl in Her Search for God*. After Charlotte had recovered and was able to travel again, she went up in an aeroplane for the first time. She was seventy-five years old. At first she was hesitant, but she was anxious to join a ship at Port Elizabeth, and flying was the only way to get there in time. Once she was airborne and could see the vast panorama spread out below, she lost her fear and was enchanted by the sense of space.

In December, 1932, the Shaws embarked on the *Empress of Britain* for a tour round the world, and in February, 1934, they were off again, this time on a cruise in the *Rangitane* to New Zealand. Charlotte looked forward to seeing the wonderful rivers, geysers and snowy mountains of that beautiful country, and she told friends later that she had greatly enjoyed her stay. She and G.B.S. visited Rotorua and the Glow Worm caves, and went to see Sir Truby King, the pioneer of modern child care; she admired the neat bungalow homes with gardens full of flowers. Charlotte told the St. John Ervines on her return that G.B.S. was happiest in New Zealand, and that it was the one country abroad she would have liked to live in.

Barry Jackson had established the Malvern Festival, which was mainly a Shaw festival, at the end of the nineteen-twenties, and G.B.S. and Charlotte went every year, when they were not travelling abroad. Charlotte, as usual, stayed in the background as much as possible when the photographers, journalists and idolizing crowds were about, but she took a close interest in the productions themselves, and liked hearing them discussed at the private parties which Barry Jackson gave at his house near the British Camp, in the Malvern Hills.

She was ready to voice her own opinions about her husband's plays to their friends. When *Too True to Be Good* was produced, and St. John Ervine criticized it at length in the *Observer,* Charlotte wrote to him:

"I, who am G.B.S.'s severest critic, specially like this play. To my mind it is not pessimistic, not despondent, & not a recantation of any of his beliefs. It is a play of *revolt.* One character after another declares that this is 'not enough': that they are getting glimpses of the 'reality that was hidden': that 'their way is the way of death, & the preacher must preach the way of life'—'Oh, if I could find it!'

"Everything in the play points to the fact that there *is* a way of life—& that all these people, some consciously some unconsciously, are struggling to find it. Honestly, St. John, I do think that in the future, when things straighten out, it will be understood that this is among G.B.S.'s *big* plays. The voice of one crying in the wilderness!

"However!

"One amusing thing about Too True is that nearly all the women like it & nearly all the men loathe it!"

They were feeling old. After their return from New Zealand, Charlotte was in bed with bronchial trouble and G.B.S. was very depressed. On May 28, 1934, he wrote telling Dino Grandi, the Italian Ambassador, who had asked them to dinner, that they no longer dined out, adding:

"My wife and I have decided that the age limit for dining out is 75. Beyond that they are bores and dotards. And alas! Charlotte and I are nearer 80 than 75.

"But we can still keep up a sort of ghastly affectation of youth-
fulness until about 4 in the afternoon; and if at any time you are
giving a quiet luncheon party, and two of your guests disappoint
you at the last moment, we should not shrink from the two vacant
chairs. . . ."

G.B.S. still detested any public mention of his age. Charlotte
wrote to Trebitsch in February, 1935:

"I write to beg you not to take any notice of G.B.S.'s eightieth
birthday. The kind thing would be to pass it over in silence. It
annoys him to be reminded of it. Do you think it nice to be 80!?
One wants to forget it."

They embarked on the *Arandora Star* for a cruise in the Pacific
Ocean in January, 1936. Charlotte wrote to Sydney Cockerell that
they both felt much better than when they had left England and
were having an interesting time; they travelled to Miami and
Havana, Honolulu and San Francisco, going on to see the Grand
Canyon and then into Mexico. But in October, 1936, Charlotte was
writing to Cockerell from Whitehall Court:

"We have only just come back—exhausted by what was called
a holiday: but we shall soon pick up here . . . our last cruise did not
agree with G.B.S."

A few months later, Sydney Cockerell must have suggested a
possible theme for a play to Shaw, for Charlotte wrote to him:

"Thank you . . . for Madame Curie. G.B.S. started reading the
book at once. Whether he can 'get a play out of it' is doubtful
though we have had discussions as to whether the rule that a doctor
who discovers a healing drug, or process which can do much to
save human beings from death or suffering is bound to relinquish
the chances of making a fortune out of it. It is so obvious in the
Curies' case the money would have been so much more usefully
used in their hands than in any others.

"I fear there is not a play in it, but how interesting & useful to
have that idea thoroughly threshed out!"

G.B.S. alarmed Charlotte greatly in 1938 by becoming seriously
ill. There was no organic disease, but acute anaemia, and he had
to have injections of liver extract—about which he knew nothing
until afterwards. Charlotte, who was asked to give her consent to this

treatment, had attacks of conscience, knowing her husband's strong vegetarian views, but she thought that in this case the end justified the means. The publicity which his illness brought vexed her almost beyond endurance. She wrote to St. John Ervine:

"Poor G.B.S. just returned from death's door . . . & messenger boys arriving in motor cars, telegrams six pages long, telephone unceasing . . . G.B.S. forced to write letter after letter when he could hardly hold the pen."

Then Siegfried Trebitsch proved a further cause of anger; he sent her an article about herself, illustrated by what purported to be a photograph of herself, cut from a German newspaper. She wrote to him:

"You have hurt me greatly. This is not me. It is a very clever fake, but we know by various things such as the eyeglasses, which are different from any I have ever worn, the cut of the dress and other trifles, that it is not genuine. . . . The writer of the article does not say one true thing about me from start to finish. As you like the dreadful thing, please keep it. I shall find it difficult to forgive you."

Less than a fortnight later she sent him another letter:

"I am sorry I wrote off in such a hurry, I was so cross! Of course, everywhere I go, there are these photographers trying to get a snap, and they drive me wild. I never consent to be photographed and *never* give any sort of interview, but I am always being pestered and tormented by journalists and photographers, and that picture you sent me was a specially awful one.

"Let's forget it . . ."

It was always possible to get away from the fret and strain of life, the perpetual blare of publicity. They went down to stay with the Webbs in the country; they visited Sydney Cockerell at Cambridge, and occasionally Hugh in Shropshire. Sissy had died in 1931, and it was not the same at Edstaston, but Hugh was always pleased to see them, and it was refreshingly quiet there. They sometimes stayed at Cliveden, with Lady Astor; G.B.S. was, of course, the star turn of the house parties there, but Charlotte appreciated the qualities of their ebullient hostess, and liked her. Some of the Shaws' friends thought that Charlotte was, like Lady Astor, a Christian

Scientist, but she was, in fact, far more interested in the ideas of Ouspensky. She had gone on from Dr. Mills's "Teaching" to a study of Ouspensky's *Tertium Organum* and *Esoterism and Modern Thought,* and she copied out scores of passages from these works, and made hundreds of notes.

She led two lives in parallel during these last years. Outwardly she was Mrs. Bernard Shaw; she travelled everywhere with G.B.S., looked after him devotedly when he was ill, listened to his opinions, was still a perfect hostess when she felt well enough to entertain. They had grown very close to each other. Barry Jackson remembered calling on them unexpectedly at Whitehall Court, and, as he was an old friend, being shown in without question. He found them sitting side by side on a sofa, looking at a large picture-book spread out on G.B.S.'s knees: a picture, themselves, of calm companionship.

There was, however, the other Charlotte: and here it seems that G.B.S. had no part at all. This was Charlotte in search of God. She had for many years kept up a correspondence, at widely spaced intervals, with people she had met earlier in life who had been on the same wavelength in the realm of the spirit. One of them was Gerald Heard, sometime secretary to Horace Plunkett, whom she had met at Kilteragh. He now lived in California, and she wrote to him in 1939:

"To me P.S. & T [not identified] has been a revelation. A spark that lighted up the whole pile of little personal discoveries and made them glow with new lights. It just put the final pinnacle on the edifice built up by me from Ouspensky and all the others. . . .

"I have been more or less studying all this since before I gave you the little Gita at Kilteragh, and I so soon found out all you say about its demanding *everything*. At first one thinks it means a quarter of an hour a day, and soon one finds it means all one's life and being and loyalty, then soon one realises that this is not enough. There was a time when if I had been free, I would have given up everything else for it. But I was not free . . ."

The outbreak of war found the Shaws at Frinton-on-Sea. They motored back to Ayot, and Charlotte spent the few remaining years of her life there, except for visits to friends. She and G.B.S. decided to remain at Ayot and not go to London; Blanche Patch, Shaw's secretary, would stay at Whitehall Court and deal with all necessary business. On October 10, 1940, Charlotte wrote to Beatrice Webb:

"We were so glad to have news of you through Miss Patch. She will have told you she is staying with us at Ayot & that we are living here together for the present. She found she could not stay in London, it was too nervy. We are comparatively safe here, though bombs are continually dropped quite near. We are both well & perfectly well & unalarmed. I suppose it is our age. We feel we have lived our lives, & had a very good share of the best that was going, & now perhaps a bomb would be the easiest way to end—if only one was sure of its making a complete job.

"Our servants are marvellous. In fact I am greatly impressed by the way the English, as a whole, are going through this ordeal. They are splendid. By the way, my pluckiest maid is *Irish*."

Charlotte was growing very bent. The doctors diagnosed lumbago, but G.B.S., writing to Sydney Cockerell in 1942, told him:

"We have just spent three weeks with the Astors at Cliveden and the Canadian medical service at the military hospital here took her on for a thorough overhaul in a businesslike way: X ray, blood sample, life history all complete. Verdict: suffering from the effect of an accident in her teens, and incurable because the only treatment—steel corsets, plaster jacket, immobilisation for months—is bearable by men under 40 only. No danger to her life beyond that of all octogenarians; but she will be an invalid as far as medical science goes: a sentence of lumbago for life."

And early the following year to Beatrice Webb:

"Charlotte is so crippled and invalided with this wretched osteitis deformans that there is not much joy in life for her. The doctors can do nothing."

G.B.S. cared tenderly for her. She had grown difficult, but his gentleness never faltered. Every evening he played the little piano which had been put in the hall so that Charlotte could hear the music: he sang arias from operas, Irish airs, songs he had heard his mother sing. Charlotte lay upstairs and listened, hunched, often in great pain . . . but who knows what resources she had within herself?

Charlotte died on September 12, 1943, at the age of eighty-six. G.B.S. wrote to Sidney Webb, who had recently been bereaved by the death of Beatrice:

"I also am a widower. Charlotte died this morning at 2.30. Her long illness had changed her greatly, and was very distressing (she was troubled with hallucinations) but at the end the distresses cleared off; and her last hours were happy. As she lies now she is not a crippled old woman; she is just like the portrait Sartorio made in Italy when she was in her first youth. The change is inexpressibly touching."

G.B.S. wrote accounts of Charlotte's death to several intimate friends, but he described only the outward signs. He was later to say in a letter to C. H. Norman:

"To become a widower is a curious experience; for it is only then that one discovers how much one's life is governed by one's wife, if the marriage has been a success."

It is probable that the real Bernard Shaw told the real truth about his long relationship with Charlotte in a letter which he had sent seven years earlier to an old friend, Mrs. Bannister, to whom he and Charlotte were much attached. Mrs. Bannister had just lost her husband, and Charlotte and G.B.S. wrote a joint letter to her which contained this passage:

"Finally a marriage consolidates itself until the two lose all sense of separateness, and the married life becomes one life."

Separate they had been in many ways: Shaw with his pen, Charlotte with her ceaseless searching for the Infinite. But, as G.B.S. had once said, he could never have married anyone else.

And Charlotte? One wonders.

CHARLOTTE SHAW'S WILL
Repercussions

Charlotte Shaw's will caused something of a sensation when it was published. Most of her estate was bequeathed to G.B.S., there was a substantial legacy to her niece, Cecily, and her servants and some former servants received legacies and annuities. Item 19 of the will was the one which roused a great deal of indignation in Ireland:

(i) WHEREAS

(a) I am desirous of promoting and encouraging in Ireland the bringing of the masterpieces of fine art within the reach of the Irish people of all classes so that they may have increased opportunity of studying such masterpieces and of acquiring a fuller and wider knowledge thereof, and

(b) In the course of a long life I have had many opportunities of observing the extent to which the most highly instructed and capable persons have their efficiency defeated and their influence limited for want of any organised instruction and training for the personal contacts whether with individuals or popular audiences without which their knowledge is incommunicable (except through books) and how the authority which their abilities should give them is made derisory by their awkward manners and how the employment in positions for which they have valuable qualifications is made socially impossible by vulgarities of speech and other defects as easily corrigible by teaching and training as simple illiteracy and whereas my experience and observation have convinced me that the lack of such training produces not only much social friction but grave pathological results which seem quite unconnected with it and that social intercourse is a fine art with a technique which everybody can and should acquire

(ii) Now with a view to furthering and carrying out the objects which I have at heart I HEREBY DECLARE that the Irish Bank shall stand possessed of the Ultimate Trust Fund as and when so transferred to and vested in the Irish Bank upon the trusts and with and subject to the powers and provisions that is to say:

[There follow paragraphs (a) and (b) providing for a Trust Fund, the income of which was to go in perpetuity "to in or towards all or any one or more of the following objects and in such proportions and in such manner as the Irish Bank shall in its absolute discretion from time to time think fit that is to say:—"]

(c) The making of grants contributions and payments to any foundation corporate body institution association or fund now existing or hereinafter coming into existence within the special period hereinafter defined having for its object the bringing of the masterpieces of fine art within the reach of the people of Ireland of all classes in their own country provided that no such foundation corporate body institution association or fund shall be eligible as an object of these trusts if

(i) it is not of a public character or

(ii) In the case of a foundation corporate body Institution or Association it is at liberty to pay or distribute any profits to or among any of its members subscribers contributors or benefactors or the fund or any part thereof or any income therefrom may be so paid or applied or

(iii) any of the members subscribers contributors or benefactors would have any right to participate in the assets or in the fund in the event of its dissolution or distribution

(d) The teaching promotion and encouragement in Ireland of self-control, elocution, oratory, deportment, the arts of personal contact, of social intercourse, and the other arts of public, private professional and business life.

(e) The establishment and endowment within the special period either solely or jointly with any person or persons or any other corporation or any educational institution or any Chair or Readership in any University college or Educational Institution now existing or coming into existence within the special period in Ireland for the purpose of giving instruction in or promoting the study by the general public of the subjects mentioned in this Clause 19 or any of them Provided that no such College or Educational Institution has for its sole object the exclusive or complete training in any single profession or calling.

(iii) I declare for the purpose of this my Will the expression 'Masterpieces of fine Art' means and includes works of the highest class in the fields of orchestral and classical music painting sculpture fine printing and literature produced or originating not in any one country exclusively but in any country in the world and by or among people in any age period or date whether Ancient or Modern.

[The "special period" was to be taken to mean "the lives of the issue now living of his late Majesty King George the Fifth and the

life of the survivor of them and 21 years after the death of the
survivor of them." The expression "Ireland" wherever used in the
Will was to denote the existing Irish Free State and any other extension of it that might take place.]

*   *   *

It is, perhaps, not altogether surprising that the publication of the Will
should have had a mixed reception in Ireland. The sections quoted here
might have been more happily phrased, but Charlotte had not meant to be
either arrogant or patronizing: that is abundantly clear. Her intentions were
of the best, and the fact that she set up such a large Trust Fund shows that
she felt very strongly about the cultural life—or lack of it—in her native
country. As far back as 1936 she had consulted Dermod O'Brien, the then
President of the Royal Hibernian Academy of Art, on the subject. There
is, among her papers, the following letter and enclosures from him:

"65, Fitzwilliam Square,
Dublin.
18 August, 1936.

"Dear Mrs. Shaw,

"Some time ago you asked me to make some suggestions as to how
you might help the arts in Ireland. You were just about to go on one of your
world tours, and I had the pleasure of having luncheon with you on the eve
of your departure, when it was hardly a convenient time for a discussion on
the arts.

"But now, when I am making a special appeal for the maintenance
of the Gate Repertory Theatre here, I am adding notes on the art conditions
of Dublin and Ireland, which may be useful if only an impression of one
who is much involved in the furtherance of all forms of art.

"But first as to the Gate Theatre, I am enclosing a letter which we
are sending out to all those who we think might be interested and helpful,
with a view to insuring the rent of the theatre at all events, which amounts
to £250 per season; and to get people to join the Playgoers' Circle nothing
could help so much if we were able to advertise the fact that your husband
would inaugurate the Sunday meetings by an address.

"As it has been proposed by the Dublin Corporation to give the
freedom of the City to him, there is a possibility of his being over in Dublin,
when, if he were willing, he might make it synchronise with an address to
the Playgoers' Circle. Is there any chance? Anyhow I hope that you will
both become members and thereby help to keep for Dublin those two actors
to whose enterprise we have had the chance of seeing performed your husband's 'Back to Methuselah' among other interesting plays. I hope you won't
be alarmed by such a budget, and please give my respects to G.B.S.

"Yours very sincerely,
"Dermod O'Brien

"The Royal Irish Academy of Music
has no endowment except for prizes and scholarships. The Professors are
paid by pupils' fees only, augmented (some of them) by fees for holding examinations at the Local Centres.

"The Dublin Corporation, with the aid of the rates, competes with lower
fees at the Municipal School of Music, and gives no assistance though having ten members on the board of the Academy, an unwieldy body of nomi-
nally some 32 people, of whom half attend fairly regularly.

"Mechanised music competes also, and lessens the number of students
and their fees.

"The Band room of the Academy is too small for trying out opera or
anything like a full orchestra: and there is no large concert hall in Dublin.
The Royal Dublin Society gives its members excellent chamber music
concerts during the winter season, but the Academy is not often called upon
to supply music. Even if the Academy could put up a reasonably good
string quartet, I doubt if the public would support it with their shillings
when so many of them can get such forms of music so cheaply at the R.D.S.
from performances of considerable celebrity.

"Having no endowment, the Academy can't command the services of any
first rate performers as professors, and we badly want a first class pianist,
violinist and 'cellist, who would not be entirely dependent on their teaching
fees. We badly want a proper concert hall, and any self respecting municipality would put one up, but the Corporation won't listen to any schemes
for building other than for the housing of the poor (who have the votes).

"The bigger theatres charge so much that it is impossible for such bodies
as the Philharmonic Society, the Dublin Operatic Society, the Music Art
Society, to make ends meet, and each of them has to make a special whip at
the end of the season among their members and supporters to try and carry
on for another season.

"There's some talk of the establishment of a 'Conservatoire' under State
or Municipal control, which would give degrees and diplomas—a function
of the Academy which would probably be absorbed by it if state-aided. But
this rumour may emanate solely from those who wish to abolish all institutions
under Royal patronage.

"As the Academy has no Charter, the changing of it under a 'Conservatoire' would make little difference except in the appointment of its
teaching staff. At the moment there's a small committee of the Board making a close examination of the affairs of the Academy, and we shall have
their findings at the end of the month, I expect.

"As Dr. Larchert (formerly director of the Abbey Theatre orchestra) is
the convenor, I fear that the recommendation may take the form of
economy in the teaching staff, getting local talent to replace the senior professors of piano and violin, which I consider would be a mistaken policy &
one not free from personal bias.

"Short of a big endowment for the maintenance of the professorial staff, it is difficult to see how the Academy, or Music generally, can be assisted, but the Academy should have a Director & be relieved of its unwieldy Board of Governors. I should like to see the Band room enlarged and a Quartet endowed, but this is because it is a form of music that appeals to me particularly.

"*The Royal Hibernian Academy of Arts*
has had no home since 1916 when its premises were destroyed by fire. Since then Govts. of all shades have been approached to aid in its rehabilitation by, at all events, giving a site at a nominal rent: and it has also been suggested that the Govt. might offer a pound for every pound subscribed, up to a specified limit, to help to rebuild & endow for overhead expenses: the Academy having no endowment except a small sum of about £40 per annum for school prizes.

"Just before the American slump, we thought that we had it all arranged & I had a plan & survey made out, but the slump produced a change of attitude and the rent asked & conditions laid down were such as it was impossible for us to accept. Among the requirements I laid much stress on the provision of post-graduate studios to enable young artists to do their work until such time as they could provide themselves with studios, there being practically none in Dublin.

"The Metropolitan (State) school of art is going to be turned into a College of Art, but I don't think that would clash with our own Academy, which I should like to make into a sort of Club for the members, associates and post-graduate students, a thing that is very badly needed.

"We also want a good travelling scholarship, that might be given from time to time, to some students who might really benefit by foreign travel and study."

Charlotte had always believed in the principle of helping accredited institutions rather than giving largely to charities. When she was a young woman she had endowed a bed in a hospital in County Cork; when she became interested in the London School of Economics and Political Science she not only gave them a good scholarship, but contributed substantial sums to their funds year after year. (It is characteristic that she took a close interest in the holders of the scholarship, writing to the Principal to give her a detailed account of each student's progress.) Her bank books and account books give some idea of the enormous number of educational and cultural bodies that she helped in her quiet way. Taken at random, the list of standing orders paid on her behalf at the end of 1936 includes:
City of Westminster Health Society, Coal Smoke Abatement Society, Commons & Footpaths Preservation Society, Society for Protection of Ancient Buildings, Dogs' Home, Battersea, Divorce Law Reform Union, Royal

Horticultural Society, National Art Collections Fund, Friends of the National Collections for Ireland, Central Asian Society, North Herts & South Beds Hospital, Society for Psychical Research, Society for Protection of Birds, Peoples' Dispensary for Sick Animals of the Poor, National Society for Women's Service, Anti-Noise League, Coleg Harlech, Friends of the Bodleian, Osteopathic Association, New Commonwealth Society, Handel Society, National Trust, London Library, Metropolitan Drinking Fountain & Cattle Trough Association, Baby Clinic & Hospital, Society for Provision of Birth Control Clinics, Aristotelian Society, and so on.

Charlotte had always been a good businesswoman where her property was concerned, and she left a considerable fortune. G.B.S. wrote to Judy Musters on January 23, 1944:

"Charlotte left me her separate property valued £150,000 for my lifetime. The net result is that without being a penny the richer, I have to pay £40,000 to the govt., and heaven knows what to the lawyers and valuers."

He also wrote to Sidney Webb on April 2, 1944:

"I have just signed a second batch of forms for Charlotte's solicitor. As they are all connected with her stocks and the sales thereof I have some hope of the legacies being paid before we are all dead. Meanwhile, if you are at all pressed, I can lend you a thousand pounds[1] as a private transaction between us without bothering about all that nonsense of an assignment which would be necessary if we did it in the form of my advancing the legacy.

"Charlotte's death has been a financial disaster for me. During our marriage her property doubled in value, as she quite unintentionally made a profit out of our arrangement by which she paid the housekeeping bills and I paid the rents, the travelling expenses and cars, and gave her £1200 a year cash. She saved and invested, with the result that whereas she had £4,000 a year when we married she had £8,000 when she died, on which I paid the supertax.

"Now as we lived on our joint incomes my inheritance of her property did not enrich me by a single farthing. But I had to pay £40,000 death duties. Altogether I have had to pay considerably more than £100,000 to the Exchequer since 1939. I have just sold out £30,000 War Loan to clear my personal overdraft; but I [am] still overdrawn heaven knows how much at the National Provincial on Charlotte's account which is a Trust.

"So much for the popular belief that I am rolling in money as a consequence of having been left £150,000. However, I am on velvet compared to many others broken by the war. I am not yet really insolvent. So enough of this."

---

[1] Charlotte had left Sidney Webb £1,000.

INDEX